How to Write

Not Your Usual
User's Guide
to the English Language

A. P. English

$$

TRUE MYSTERY CONTEST!

Sponsored by Wicked Good Books, Inc.

ARE YOU A WORD SLEUTH? Find the Conan Doyle titles hidden in *The True Mystery of Hamlet*, and you may win. Every retail paperback copy sold of *The True Mystery of Hamlet* adds one dollar to the prize fund, with no upward limit. In the unlikely event that *The True Mystery of Hamlet* sells more than 100,000 retail copies by 31 December 2017, the prize will be more than $100,000.

HOW TO WIN: *The True Mystery of Hamlet* (ed. Dotson, contains phrases that directly suggest titles adopted by Sir Arthur Conan Doyle. The first two clues occur in the first paragraph of *The True Mystery*, with the phrases, "a scandal in Bohemia" and "memoirs of Sherlock" [Homes]. All clues are in plain view. A few may be hard to spot. Find them all, or even most of them, and you may win. For contest rules, tips how to spot the clues, and an official entry form, visit Wicked Good Books, Inc., online, at www.wicked-good-books.com. Competition ends 31 Dec. 2017; the Sponsor reserves the right to extend the deadline if the prize fund by 12/31/17 has not yet reached at least $10,000. No purchase is necessary to enter.

One of the four greatest stories ever told:

The True Mystery of Hamlet, by [Thomas] Watson, edited for 21st century detectives by Alf Dotson: From the newly discovered Jamestown Shakespeare Manuscripts comes a 100% solution to the greatest mystery ever conceived by the mind of man: *Hamlet, Prince of Denmark.* The historical Sherlock Homes (not to be confused with Holmes, his fictional name-sake) investigates the deaths of Prince Hamlet's father and uncle, the queen mother, Hamlet's school chums, his girlfriend, his girlfriend's father and brother, and of the sulky prince himself. Homes plucks the heart from Hamlet's mystery long before Sigmund Freud traced the young hero's strange fixation to an unresolved Oedipal Complex.

$$$

HARD-BOILED DETECTIVE CONTEST!

Sponsored by Wicked Good Books, Inc.

ARE YOU A WORD SLEUTH? Find the Raymond Chandler titles hidden in *Othello l'Amour* and you may win. Every retail paperback copy sold of *Othello l'Amour* adds one dollar to the prize fund, with no upward limit. In the unlikely event that *Othello l'Amour* sells more than 100,000 retail copies by 31 December 2017, the prize will be more than $100,000.

HOW TO WIN: *Othello l'Amour* (ed. Dotson), contains phrases that directly reference titles adopted by Raymond Chandler (*e.g.,* "Red Wind"). All clues are in plain view. A few may be hard to spot. Find them all, or even most of them, and you may win. For contest rules, tips how to spot the clues, and an official entry form, visit Wicked Good Books, Inc., online, at www.wicked-good-books.com. Competition ends 31 Dec. 2017; the Sponsor reserves the right to extend the deadline if the prize fund by 12/31/17 has not yet reached at least $10,000. No purchase is necessary to enter.

One of the four greatest stories ever told:

Othello l'Amour, by Christopher Marlowe, edited for 21st century gumshoes by Alf Dotson: From the Jamestown Shakespeare Manuscripts comes the first hard-boiled detective story ever written; possibly, the most thrilling. In 1588, in Venice, the daughter of a white senator eloped with the commander of the armed forces, an African, and fled to the island of Crete. Her father, Signore Brabantio, hired Christopher Marlowe (1564-1593)—poet, university wit, playwright, atheist, homosexual, and government agent—to find the doll and bring her home. Here is a tough-guy case that has it all—scandal, gold, pearls, a magic totem, a doting patriarch, a husband war-hero, a cross-dressed lover, a rosy-cheeked boy, a femme fatale, a stupid constable, ethical ambiguities, and five violent deaths in one night—all five cases being solved before breakfast.

$$

TRUE ROMANCE CONTEST!

Sponsored by Wicked Good Books, Inc.

DO YOU KNOW ROMANCE? Find the paperback romance titles referenced in *The Taming of the Pooch* and you may win. Every retail paperback copy sold of *The Taming of the Pooch* adds one dollar to the prize fund, with no upward limit. In the unlikely event that *The Taming of the Pooch* sells more than 100,000 retail copies by 31 December 2017, the prize will be more than $100,000.

HOW TO WIN: *The Taming of the Pooch* (ed. Dotson), contains phrases that directly suggest titles of identifiable paperback romances. Find them all, or even most of them, and you may win. For contest rules, tips how to spot the clues, and an official entry form, visit Wicked Good Books, Inc., online, at www.wicked-good-books.com. Competition ends 31 Dec. 2017; the Sponsor reserves the right to extend the deadline if the prize fund by 12/31/17 has not yet reached at least $10,000. No purchase is necessary to enter.

One of the four greatest stories ever told:

The Taming of the Pooch, by Isabella Sforza, Lady Porcigliano, edited for 21st century lovers by Alf Dotson: From the Jamestown Shakespeare Manuscripts comes the earliest and quite possibly the greatest paperback girl-takes-charge romance of all time, witty, warm, and scrumptious. Written in 1555 by Lady Porcigliano and translated by Anne Cook Bacon, the *Taming of the Pooch* touches upon the countess's love affair with the Renaissance humorist, Hortensio Lando; but her story features the courtship of Caterina di Baptista of Padua, a romantic who teaches her Petruchio everything that every woman ever wished her man knew about love. Recovered at last from the dustbin of patriarchalist history, Lady Porcigliano's *Taming* may be the most transformative woman's romance since Adam and Eve. Also, the funniest.

First publication 2015.

Typeset in Century Schoolbook

Library of Congress Cataloging in Publication Data

English (Angelique P.), 1950–.
  Title. *How to Write*

I. English language—Rhetoric.
English, Angelique P. (1950–   ). Title.

ISBN-10: 0-9882820-1-1
ISBN-13: 978-0-9882820-1-8
LCCN: 2014960224

ACKNOWLEDGMENT

I am grateful to Jacob Weisberg for his help in documenting Capital crimes against the English language; to my students, whose zeal for excellence gives me hope for the future; and to Sarah Nelson and Philosophy Walker in particular, for their valued assistance in the preparation of my typescript.

—A.E.

Royalties from this W.G.B. book support
UNICEF
and
The WGB Scholarship Fund

Women's Works, volumes 1-4

IN HIGH SCHOOL AND COLLEGE, the curriculum in history and literature virtually ignores one half of the human race. You can now remedy that oversight on your own. Twenty-five years in production, *Women's Works* gathers together the best of the early women's tradition, from the ancient Celts to Colonial America. All early women's texts in this amazing collection have been edited in modern spelling from the original manuscripts and printed books. Works originally in Welsh, Norman French, Old or Middle English, or in Latin are provided with a parallel English translation. Historical and biographical context is supplied for all selections. Here, at last, is the education in women's culture that you never got in school —poetry, drama, autobiography, satire, women's medicine, birthing manuals, life inside medieval nunneries, witch confessions, Elizabethan cookery; legal history of rape, domestic violence, and reproductive rights; early feminists, English queens, lesbians, prostitutes, celebrities, saints—it's all here. History and literature are not just by and for *men*.

"[*Women's Works*] is a gem. It provides witty, lively introductions to a large gathering of women's writing across a range of subjects [...] the most complete and compelling collection of its kind, combining meticulous scholarship and engaging presentation with fully teachable texts. The anthology we have needed for so long has finally arrived."
—Valerie Wayne, Prof. Emerita of English, Univ. of Hawai'i

"A remarkable contribution to scholarship that is also a pedagogical treasure, *Women's Works* ... should be in every university and college library and open on the desks of everyone teaching courses on or including seventeenth-century English literature."
—Prof. Margaret Ferguson, Distinguished Professor of English, University of California at Davis, and 2014-15 President of the Modern Language Association

"This collection is a revelation, even to those of us who have long been interested in women's writing. From now on, it will be an indispensable resource."
—Phyllis Rackin, Professor of English emerita and past president of the Shakespeare Association

"As the reader for countless journals and university presses in the field, I can place Foster in a rather wide range, a rather huge number, of Renaissance scholars. And he is surely one of the best: learned, bright, witty, winning – compelling in his argumentation and attractive in his style and presentation. ... *Women's Works* is simply breathtaking. Not in its concept – we have long needed, and said we have needed, a thorough anthology of the best writing of Medieval and Renaissance English women ... – but in its execution. ... And he has prepared, for the first time, a work that is authoritative and comprehensive, complete and final. It will not, because it cannot, be superseded."
—Arthur F. Kinney, Thomas W. Copeland Professor of Literary History and Director of the Center for Renaissance Studies at the University of Massachusetts

Women's Works, vol. 1 (900-1550). 440 pp. illus. $29.95.
Royalties support the Society for the Study of Early Modern Women.
Women's Works, vol. 2 (1550-1603). 440 pp. illus. $29.95.
Royalties support the Society for the Study of Early Modern Women.
Women's Works, vol. 3 (1603-1625). 440 pp. illus. $29.95.
Royalties support the Society for the Study of Early Modern Women.
Women's Works, vol. 4 (1600-1650). 440 pp. illus. $29.95.
Royalties support the Society for the Study of Early Modern Women.

For the tables of content and free pdf extracts, visit www.wicked-good-books.com.

Coming soon from Wicked Good Books:

THE PLAYER'S SHAKESPEARE

Strange but true: until The Player's Shakespeare came along—four centuries overdue—directors, actors, and drama students have had to depend on editions of Shakespeare's plays that were prepared by literary scholars for use in English classes. Each new volume, whether in cloth or paperback, has tended to repeat the mistakes made by previous editors. Entrances and exits are mismarked. Speeches are sometimes assigned to the wrong character. Bodies of the slain are left on stage with no signal given when the corpse is to be carried off. No thought is given to the relationship between the Shakespearean script and the venue in which the play may be performed. Laugh-lines are overlooked, becoming throwaway lines. The editorial "glosses"—those definitions and paraphrases at the bottom of the page—are often wrong, usually reductive, and always conservative. Dramaturgy, staging, set design, casting, doubled roles, cross-dressing, costume notes, landmark productions, receive at best a few perfunctory remarks from Shakespeare's literary editors. Readers learn instead about themes, poetic justice, patterns of imagery. (Do you go to see *Hamlet* for its metaphors of an unweeded garden? for its "theme" of revenge? Or do you go to the theater because, when well acted, it's a great show?)

The Player's Shakespeare—in the pipeline for 2017—will present Shakespeare's most popular plays in script format, in a reliable text, with notes on meter and delivery, staging, and stage history. Illustrations from past and recent productions appear on the verso (lefthand page), together with the notes. The glosses and stage directions—based on 400 years of experience in the theater—are fresh, helpful, and accurate, but never prescriptive.

The Player's Shakespeare, collaboratively edited by a team of experts—scholars, dramaturges, and actors—promises to supply the definitive acting script of Shakespeare's plays for today's theater, and for generations to come.

Visit wicked-good-books.com for more information.

Using this gift from heaven

How to Write comes in four sections, beginning with part one, the "Ten Commandments." Memorize them. Then just follow the easy steps (also supplied) for writing original works of incredible genius.

Part two, "How do they *do* that?" unfolds the wisdom of the ages concerning the kinds of writing you are most often asked to do for others, whether in the classroom or at work.

Part three, "Write or Wrong," is a guide to words, thereby to prevent you from emulating the many scholars, athletes, and presidents before you who have made fritters of the English language.

Part four, "Index and Ready Reference" directs you, in a jiff, where to go for the help you need.

Yeah, write

AT THE FAMILY DINNER TABLE, and in school corridors, and even around the office water cooler, one sometimes hears the remark, "My teacher ["boss," "editor," "girlfriend"] *just doesn't like my writing style.*" Yada-yada-yada.

Think again, Sparky! Some writers have style. Some don't. You don't, not yet, but help is on the way because here's *How to Write.* Your parents would not have given you this guide to good writing had they not seen your sparks of genius. Your teacher would not have asked you to read it if you were beyond hope. Your boss would not have supplied you with an office copy if she thought you could not learn how to communicate.

In any professional field—education, law, medicine, journalism, commerce, the arts—those individuals who best succeed are those who are best able to express themselves. Okay, not always—some U.S. presidents cannot speak or write, and many supermodels have no need—but if you lack the party machinery or family connections to propel you into the White House, and if God has neglected to give you a body fit for the cover of *Cosmo* or *Planet Muscle*, then your next best bet is to use words and to use them well. Learn to say what you've got to say as it needs to be said. All the rest (an A+ in English 101, a desk job, a promotion, a good-looking lover, a Jaguar, a Nobel Prize for Literature) is then just icing on the cake.

Writing ability is not a "gift." You have to work for it. No one comes out of the womb discoursing wonders, or explicating *Hamlet*, or even telling a well-crafted joke. Babies are born, they want to be heard, they squawk. Intelligible speech comes with observation and practice—without which, those inarticulate cries will soon become tiresome even to the ears of a doting mother, and ineffectual as well for the child who does the squawking. Composition, like speech, is an activity that can be learned, with time, attention, and practice, by virtually anyone. But no one can develop facility in writing without a thoughtful commitment to excellence.

The English language is a wonderful instrument. *How to Write* is your user's manual. Read it. Study it. Take it to heart until you can recite whole chapters in your sleep. It's time, kiddo, to spread your wings and fly. It doesn't take a literary genius (or a scholar, journalist, or secretary) to write well. You may be a high school football lineman who doesn't know his nouns from his verbs, or his *like* from his *as,* or his *nevertheless* from his *but.* Not to worry. You, too, can learn to write like an angel—clearly, correctly, concisely, and creatively—but only if you give a damn.

—A.E.

How to Write...

Part 1:

TEN COMMANDMENTS

1. Be Interesting

2. Be Specific

3. Be Organized

4. Be Clear

5. Be Concise

6. Be Choosy

7. Be Accurate

8. Play By The Rules

9. Do Not Steal Much

10. Just Get it Right

Ten Commandments

1.1. BE INTERESTING

1.1.1. Angle: *Find your best hook, line, and bait*

> *There are no dull subjects. There are only dull writers.*
> —H.L. Mencken [1]

1.1.1a. *Begin with a bang, not a whimper.*

Your writing—whether it's for school, a broker's office, police department, law firm, sales force, op-ed page, professional conference, Women's Online Bible Study, or a restroom stall—must compete for attention and credit with the work of other writers. Professional journalists know that they need to hook the reader's interest in the first two sentences or their story will not be read. The same goes for you. If you do not have a good lead, only your mother, sweetheart, and best friends will follow you onto page two.

1.1.1b. *Choose a subject that grabs you.*

If your teacher or boss or editor has assigned you a boring topic— "The Semicolon," let's say—and you are not a boring person, find a way to make the subject interesting not just for yourself but for your readers. If your task is to review a book or a show or a Hollywood film, read published reviews to see how it's done. If it's to be a research project, become an expert on your subject. If it's an opinion paper, be persuasive. Don't just stand there dribbling, take the ball and run with it. If nothing really interests you, then try writing about the benefits of a career in fast food or telemarketing.

1.1.1c. *Find a title that will interest your intended readers.*

Subscribers to *Cosmo* are more likely to read an article on "Bedroom Gymnastics" than if the same piece were called "Family Circus." Students of literature may take more interest in an essay called, "'You base football player': Oswald and Defective Masculinity in Shakespeare's *King Lear*," than in a paper on "Shakespeare's Sports Knowledge." And your history teacher may form a better first impression of a classmate's eight-page paper titled, "Making the A-List: Adultery among the Puritans" than of your own ten-page paper, which is labeled: "Midterm Essay."

Before brainstorming for a title, consider your genre, your subject, your designated audience. The title for a work of fiction or for an op-ed piece should catch interest even if your reason for having chosen it

remains unclear until well into the narrative. The title for an academic essay (or, more succinctly, for a news story) may or may not be
interesting, but it should always signal to your intended readers what
the essay or article is about.

1.1.1d. *"Fit audience find, though few"* (*Paradise Lost*, 7.31).

Or, as John Milton might say if he were alive today, don't just fling
it—pitch it to someone who can catch. Milton knew that his writing
could not be all things to all people, not even when writing a lofty
Puritan epic in blank verse, or a prose defense of political
assassination. What's clear, direct, and compelling for one reader may
be too elementary for a second, impossibly difficult for a third. Know
for whom you are writing: to talk down to an informed audience can
be as ineffective as talking over the heads of the uninitiated.

For each particular writing task, envision your ideal readers—local
taxpayers, high school athletes, state legislators, Southern Baptists,
Uncle Ralph, an impatient creditor, the NPR crowd—someone other
than your English teacher. Find the best angle, the right level and
tone, for those intended readers. Whom will your chosen subject
concern? Who needs to consider what you intend to say? Who will be
informed or persuaded or best entertained? Direct every remark to
your imagined set of ideal readers, even if they are unlikely ever to
read what you have written.

Are you addressing an audience of men and women? Then do not
use *men* or *he* as if it meant everyone, including women. An essay on
drunk driving addressed to emergency medical teams will have little
in common with a paper on the same subject addressed to members of
the Teamsters Union. Writing a classroom essay? Imagine yourself
performing for other bright students in the course who would like to
write as well as you can do. Whether addressing children or adults,
follow the example of Jesus: if your audience is hungry, feed them. If
grieving, console them. If ignorant, inform them. If skeptical,
convince them. If hostile, outfox them. And when you need to make a
point, make it through examples, figurative speech, and story-telling.
Your opponents may nail you anyway, but at least you will not have
deserved it.

1.1.1e. *Exhibit some gusto.*

Having settled on a topic and an approach, let your voice be heard.
Be assertive. Be bold. Be definite. Take a position. Make us give a
damn. Writing, like courtship, is a performance art. Think of every
writing assignment as a blind date with beautiful minds. Be
prepared to show them a good time.

1.1.1f. *It's not really about you.*

Take your eyes off your navel. Estimate how many people on the planet Earth are interested in your topic, and how many are interested in you as a person; adjust your focus accordingly. Most writers should be heard and not seen. Except in a diary, an autobiography, a résumé, or a letter to Mom, avoid making yourself the subject of your own writing. Use "I," "me," and "my" as needed, but don't overdo it: your readers, after all, may not share your conviction that you are a uniquely interesting specimen of the human race:

• *This may sound a little West Texas to you, but I like it when I'm talking about—when I'm talking about myself, and when he's talking about myself, all of us are talking about me.* (President George W. Bush.) [2]

It may be great fun to talk and write about yourself but unless you are a celebrity, the audience for whom you are writing will be more interested in the performance than in the performer.

Don't tell us the fascinating story of how you settled on a topic ("As I was reading *Clarissa,* feeling rather bored with the slow pace of the action, it occurred to me that Mr. Lovelace's big sword is a phallic symbol...".)

Your topic may be earthshaking or even catastrophic but that is no reason to interject your feelings about it:

• U.S. Vice President Dan Quayle, on a California quake that killed sixty-two people: *I could not help but be impressed by the magnitude of the earthquake.* [3]

• President George W. Bush, on his response to seeing a hijacked commercial jet crash into the World Trade Center: *I saw an airplane hit the tower—the TV was obviously on, and I used to fly myself, and I said, "There's one terrible pilot."* [4]

Address the problem at hand in a fresh way without pausing to narrate your own mental activity.

When applying for a job or for college admission, be matter-of-fact in presenting your particular skills, experience, and intellectual interests, without dwelling on your sorrows, anxieties, hopes for the future, and shoe size. Write from your own experience, but let the reader take interest in your writing, not in your subjectivity. Show us something we haven't seen before—new information, a fresh insight, a surprising truth—but don't show us the inner workings of your mind.

1.1.1g. *If you want to write well, be well read.*

Read widely. Read attentively. Read thoughtfully. On a few special topics, read deeply. If you read nothing but online chat, or technical manuals, or your own diary, or biology textbooks, or Shakespeare, don't feel injured when no one wants to talk to you at a party, much less read something you have written. Flowers don't grow well in rocky ground. Nor do they grow well in over-fertilized peat moss. To bear good fruit, the human brain requires some cultivation.

1.1.2. Tone: *Stay on pitch.*

> *I will roar, that I will do any man's heart good to hear me. I will roar, that I will make the Duke say, "Let him roar again! Let him roar again!"* —Bottom the Weaver [5]

1.1.2a. *Be confident.*

A common fault of insecure writers and bad speakers is the introductory disclaimer. When a presidential candidate begins his talk with the caveat, "I don't feel like I've got all that much too important to say on the kind of big national issues," why listen to him? [6] So, too, for essay writing. Humility is a virtue. Ignorance is not. Don't undermine your own authority or discard your right to be heard. Never tell us that you have no clue what you're talking about. Let us make that discovery for ourselves. Strike out such remarks as "I may be wrong, but—." Speak and write as an authority. If you do not know the answers, find them. If the answers escape you, ask different questions.

You can be assertive and yet avoid sounding like a know-it-all by stating the facts plainly, without gloating, without puffing, without belittling your adversaries, and without roaring. Note where your opinions or conclusions differ from those of other writers and public speakers, but do not abuse those who addressed the same subject before you came along. Your readers will give you more credit for having surpassed the great thinkers who preceded you than for having exposed the mistakes of a fool.

Rarely is there a need to write, "I think," or "I believe," or "In my opinion," or "It seems to me that..." Unless you are a notorious liar, or a well-known nincompoop, we will take it for granted that your writing represents what you think.

1.1.2b. *Don't lecture.*

If the force of your narrative, argument, and examples cannot persuade your readers of the truth, or move us to act, then preaching at us will not help. If you want to sound like a tour guide or a pedant, write sentences that begin, "Compare," "Consider," "Keep in mind," "Look at," "Note that," "Remember that," or "Take." Otherwise, don't.

1.1.2c. *Don't be pretentious.*

When tempted to pluck fancy words from a thesaurus, such as *quotidian* or *praetertranssubstantiationalistically,* first go take a cold shower. Then dry off and use the words we already know. Go easy also on the conjunctive adverbs (such gluey words as *consequently, however, nonetheless, otherwise, therefore*). *Thus* is rarely necessary. *Thusly* is comical. Simple words, short sentences, active verbs, and a plain style will hold your reader's interest. Textbook prose will not.

Some professional scholars and many ambitious students write over-long sentences glutted with abstract nouns, inflated with pretentious diction, and no active verbs. Their idea of good writing resembles the Christian's idea of Heaven: inaccessible except to the chosen few; it goes on forever; and nothing happens.

1.1.2d. *Decode the technobabble.*

Many technical writers and scientists are addicted to irregular noun clusters, producing such leaden waste as *army lab scientists' biosafety cabinet procedures manual,* or *all-wheel drive sport utility vehicle,* or an *IBM mainframe computer database users group newsletter.* If it is your job to tell consumers that "Hexnuts and lockwashers (fig. 3) must secure top frame angle bracket to wing sprocket flange grommet," first learn some English verbs. Such prose is the stylistic equivalent of chronic constipation. Verbs are the fiber that will get your ideas (or your technical instructions) moving again, no matter what your assigned topic may be.

1.1.2e. *Don't be glib.*

Even in papers or talks that are witty or amusing, your seriousness of purpose should be evident.

1.1.2f. *Don't be quaint.*

When you feel inclined for cuteness' sake to use such archaic words as *lo and behold, doth, hath, quoth, saith, thou, verily,* and *wherefore,* resist the temptation. Shakespeare, who was born in 1564, can be forgiven for writing like an Elizabethan. You have no excuse.

1.1.2g. *Avoid cuteness.*

Unless you have a deft wit and good occasion to use it, don't be jokey. "Surprise, surprise" is more irritating than funny. "Ho, ho," is fine for Santa Claus because Santa is not a writer. Don't say "no pun intended" if your pun was intended. Better yet, don't say it at all. Judicious punning can be a mark of fine writing but not when you draw attention to the ambiguity.

1.1.2h. *Avoid sentimentality.*

"The tiny cancer victim raised her precious little hand to wave goodbye, just as a lone sparrow took wing over the treetops" (student novelist). "Every once in a while, you let a word or phrase out, and you want to catch it, and bring it back. You can't do that. It's gone— gone forever!" (Vice President Dan Quayle). [7] "It's rural America. It's where I came from. We always refer to ourselves as real America. *Rural* America, *real* America. Real, real, *America*" (Dan Quayle, again). [8] Do not hint at sentimental solutions for problems of international conflict, economic crisis, or realpolitik: "I couldn't imagine somebody like Osama bin Laden understanding the joy of Hanukkah" (President George W. Bush). [9] Make us feel sad if you must, or warm and fuzzy inside, but hold the slop, we're not really that hungry.

1.1.2i. *Take responsibility for your own conclusions.*

Avoid heaping up quotations from other writers who think as you do. Let the force of your argument, the value of your information, and the liveliness of your own prose carry the day.

1.1.3. **Variety:** *Get out of the rut.*

> Not chaos-like together crush'd and bruis'd,
> But, as the world, harmoniously confused:
> Where order in variety we see,
> And where, tho' all things differ, all agree.
> —Alexander Pope [10]

1.1.3a. *No drumbeat repetition.*

Repetitious vocabulary and repeated phrases will cause your audience to tune you out, even if you are the President of the United States:

This is a world that is much more uncertain than the past. In the past, we were certain. We were certain it was us versus the Russians, in the past. We were certain, and therefore we had to keep the peace. That's what we were certain of. [...] You see, even though it's an uncertain world, we're certain of some things. We're certain that even though the evil empire may have passed, evil still remains. We're certain there are people that can't stand what America stands for. [...] We're certain there are madmen in this world, and there's terror, and there's missiles. And I'm certain of this, too: I'm certain, to maintain the peace, we better have a military of high morale—and I'm certain that under this administration, morale in the military is dangerously low. —President George W. Bush [11]

Every writer has pet words that he or she uses repeatedly. Watch out for your pets, taking care not to kick them senseless. No one, of course, can write without repeating common function words, such as pronouns (*him, its, she, who,* etc.), prepositions (*for, from, in, on, to*), and conjunctions (*and, but, or*). It is actually better to repeat *and* and *but* than to clog your prose with *moreovers* and *howevers*, and better to repeat *he said* or *she said* than to write "he retorted," "he opined," "he commented." But it is good to avoid unneeded repetition of any word or phrase. First do your cuts and phrase-tightening. Then find accurate but simple substitutes for the repeated terms. *Novel, narrative, story,* and *text* may be useful synonyms for *book,* but *tome* is pretentious. When writing a business report, *staff, workers,* and *personnel* may sub for *employees,* but *breadwinners* is trite, and *workmen,* sexist.

1.1.3b. *Vary your sentence structure.*

Vary the beginnings of your sentences and paragraphs. Vary their length. Vary their structure. Chant, sing, or shout, dance or march, but do it gracefully. A procession of clunky sentences having mechanical symmetry soon cloys. If every sentence has a dozen words and every paragraph five sentences, or if half of your thoughts begin with the same dreary formula, you are being tiresome.

Here are four drab ways to begin an English sentence:

• *There is/are/was/were/will be ...* ("There is a problem with...." "There are many characters who..." "There will be funding for...")

• *This is/was/has been/will be ...* ("This is a story about..." "This has been a good season for..." "This will be the second time that...")

• *It is/was/has been/seems ...* ("It is interesting that..." "It is important to note that..." "It has been said that..." "It seems like only yesterday that...")

• *One of the ...* ("One of the most serious problems is that..." "One of the most memorable experiences I ever had was..." "One of the best examples I can think of is...")

If you like, choose one of these models to begin a novel ("It was the best of times, it was the worst of times..."), or a poem ("There is a Yew Tree, pride of Lorton Vale,..."), or a joke ("There was this blind dwarf who...")—but do not heap them in the same paragraph. One too many slices of processed cheese can wreck a perfectly good burger.

1.1.3c. *No gimmicks.*

Consider this, as a title, topic, and introductory paragraph:

Oedipus Rex: Tragedy or Comedy?

By I. M. Tedious

Webster's Dictionary defines *tragedy* as "a serious drama typically describing a conflict between the protagonist and a superior force (as destiny) and having a sorrowful or disastrous conclusion that excites pity or terror."[12] Consequently, *Oedipus Rex*, by Sophocles, can be classified as a very disastrous tragedy because the protagonist, your typical Greek, has seriously killed his own terrified father and married his own compassionate mother....

If you bore your audience with such stuff as "The dictionary defines [*blank*] as—," then your fate, when destiny strikes you down, will excite pity in no one. Think before giving your readers a lesson in vocabulary. Rarely is it necessary to quote Webster's or any other fellow's dictionary. On those rare occasions when you must use terms or technical jargon with which your intended readers are unfamiliar, just say in plain speech what you mean by the specialized vocabulary, and move on. If usage has changed over the years so that you need to mention what a word meant long ago, then reference the *Oxford English Dictionary*. But do not annoy us with a writing gimmick that has appeared already in tens of millions of grade school reports and in far too many college essays.

1.1.4. **Vitality:** *choose lively verbs.*

> *Alice was too much puzzled to say anything, so after a minute Humpty Dumpty began again. "They've a temper, some of them—particularly verbs, they're the proudest—adjectives you can do anything with, but not verbs."*
> —Lewis Carroll, *Through the Looking-glass* [13]

1.1.4a. *To be or to do?*

As Hamlet learns, to be is less noble than to act. No one wants to watch the prince of Denmark sit on his fanny with nothing to do. So, too, for the English sentence. Without robust, lively verbs, your essay or story will remain a desert, a mudhole, a waste dump. Granted, no one can write with without using such helpful words as *am, is, are, was, were* (as in the first sentence of this paragraph). Your first draft in particular may suffer from a glut of inactive verbs. You will dash off far too many sentences beginning, "It is," "There is," "This is," "He was," "They were." In revision, recast most of those lifeless verbs. Make the subject of every sentence actually *do* something and you'll be surprised to see your prose rise off the couch and stir to life.

- Verbs of being: *It was a pleasant day. There was a cool breeze. Ocean smells were in the air.*

- Active verbs: *A cool ocean breeze lifted the curtains, filling our room with the smell of suntan lotion, salt air, and dead fish.*

Active verbs usually sound more thoughtful, more intelligent, than verbs of being:

- Verb of being: *The benefits of helping somebody* is *beneficial.* (Pres. George W. Bush.) [14]

- Active verbs: *The only justification we have* to look down *on someone is when we* stop to help *them up.* (Rev. Jesse Jackson.) [15]

1.1.4b. *Prefer the active to the passive voice.*

In an active sentence, the subject performs the action of the verb: "I ate my fried squid." In a passive sentence, the action is performed without direct agency: "My fried squid was eaten." Active verbs move, strike, carry, and persuade. Verbs in the passive mode (*is moved, was struck, will be carried, are persuaded*) slow the pace and deplete the energy of your work. Active voice is more direct, less wordy, than the passive:

- Passive: *The passive voice is to be avoided.*
- Active: *Avoid the passive voice.*

- Passive: *It was arrived at, it was seen, it was defeated.*
- Active: *I came, I saw, I conquered Iraq.*

Active voice is more visual, more immediate to the imagination, than the passive:

- Boring: *Although I worked at the circus for only three months, much was learned.*
- Better: *While working last summer for the Apple Family Circus, I taught the lions and tigers some astonishing gymnastic tricks, including my world-famous ten-cat pyramid.*

Save the passive voice for those rare occasions when the object of the action is more important than the doer—

• *In Illinois, Minnesota, and Montana, dentures* are required *by law to bear their owners' Social Security numbers. No penalty* is prescribed *for dentures that do not comply with the ordinance.*

—or when you want the important noun to come at the end of the sentence: *Did you know that the automatic telephone-dialing system was invented by an undertaker?*

The passive voice is to writing as steamed cabbage is to a bowl of fresh fruit. Keep your writing active. Remember the Nike motto: *Just do it.*

1.1.5. Freshness: *Be inventive.*

> *In my sentences I go where no man has gone before.*
> —President George W. Bush [16]

1.1.5a. *Avoid clichés like the plague...*

Or like a herpes rash. Or like a bus station restroom. Or like someone else's used Band-Aid. Or not. An overworked phrase is no worse, nor any better, than an old hat. If there were something wrong with it, the phrase would not have come to feel so comfortable in the first place. Such off-the-shelf expressions as "gravy train," "green light," "landmark decision," "uneasy peace," "well-placed insider," may be exactly the right phrase to express your purpose. But if you find yourself using them only because you have heard them elsewhere, not because they are perfectly suited to the context, you should find another way to say it. Threadbare expressions— "meaningful discussion," "what it means to be human," "the lion's share," "One thing is certain," "The bottom line is that"—make for stale prose. Be inventive. Be imaginative. If you find that overused or musty phrases have crept into your first draft, line out the musty language and put something fresh in its place. Moldy language makes for dull reading.

1.1.5b. *Avoid over-familiar figures of speech.*

No matter whether you are a novelist or a meteorologist, spare your audience from one more "dark and stormy night." If you are a newswriter, and are tempted to say that "Shoppers will have to dig deeper in their pockets this year," etc., dig deeper into your pocket or manure pile for a fresh metaphor. Tired phrases can spoil even the most dramatic subject, such as homicide:

• *The man brandished a gun. Shots rang out, striking terror into the hearts of innocent bystanders. Two were gunned them in cold blood. The killer then turned the gun on himself. He was rushed to a hospital, where he is fighting for his life. Neighbors say that Yusef Chin, the alleged shooter, is a quiet man who always minded his own business, but his own mother says nothing could be further from the truth. He was a walking powder keg, a disaster waiting to happen. Police are monitoring the situation.*

Unless you are a creative genius of inexhaustible originality, dead phrases and moribund metaphors will creep into your writing. One or two per page may escape notice or, if aptly chosen, add color and interest to your work. Cut the rest. Don't bore us to tears, don't bore us to death, don't bore us stiff. Give tired language a rest.

1.1.5c. *Consider the sense of every trite phrase.*

Many familiar phrases are so old and hoary they have lost their common sense. When a kitchen or shop has been cleaned up, "spic and span," every *nail and chip* has been swept away. If Joe takes Mary's story "with a grain of salt," he swallows it with the extra flavoring that Mary threw in by way of exaggeration or evasion. (It is the speaker or the writer, not the audience, who gives the story a dash of seasoning.) To "toe the line" is to come as close to breaking the rules as you can without actually crossing over. To "beg the question" means neither *raise a question* nor *evade the answer.* You *beg the question* when you present an argument whose conclusion assumes the truth of the very conclusion that your argument is designed to produce ("All civilized people agree that murder is wrong; therefore euthanasia must not be legalized"). When former Second Lady Marilyn Quayle states that "Most women do not want to be liberated from their essential natures as women," her thesis begs two questions: what does she mean by women's "essential nature?" and how does she know that most women are therefore opposed to the women's liberation movement and the Equal Rights Amendment? [17]

Browse on clichés if you must. Do not butcher them. An invading army *wreaks* havoc; "reeking" havoc is what you smell during the sixth week of a summer strike by city garbage collectors. If a presidential candidate praises his running mate as a "sounding rod," he means either a *lightning rod* or a *sounding board*; when he deplores "these hateful few who have no conscience, who kill at the whim of a hat," the intended phrase was *on a whim* or *at the drop of a hat.* [18] When Vice President Dan Quayle applauded the retiring White House Chief of Staff, saying, "This isn't a man who is leaving *with his head between his legs,*" the contorted cliché invoked (among the cynical press corps) an unwelcome mental image of erotic yoga. [19]

Car accidents, though interesting, usually result from bad driving: so, too, for language mishaps. When you perform bodywork on a familiar phrase, making inventive twists, let your remodeling be creative, not accidental or catastrophic. Familiar phrases weirdly altered will strike your readers as less wise than amusing:

• *The senator has got to understand he can't have it both ways. He can't take the high horse and then claim the low road. [...] And my case to the American people is, if you're happy with inactivity, stay with the horse. The horse is up there now.* (George W. Bush.) [20]

• *Families is where our nation finds hope, where wings take dream. Families is how we pass values from one generation on to the next.* (George W. Bush.) [21]

Deadly imprecision in the handling of clichés is a feature of much bad writing, whether in a school classroom, corporate boardroom, or public restroom. I quote the following homicide report verbatim, from a short story by a student at UC Santa Barbara:

• *He struck her once again, till she lay on all four hands and knees. There now, in peace and in an ocean of the most impassioned blood, lay the inefficient cadaver.*

Many threadbare phrases have started to unravel altogether. As a *case in point* (not "case and point"), the phrase, *all intents and purposes* is commonly misspelled "all intensive purposes," A *dog-eat-dog world* is often domesticated as a "doggy dog world." You may write glibly, *tongue in cheek*, but it's tough to write with "tongue and cheek." To *seize the day* (Carpe diem!) is to use time wisely; to "cease the day" is to go to bed early. To *whet your appetite* is to sharpen it; to "wet your appetite" is to drink or drool before dinner. A *cardsharp* may deal himself four kings; a "card shark" with a whetted appetite will eat them. To leap the fence or cross the border is to go *beyond the pale*; to go "beyond the pail" is an accident involving either Jack and Jill, or the stomach flu. A *hair's breadth* is narrow; for "a hair's breath," ask your cat to hock up a furball; or, if it's "a hare's breath" you want, eat carrots. A *hare-brained* fellow is as dumb as a rabbit; a "hair-brained" man has unusually deep roots.

If you're so suave you've got it made, you are *in like Flynn* (Errol Flynn); only an Indian arrowhead goes "in like flint." When you feel anxious, watch with *bated* (held) *breath*; for "baited breath," gargle with an aphrodisiac. If you feel like a farmer in springtime with forty acres and no tractor, you have *a long row to hoe*; if you have "a long road" to work on, find some other tool than a hoe. When you buy something off the shelf, it is *brand new*; use "bran new" for constipation. What's *coming down the pike* will arrive shortly; what's "coming down the pipe" has just been flushed, so look out below. Speaking of which, the Titanic suffered *wrack and ruin*; "rack and ruin" denotes a form of Christian discipline administered by the medieval Church to Jews, Muslims, and to non-ecclesiastical sex offenders.

If you think you can mangle clichés with impunity, you have another *think* (*not* another "thing") coming. Unsure how to use a familiar phrase? *Home in on* a dictionary. Do not "hone" in on one.

1.1.5d. *Reinvigorate tired language.*

Revised clichés may make for lively writing, as in the legend of the first-grade teacher who gave each child in her class the first half of a proverb known to most adults. Instructed to complete the thought, her student writers, unacquainted with her proverbial chestnuts, made them fresh: "Strike while the *bug is close.*" "Don't bite the hand that *looks dirty.*" "A miss is as good as *a Mr.*" "The pen is mightier than *the pigs.*" "A penny saved is *not much.*" "You get out of something what you *see pictured on the box.*" "When the blind lead the blind, *get out of the way.*" "Better to be safe than *punch a fifth grader.*"

If a first-grader can inject new life into a cliché, so can you. It is hardly necessary, or even possible, to eliminate every familiar phrase from your writing. Shuffle, cut and choose. The master stylist George Orwell put it this way: "A newly invented metaphor assists thought by evoking a visual image, while on the other hand a metaphor which is technically 'dead' (e.g., *iron resolution*) has in effect reverted to being an ordinary word and can generally be used without loss of vividness. But in between these two classes there is a huge dump of worn-out metaphors which are merely used because they save people the trouble of inventing phrases for themselves." [22]

That middle zone is your playing field, the fallow ground on which to cultivate your style. When you revise, look for phrases often seen elsewhere. Such terms as *ice-cold, snow-white, coal-black,* and *rock-hard* may be doing their job. If so, let them stand. *Iron resolution* is hardly strengthened by calling it "steely determination," but *jet-black* is an unhelpful term if it conveys an image of black airplanes instead of the dense black mineral, lignite (a.k.a., *jet*). Don't offer to put your reader "on tenterhooks" if you don't know a tenterhook from a meathook. Any proverb, simile, or metaphor that has lost its point should, like a pencil, be sharpened or discarded. Wipe out lame duck metaphors and strive for a phrase that can truly spread its wings and float, taking pains not to mix metaphors into a pea soup of discordant images as I have done in this ridiculous sentence.

When revising, patch threadbare phrases with an extra word, a synonym, or an inventive twist:

• *When the chips are down, the buffalo is empty.*
• *Best to let sleeping alligators lie, and to kick a dead dog if you can find one.*
• *Grandpa's enthusiasm and shorts were dampened by bladder trouble.*
• *It's time for our principal to read the writing on the wall of the Boys' Room.*
• *Every Monday after school the Computer Club guys meet in Room 212 to share their deep dork secrets.*

For "It's a dog-eat-dog world," try something like "It's a pitbull-eat-Pekingese world" or "Democracy is two wolves and a sheep voting on lunch." Better yet, follow the example of original thinkers. Abandon the hackneyed phrase altogether for some freshly minted expression of your own, after the manner of Johnson, Shaw, and Churchill:

• Tired: *Criticism rolls off me like water from the back of a duck.*
• Fresh: *A fly, sir, may sting a stately horse and make him wince; but one is but an insect, and the other is a horse still.* (Samuel Johnson.) [23]

• Tired: *1. The road to hell is paved with good intentions. 2. Don't judge a book by its cover.*
• Fresh: *The road to ignorance is paved with good editions.* (George Bernard Shaw.) [24]

• Tired: *When the going gets tough, the tough get going.*
• Fresh: *If you're going through hell, keep going.* (Winston Churchill.) [25]

1.1.6. Image-ination: *Be visual.*

> *Show, don't just tell.*
> —advice to young Homer from the oracle of Apollo [26]

1.1.6a. *Picture it.*

Your writing need not always be so bone-headedly literal. "Imagination" refers, quite literally, to your power to make *images,* using words alone, without such commonplace aids as a movie or television screen. Your original figures of speech—metaphors (*A is B*), similes (*X is like Y*), and other such writerly flourishes—can help to make a point more visually, eloquently, or sweetly than through bald assertion. Robert Burns likens his love to a red, red rose. Shakespeare compares his love to a summer's day. King Solomon compares his lover's eyes to fishpools, her nose to the tower of

Lebanon which looketh toward Damascus, and her belly to an heap of wheat set about with lilies. Each lover, each topic, may suggest apt similes to your fecund imagination. Find original imagery that works.

- Dull: *Democracy is an inefficient form of government run by fools.*
- Metaphor: *Democracy is the art and science of running the circus from the monkey cage.* (H.L. Mencken.) [27]
- Dull: *When passing new legislation, our elected representatives often engage in costly and self-serving backroom negotiation.*
- Simile: *Laws are like sausages. It is better not to see them being made.* (Widely attributed to Otto von Bismarck.)

Keep in mind that original similes and metaphors, like children, often turn out badly, especially when pureed in a blender:

- *Security is the essential roadblock to achieving the road map to peace. [...] I am determined to keep the process on the road to peace. [...] I mentioned early on that I recognize there are hurdles, and we're going to achieve those hurdles.* (President George W. Bush.) [28]

- *I think we need not only to eliminate the tollbooth to the middle class, I think we should knock down the tollbooth.* (George W. Bush.)[29]

- *We want our teachers to be trained so they can meet the obligations, their obligations as teachers. We want them to know how to teach the science of reading. In order to make sure there's not this kind of federal—federal cufflink.* (George W. Bush.) [30]

    Let your pictures do the talking. With figures of speech, as with telling of jokes, it is better to hold your tongue than to offer one that requires explanation:

- *Votes are like trees, if you are trying to build a forest. If you have more trees than you have forests, then at that point the pollsters will probably say you will win.* (Vice President Dan Quayle, on how to win an election by building more trees than forests.) [31]

- *I have said that the sanction regime is like Swiss cheese. That meant that they weren't very effective.* (President George W. Bush, arguing that economic sanctions [ineffective cheese] cannot bring down an unfriendly government as quickly as a U.S. military invasion). [32]

- George W. Bush, on economic theory: *We ought to make the pie higher.* [33] (Later, by way of explanation:) *It is a very complicated economic point I was making there. Believe me, what this country needs is taller pie.* [34] (Later still, by way of reduced expectations:) *Over time, our economy is going to be just as strong as the American spirit, and so I'm very optimistic about the economy. How long it will take to recover, to the levels that we hope, is just—is beyond my pay grade.* [35]

Be thoughtful. Do not shoot similes at your reader rapidly, like bullets from a machine gun, nor clunkily like spuds from a potato cannon, nor clamorously, like a shower of cats and dogs. Create images deftly, as with an artist's brush, or not at all.

1.1.6b. *What's your story?*

One memorable anecdote is worth a thousand essays. To focus your reader's attention (in a college admissions essay, let's say), or to enliven a dull subject (such as investment advice), or to disarm a potentially skeptical audience (a letter from management to unsalaried workers)—include a thoughtful anecdote. A short, self-contained story or example can lend a human touch to your discussion and make a point stick where a more clinical or abstract treatment would fail.

For example: Your job is to train Emergency 911 operators. You want to impress upon your trainees the importance of clarity when answering a panicked caller's questions. They seem not to be getting it, so you share an anecdote:

A couple of New Jersey hunters are out in the woods when one of them falls to the ground. He doesn't seem to be breathing, his eyes are rolled back in his head. The other guy whips out his cell phone and dials 911. He gasps to the operator: "My friend is dead! What can I do?"

The operator, in a calm, soothing voice says: "Just take it easy. I can help. First, let's make sure he's dead." There is a silence, then a shot is heard.

The guy's voice comes back on the line. He says: "Okay, now what?" [36]

Your readers will recall the point of an apt anecdote long after they have forgotten your opinions and generalizations.

Just as a well-chosen joke, or a personal recollection, may secure audience-interest in a serious speech or lecture, an historical or literary anecdote may serve as the hook for an essay in the humanities, or illustrate a key point along the way. There are untold stories everywhere, tragic or comic, inspirational or devastating, trite or profound, that are just waiting for someone like you to come along and make sense of what such narratives may tell us about our past, our culture, our selves.

1.2. BE ORGANIZED

1.2.1. Foundation and structure: *Sketch out a plan.*

> *Design informs even the simplest structure, whether of brick and steel or of prose. You raise a pup tent from one sort of vision, a cathedral from another.* —E. B. White [1]

1.2.1a. *Architectural vision.*

Begin your writing project with a clearly defined goal but without a detailed outline. No one can write well from a straitjacket. Despite what they told you in middle school, it's tough to write from an outline, a device that can have essentially the same effect on your otherwise spontaneous expression as overtight underwear. Even if you remember how to construct one of those elaborate grammar-school structures with Roman numerals, Arabic numerals, capital letters, and lower case letters (to signal your main points, subheadings, paragraph topics, and examples), why relive the horrors of seventh grade? But before you start writing in earnest, you should at least be able to state what it is that you intend to show. That is harder to do than it sounds. For expository or persuasive essays, it is not enough to have a topic. The essay will flop unless you have a *thesis*—a controling idea that you can express with entire clarity. If you cannot say what your thesis is, you have not yet thought hard enough about your topic.

1.2.1b. *Say goodbye to the "five-paragraph" theme.*

You can also forget what you learned about the "five-paragraph theme," the standard model for student writing in the lower grades. In its most mindless incarnation, the writer announces in the first paragraph that he has an idea: "Marijuana should be legalized." "Ferrets are fun pets." "Nintendo is cool." The writer serves up three reasons why this is so, with one paragraph for each of the three points. The fifth paragraph tells the reader what has just been said in paragraphs 2, 3, and 4 in case he or she missed it the first time around. The five-paragraph, three-point, essay is a useful pedagogical device, for it helps children learn the rudiments of an argument. But if you have not unlearned this simple trick by the time you reach college, you're in trouble. (A college English teacher was once asked: Do you think that the five-paragraph theme ruins young writers? "It doesn't ruin enough of them," was the professor's weary reply.) A persuasive or expository essay should have as many well-developed paragraphs, or as few, as are needed for a successful argument.

1.2.1c. *Write* **toward** *an outline, not* **from** *it.*

When you begin a new writing project—a report, story, essay, or speech—know where you stand and where you intend to go. Complete a first draft. Number the sections or paragraphs. Then make a simple list, on a separate sheet of paper, of what you have already written, and note the trouble spots— repetitions, omissions, digressions, ineffective organization, lame transitions. Ensure that your sentences follow one another like clockwork, not like pigs in a chute.

In subsequent drafts, improve continuity and economy. Move things around. You have a cut-and-paste function on your word processor. Use it. Move, cut, shuffle, re-deal. Find your best lead, from what you've got so far, and move it to the top. Arrange your 'graphs sensibly, constructing artful bridges between the various sections of your argument (or explanation or sales pitch). Find paragraphs that are soul mates and put them together. Repeat the procedure after you have completed a second draft. Structural problems can be fixed as you go.

1.2.2. Research: *Reading precedes Writing.*

> *Research is formalized curiosity. It is poking and prying with a purpose.*   —Zora Neale Hurston [2]

1.2.2a. *Get to know your library.*

Ask questions of your friendly reference librarian. Find dependable sources. Learn where and how to look, whether in the reference section, open stacks, periodicals room, microforms, or digital archives. To conduct primary research on the Internet without visiting a library is like searching for your lunch in the swamp across the street from the restaurant.

1.2.2b. *Keep organized notes.*

When conducting research use notecards if you must, a laptop if you can get your hands on one. Better to take notes directly onto a computer than to fill out and file 3x5 notecards or multi-colored Stickie notes.

Check and double-check the accuracy of quoted material, to ensure that every word, every comma, is reproduced exactly as in your source. Remember to record full and accurate bibliographic information for each source consulted, including the library shelfmark, to save time later on.

1.2.2c. *Trace information to its source.*

In your final draft, don't quote anybody's quotation of somebody else. Assume that all secondary sources are mistaken, as indeed they often are. When you find the original source, you can speak with confidence, assured that you are not passing along misinformation. Those originary sources may also contain fascinating material that others have not considered when tackling your particular topic. Library research is like a treasure hunt, and quite satisfying when you find a gem that others have overlooked. Remember the gospel, *Mankind shall not live by Google alone.*

1.2.2d. *Discover your approach and argument as you go.*

Don't wait until you have finished your research to construct your argument, or you will be facing a deadline with a heap of notes, no fresh ideas in your head, and no fire in your gut. Your argument, or story, or report, should take shape in your mind long before you begin your first draft.

1.2.2e. *Know when to quit looking.*

Few writers have the time and resources to gather all of the evidence they'd like to have on hand before submitting a final draft. Some data may be unavailable. The library book you most need may be checked out. Some interviews may be hard to get. Deadlines may curtail your research. But beware of the "Ready, aim, aim, aim," syndrome, squinting all week long at your target without ever firing a first shot. Why spend all of your research time trying to draw a bead on the one rabbit that keeps eluding you? State the facts at your disposal and be modest enough to acknowledge the limitations of your data. Set aside for another occasion the questions you cannot yet answer.

1.2.3. Introduction: *Jumping in.*

> *We* [*must*] *continually be jumping off cliffs and developing our wings on the way down.*   —Kurt Vonnegut [3]

1.2.3a. *Find your point of departure.*

Each kind of writing—journalism, literary criticism, a sociological study, a lab report, prose fiction, a technical manual—has its own conventions for getting started. Work within the genre. Study how other writers have jumped into their topic when doing the kind of writing that you must do. Follow the trajectory of those authors who grabbed your attention most quickly, and who kept you focused on their performance until the final touchdown.

1.2.3b. *Don't dawdle.*

When writing your first draft, you may need a while, perhaps several pages of pre-writing or free association, just to get all of your baggage in one place. In your second draft, unpack and start over. Cut the introductory blather to the barest minimum and move straight into your subject. Don't bore your readers with idle chat. When reading your essay or letter or story we should not feel as if you are dragging us slowly into cold water or into a stagnant lagoon. Catch us by surprise: push us from behind into a hot Jacuzzi. Don't begin with a tiresome meditation on how art and life are a lot alike, or by observing that Shakespeare was a genius. Don't waste our time talking about how you happened to settle on a topic. Don't serve up a tedious general survey of the issue at hand. Don't inform us that your subject is important or that you have a unique point of view. We can decide that ourselves, from your performance. Just go. Jump off the cliff and show us how well you can fly. If, after jumping off, you and your thesis take a long vertical drop and splatter on the rocks below, well hey, at least you tried.

1.2.3c. *If you get stuck, come back later.*

Many writers find they cannot write a snappy introduction until the essay is all but finished. That's okay. In the meantime, let your first two paragraphs indicate your topic, tone, and point of view. As your story or essay moves forward, give us a sense of your route and destination, but subtly. Don't make us eat the map ("In this essay I will argue three main points, the first of which is that..."). Let your points seem obvious without making them so.

1.2.3d. *Pace yourself.*

Rarely will you need to make statements in your introduction that will be repeated later on. Above all, do not spend all of your sweet breath, or spill all of your beans, on that first page. Experienced writers, like seasoned performers, will save some of their best magic and brightest fireworks for the end. Paul Newman tells the story of two bulls, one old and one young, who were grazing on a hilltop when they spotted a herd of cows. The young bull said, "Let's run down there and do one of those cows!" "No," said the other bull. "Let's walk down, and do all of them." Your first few pages may be interesting, or funny, or sad, or helpful, or thrilling. That's great. But if you cannot keep it up, then start out slower or quit sooner.

1.2.4 Navigation: *Get past false starts and detours.*

It's like driving a car at night. You never see further than
your headlights, but you can make the whole trip that way.
—E. L. Doctorow

1.2.4a. *Dig and hurl.*

Staring in terror or depression at a blank page or at a blank computer screen will take you nowhere. One of the best methods to get a first draft completed is the unmethodical dig-and-hurl technique: read up on your topic, or read around in your primary text, until you have about a shovelful of material. Find a blank piece of paper, or a computer. Now: *hurl!* Don't pause to make your first toss neat, polished, or artful. Your Bavarian sandcastle can take shape later. Go back for another scoop. Now: *hurl!* Back to your source, and *hurl!* When you have accumulated a pile of loose but pretty good stuff, you will have something to work with. The writing will come a lot easier.

1.2.4b. *Keep moving forward.*

Or, to adopt another metaphor, take your eyes off the ground. Cruise with your eyes on the road ahead. Rack up the mileage markers, in that first draft, with as much speed as you can get away with. One big difference between experienced writers and novices is that students and other would-be writers tend to compose anxiously, striving to avoid "mistakes" as they go. They get bogged down, moving or revising or counting sentences, or proofreading and spellchecking. Such nitpicking tortoises will do well to remember the sad fate of Alexander Cruden. Born in 1700, Mr. Cruden is best known for his painstaking *Concordance of the Bible,* compiled almost two centuries before that digital age when a computer could have done the whole job in two minutes. A fastidious scholar, Cruden called himself "Alexander the Corrector." Grown slightly mad from a disappointment in love, he took daily walks through his home city of Aberdeen, Scotland, to calm his troubled soul; but he could never pass by the least graffito on a wall without pausing to efface it: which made his daily walks rather tedious. Mr. Cruden died in 1770, a harmless imbecile.

Experienced writers allow themselves to write badly, to resist self-erasure and correction in their first and second and third and fourth drafts. They know there are as many good ways as bad ways to express a thought, or to develop a paragraph. The key to success is revision. In those early drafts, don't sweat the graffiti. You cannot get your thoughts and style exactly right in your first draft, so don't try. Just get some blocks of text saved to disk so that you have plenty of material to revise later on. If you're serious about your work, you will return to each paragraph many times before letting it stand.

1.2.4c. *Transitions.*

When reviewing early drafts, watch for whiplash transitions. Each change of direction or topic should be smooth, like taking a cloverleaf, not like falling off the overpass onto the road below.

Refrain from using "Another" and "Also" and "However" like hot glue, to paste together ideas or whole paragraphs that do not belong together. Each sentence, each paragraph, each section should follow inevitably from the preceding and lead inevitably to the next. In your final draft, it should be impossible to move or remove a single sentence without doing damage to the whole.

1.2.4d. *Wrong turns.*

When you hit unexpected bumps, you have probably taken a wrong turn and gone off track. Don't meander back. Don't drive in circles. If you find yourself writing "as I said before," "as I discussed above," "we have already seen that," then you have got a problem with your organization. In your next draft, pinpoint where you went off course, and resume. Experiment a little: before deleting a sentence or paragraph that seems out of place, try pasting it elsewhere in your piece. Look for a better fit. If that doesn't work, kill it.

1.2.4e. *Footnote detours.*

When you catch yourself in a digression that slows the pace, drop the digressive material to a footnote and deal with it later, usually by omission. A "content footnote" is an academic euphemism for digressive material that you were either too lazy to integrate into your text, or too self-indulgent to discard. Be ruthless in cutting discursive footnotes from your final draft. You may think the explanatory footnote wonderfully convenient; your readers will find it a nuisance. If you doggedly ring your neighbors' doorbell while they are upstairs in the throes of making love, they may well become annoyed with you. Pestering your readers with content footnotes during a fine composition will have much the same effect.

1.2.4f. *Writer's block.*

So you have been staring, for hours, at a computer screen, and you can't get started? or you have started but have stalled out? Turn off the music, online chat, computer games, and cell phone. Put your transmission in reverse, back over those last few bad paragraphs, and start again. Or leave a gap and move on. Or write garbage and move on. Eat. Take a nap. Stop to read someone else's writing for a while.

Then return to the keyboard. If your writer's block is chronic, it may be a symptom of something else, either medical (*Clinical Depression, Chronic Fatigue Syndrome, Attention Deficit Syndrome*), emotional (*stress, lack of confidence*), or a character issue (*just too damned lazy*). Seek help.

1.2.4g. *The insurmountable roadblock.*

Writer's block is something you do to yourself. A roadblock is something that gets in the way of your argument. William Strunk's advice—"Choose a suitable design and hold to it"—is a good trick, if you can do it. [4] But as you undertake your research (or, sometimes, long after you have begun writing), you may find that your original design needs tweaking. Perhaps you have set out to prove that Desdemona really *did* make whoopee with Cassio, or that Shakespeare's *Romeo and Juliet* is indebted to Leonard Bernstein's *West Side Story*, or that starting the Iraq War was a good idea. The essay is now half written, it's due tomorrow, and in the course of developing your argument you have run into a few serious and unforeseen objections.

When you find yourself in a hole, it may be unwise to continue digging. Having discovered an inconvenient fact, accommodate your research to any new information that invites you to climb out and start over. Don't try to sweep the problem away. Sometimes, your whole argument may be wrong-headed, or built on faulty assumptions. In writing, as in business, to escalate your commitment to a wrong idea is a formula for failure. If the donkey you have saddled so carefully and have driven so gently just won't go, no matter how hard you try, stop kicking. Or, to put it another way: if the horse is dead, get off. The word, *essay*, means a "try" or "attempt." Some essays don't work out. It happens to everyone. Get over it. Start again.

1.2.5. Development: *From sketch to masterpiece.*

Prose is architecture, not interior decoration.
—Ernest Hemingway [5]

1.2.5a. *Paragraph development.*

The paragraph is a unit of thought, not of verbal distance. Length may vary. In expository writing, a half page, double-spaced, is the norm, but each paragraph should be just long enough to make a telling point before you move on to the next. If you find yourself writing a lot of one- or two-sentence 'graphs, you are probably scrimping on the kinds of detailed argument or specific description that makes for lively writing. If you find that your paragraphs often drag on for a page or more, find a convenient break and insert a carriage return.

A good paragraph is as tightly crafted as a sentence, advancing the story, argument, or report without wasting words. One fault of much student writing is a tendency to begin a paragraph with a general assertion, and then to paraphrase the general assertion, and then to paraphrase it again and again, before moving on to a new 'graph and pulling the same stunt again with a new and different topic sentence, thrice-repeated. The more effective model begins with no more than one broad statement or assertion before downshifting to the specific and concrete. It may be that a reader can get the gist of your argument just by skimming the first sentence of every paragraph, but that's not what you want. None of your topic sentences is likely to contain an original thought or interesting observation. It is precisely your selection of details—quotation of the literary text, opinion of an authority, remarks by an eyewitness, legal precedents, new data, funny anecdotes, possible objections—that will set your work apart as a text worth reading in full.

Three is a goodly number of points to make in a Sunday sermon, though not always in an essay. The number of main points required may vary widely from one writing assignment to the next. The number of paragraphs needed to develop just one topic sentence may vary as well. There is no universal formula for what constitutes a developed essay, and there is only one rule: do whatever works.

1.2.5b. *Experiment.*

Keep your readers in mind. Take some chances. Keep us awake. Take us someplace we haven't been before, or at least get us to familiar ground by a new, more scenic route. Diversify. Innovate. Tell us something we did not already know. Help us to understand a familiar problem in a new way. Show us a little razzle-dazzle. Sharpen your points. Dance like a fencer. Make your vorpal blade go snicker-snack. Stand, thrust, parry, strike home. Finish with a deft *tuchet!*

1.2.6. Conclusion: *Draw down the curtain.*

> *If well thou hast begun, go on;*
> *It is the end that crowns us, not the fight.*
> —Robert Herrick

Ending well is hard to do. The quickest way to end a war is to lose it. The quickest way to end an essay or short story, though not the best way, is to stop thinking. But neither should you go off on a tangent at the last moment, or introduce some new fact that should have been mentioned earlier. A conclusion should achieve a sense of completion, of closure, of aesthetic satisfaction. Your final paragraph may be modest, or subtle, or courageous; abstract or personal; general or specific; funny or sad. You may close with a pinprick of wit or by dropping the Big One. The object is to do whatever provides the best fit with all that has gone before.

Conclude, don't just repeat. Tie your ideas together, seamlessly, leaving no loose ends. After completing a draft, review your introductory and concluding paragraphs: if they seem interchangeable, one or both of them can be deleted. There is no need to repeat what you have already said unless to add an unexpected twist. Neither will you need to restate your main points unless they have been badly expressed, in which case it is not yet time to write a conclusion, anyway.

A writing trick that most of us mastered by the seventh grade is the "summary conclusion": *In this essay/speech/letter I have tried to show that...*. You're grown up now, and should know better. A summary conclusion is about as thrilling, for your victims, as a summary execution would be. Readers do not need to be told again, on page 6, what you said on pages 1-5 unless you are writing for Alzheimer's patients.

The object of the final paragraph is to bring closure to your performance. Make the ending personal if you like, or anecdotal, or inspirational, so long as you are attentive to the conventions of the genre in which you are writing. Use your final paragraph to set up a pithy quotation and close with the quotation. Or show us why your information improves upon what we knew before, or thought we knew. Show us why your thesis may be usefully extended to other problems, or situations, or texts. When you're writing, you get to have the last word, so make it a good one. End with a bang, or with a funny anecdote, or with a singing fat-lady, but do not end with a whimper.

1.3. BE SPECIFIC

1.3.1. *The life is in the details.*

> *I keep six honest serving-men*
> *(They taught me all I knew);*
> *Their names are What and Why and When*
> *And How and Where and Who.*
> —Rudyard Kipling [1]

ALL GOOD WRITING—whether for a news story, fairy tale, college essay, technical manual, résumé, campaign speech, lab report, or epic poem—draws its life from the details. Sweeping generalities, vague abstractions, and vacuous opinions are a bore. Follow each broad statement with a specific example. The remark that "Thousands of American children have become addicted to computer games" will have more force if you can supply dependable statistics, or can cite a recent study, or can tell us the heart-wrenching story of a single young computer-game addict whose adolescence was wasted on *Doom* and *WWE Smackdown*.

Scout about for facts and vivid examples that other writers may have overlooked. Interview people in the know. Read the latest academic research. Supply an anecdote. Give your readers new information, a new perspective, or a good story, to illustrate each main thought.

1.3.2. *Say who?*

> *Abbott*:   We have *Who*'s on first, *What*'s on second,
>   *I Dunno*'s on third.
> *Costello*:   That's what I want to find out.

1.3.2a. *Kill "people."*

People is a fun magazine but it is not always a fun word for the reader of your office memo or history essay. For most purposes, *people* is a better word than *humans* or *human beings*, and a much better word than *persons*. The world must be peopled, but not overpeopled, so when you feel the urge to *people* your page, exercise a little self-restraint.

When observing what "people" say, or think, or do, make clear whom you have in mind. Frank Rizzo, a former mayor and police chief of Philadelphia, once remarked: "The streets are safe in Philadelphia, it's only the people that make them unsafe."[2] Having popped "people" into an essay for your English teacher, line it out and narrow your reference is to modern readers, or to the author's contemporaries, or to characters in the fictional text, or to Philadelphians. To say, in a letter to the editor, that "Most people are not really prejudiced against Latinos" is itself a prejudicial statement, for it presumes that Latinos are not people. The individuals, groups, and nations that constitute *Homo sapiens* are surprisingly diverse, many of whom do not look, think, or speak as you do. Don't speak of "people" as if it meant everyone. Besides: if what you have to say is true for everyone, then you have picked the wrong topic to write about because that leaves precisely no one who needs to hear what you have to say.

1.3.2b. *Says who?*

No matter what the task at hand—a news story, fiction, history, criticism, a sermon, a friendly letter—you cannot write in a lively way without engaging additional voices—an eyewitness, a tragic protagonist, a medieval king, a feminist, an apostle, a fellow Hemingway critic. Make clear who voices every opinion, every sentence, each phrase, in your text. Most of those beliefs and statements, of course, will be entirely your own. Don't be coy. When you write such stuff as "It has been said that—," or "Many authorities believe that—," or "Many critics suppose that—" your reader will not be fooled: What you really mean to say is: "I think I may be right, but I haven't bothered to look up the reference." Do your homework. If you cannot find any authority who agrees with you, don't try to imply otherwise with a vague passive, or by enlisting a hypothetical third party.

1.3.2c. *Always attribute.*

When quoting, or when writing dialogue, use "said" as often as necessary, giving each new speaker a new paragraph. By following these useful conventions, you save the reader from getting lost in a confusing welter of who said what:

"Sometimes," said President Bush, "words have consequences you don't intend them to mean." [3]

"When I use a word," Humpty Dumpty said, in rather a scornful tone, "it means just what I choose it to mean—neither more nor less."
"The question is," said Alice, "whether you can make words mean so many different things."
"The answer is," said Humpty Dumpty, "which is to be master—that's all." [4]

When citing an authority or someone's opinion, always identify your source. *Who* believes it? *Who* has said it? Some writers serve up quotations on a platter without attribution: "Cheerios reduce cholesterol." "Giving money and power to government is like giving whiskey and car keys to teenage boys." "The wages of sin is death." The news media "misunderestimated" the president."[5] Quotation without attribution is an annoying habit. Each reference should be introduced, or followed hard after, by the person to whom those quoted words or borrowed ideas belong. When the rest of us read your work, we should not have to stop and puzzle out who says what, or riffle through the endnotes to discover whose opinion or statement is being cited. Just tell us.

If your quoted statement is a universal Truth no matter who said it or how it is expressed—"It is a bad idea to commit incest"—then put the thought in your own words and omit the quotation marks. When paraphrasing or summarizing ideas that are not entirely your own, just be frank about what belongs to whom. Don't seem to claim credit for ideas or language that you have borrowed from someone else. (Remember the tenth commandment: *Do not steal much.*)

1.3.3. *Say what?*

Costello:	*Who* picks up the ball and throws it to *What, What* throws it to *I Dunno, I Dunno* throws it back to *Tomorrow*—triple play.
Abbott:	Yes.
Costello:	Another guy gets up—it's a long fly ball to *Because.* Why? [6]

1.3.3a. *Show, don't just tell.*

No matter what your writing task, the telling usually comes first, in a general observation or topic sentence, but the showing is always more important. Be visual and particular:

- Telling: *Don't be a copycat.*
- Showing: *If one synchronized swimmer drowns, must the others drown, too?*

- Telling: *There was a scary-looking dog in the yard.*
- Showing: *A Rottweiler, tied to a stake near the sidewalk, strained at her leash.*

- Telling: *Emotion clusters about common things. The pathetic often stimulates the imagination to new patterns.* (William Carlos Williams.) [7]
- Showing: *So much depends upon a red wheel barrow glazed with rain water beside the white chickens.* (William Carlos Williams.) [8]

1.3.3b. *Prefer the concrete to the abstract.*

Hunt down and kill vague expressions, substituting words that will convey a precise image. Use specific, concrete adjectives or none at all. "Big" and "little," "good" and "bad," "positive" and "negative," are so thin as to convey scarcely any meaning at all:

• *You cannot lead America to a positive tomorrow with revenge on one's mind. Revenge is so incredibly negative.* (George W. Bush.) [9]

"Positive" thoughts may be optimistic ones, such as your upbeat approach to that thousand-dollar loan you once made to your brother-in-law, or your hopes for a bon voyage aboard that discount cruise in the Caribbean during hurricane season. Conversely, "negative" statements—from your stock analyst, doctor, or your son's math teacher—may be cause for alarm. But the terms, "positive" and "negative," are best reserved for the poles of a battery. Find words that will convey some more colorful image to the mind's eye than a plus or a minus sign.

1.3.3c. *Destroy things.*

Thing may be the most tired thing in the English language:

• *Things have never been more like the way they are today in history.* (President Dwight D. Eisenhower.) [10]

• *Things are more like they are now than they have ever been.* (President Gerald Ford.) [11]

• *Well, on the manhood thing, I'll put up mine against [Mondale's], any time.* (Pres. George H. W. Bush.) [12]

• *We are doing the right* thing, *and we do not see the bad* things. [...] *I hope there's some respect and dignity for* things *I did not do.* (Vice President Dan Quayle.) [13]

• *See, we love! We love freedom. That's what they didn't understand. They hate things. We love things.* (President George W. Bush on the 9-11 terrorists.) [14]

• *One of the things we've got to make sure that we do is anything.* (George W. Bush on the violence in Israel and Palestine.) [15]

You can find a more specific word than "thing," almost always.

1.3.3d. *"The situation" always needs help.*

No one has ever written a good sentence ending in "the situation."

I take it back: that was the first one good one ever, in the entire history of the language. But it is usually better, when such lame phrases as "the situation" creep into your work, to strike them out and to fill the gap with something specific. If you ever catch your fingers typing the ill phrase, *"this* situation," slap them. If they should type "this situation" twice on the same page, break your left pinkie as a warning to the other nine not to do it again. If you cannot say what "this situation" is (*a crux in the text, a budget crunch, poor voter turnout, oily skin*), then don't waste our time writing about it.

1.3.3e. *"This," "these,"* and *"that"*: *Just say no.*

If your goal is to write vivid, specific prose, then your helpless addiction to *this, these,* and *those* may be your worst enemy. Such words, much overused, are best saved for the captions beneath pictures and museum exhibits ("This portrait of Sir Philip Sidney, by an unknown artist, was completed in 1576." "This woolly mammoth was discovered in 1813.") The demonstrative pronoun may be a time-honored convention of American joke-telling ("There was this blind man, and he walks into this bar..."), but *this* and *these* rarely facilitate lively, serious, or even comic prose style.

This and *these* are words that pepper the speech and writing of speakers and writers who don't really know who or what they are talking about:

• *The Holocaust was an obscene period in our nation's history—I mean,* in this century's history. *But we all lived in* this century. *I didn't live in* this century. (Vice President Dan Quayle.) [16]

• *The true threats to stability and peace are* these nations *that are not very transparent.* [...] *The true threat is whether or not* one of these people *decide, peak of anger, try to hold us hostage, ourselves; the Israelis, for example, to whom we'll defend, offer our defenses; the South Koreans.* (George W. Bush.) [17]

• *[T]he vast majority of Iraqis want to live in a peaceful, free world. And we will find* these people *and we will bring them to justice.* (George W. Bush.) [18]

That, when used as a demonstrative pronoun like *this* or *these,* is no less subject to vagueness or confusion:

• *It has been said by some cynic, maybe it was a former president, "If you want a friend in Washington, get a dog." Well, we took them literally—that advice—as you know. But I didn't need that because I have Barbara Bush.* (George H. W. Bush.) [19]

Here, the second "that" evidently denotes "a friend" and not "that advice" to get a dog.

Never use "this" where *the, his, her,* or *my* would be more direct or personal. A demonstrative pronoun is the lazy writer's way to avoid coming up with varied phrasing to denote the same object of discussion. Instead of reporting what "Shakespeare says in this play," explicate what is said by Claudius or Ophelia in Shakespeare's *Hamlet.* Find synonyms: not "this play," "this play," "this play," "this play," but *"Titus Andronicus,* the bloodiest of Elizabethan revenge plays," "such violent dreck," "macabrely wretched excess," "Shakespeare's least digestible tragedy." Instead of saying "this problem," "this employee," "this campaign," find alternatives: "the government's unwelcome interest in our creative accounting," "Ms. Greer's trusted assistant," "the candidate's primrose path to bankruptcy."

Never use "this," "these," or "that" to refer vaguely to some preceding idea. *(This is because it's bad writing.)* To work at all, a demonstrative pronoun needs an obvious and direct referent. If your "this" is followed immediately by "is," and not by a specific noun or phrase ("this pipe bomb," "this unlikely hero," "this unexpected gift of flowers"), then rewrite the sentence. Thomas Jefferson provides a useful model: "We hold these truths to be self-evident: that all men are created equal; that they are endowed by their creator with certain unalienable rights"—but your right to alienate readers with a vague pronoun is not one of them. Nor is Thomas Jefferson to blame for your unthinking addiction to "this."

Used sparingly, demonstrative pronouns may be clear, concise, and pointed. One may hardly improve upon the immortal words of Thomas Paine, though many statesmen have tried:

- Memorable: *These are the times that try men's souls.* (Thomas Paine.) [20]
- No better: *There may be some tough times here in America. But this country has gone through tough times before, and we're going to do it again.* (George W. Bush, on his economic policy.) [21]

So, too, for the words of I Corinthians 13:13—

- Memorable: *Now abide faith, hope, love, these three: but the greatest of these is love* (1 Cor. 13:13).
- More concise: *Faith, hope, and love remain, but love is the grandest.*
- More particular: *There's only one person who hugs the mothers and the widows, the wives and the kids, upon the death of their loved ones. Others hug, but having committed the troops, I've got an additional responsibility to hug, and that's me, and I know what*

> *it's like. [...] People say, how can I help on this war against terror? How can I fight evil? You can do so by mentoring a child; by going into a shut-in's house and say "I love you."* (George W. Bush.) [22]

The second, anonymous, version is more concise than I Corinthians 13:13, but dull. The third, by President Bush— with its imagery of evil-fighting hugs, compassion, and a mentor's "I love you"—is more specific, but sappy.

Reserve "this" and "these" for special occasions, as for informal communications where your intended audience will know exactly what you mean. *Case in point*:   in April 1986, the *Wall Street Journal's* bureau chief, Al Hunt, predicted (wrongly) that George H. W. Bush would lose the Republican nomination. His son, George W. Bush, responded concisely, and with complete clarity:

• *You* [unprintable expletive] *son of a bitch. I saw what you wrote. We're not going to forget this.* [23]

The sentiment can be more vividly expressed—("You [*unprintable expletive*] son of a bitch. Hereafter, when the *Wall Street Journal* comes crawling to us for a sound bite, we'll be giving our best stories and mentor's hugs to the *Washington Post,* not to you")—but for the immediate occasion, "this" was clear enough.

For every writer who uses *this* and *these* to good effect, you will find myriad others who use these words as crutches, to prop up a lame sentence. More than two demonstrative pronouns per page is overdoing it. If, like many first-year college students, you use 6-10 of them per page of double-spaced text, you're an addict—a chronic avoider of the specific phrase. Make it a habit, when revising, to substitute a concrete image or idea for every "this" and "these" in your preceding draft. The changes will add power and interest to your prose:

• First draft (C+): *In this poem by Howard Nemerov there are two young lovers. They are confronted by a reminder of their mortality. This memento mori appears in the form of a dead fish. This fish seems to grin at these lovers as they stand and embrace on the beach.*

• As revised (A-): *In Howard Nemerov's poem, "The Goose Fish," two young lovers are confronted by a memento mori in the form of a dead fish, which seems to grin at them as they stand embracing on the beach.*

1.3.4. *Where and when?*

> *Costello*: The pitcher's name?
> *Abbott*: *Tomorrow.*
> *Costello*: You don't want to tell me today?
> *Abbott*:   I'm telling you now.
> *Costello*: Then go ahead.
> *Abbott*: *Tomorrow.*
> *Costello*: What time? [24]

1.3.4a. *When did it happen?*

Student writers of small ambition and no intellectual curiosity love such phrases as "a long time ago," "at the time," and "during the period when." (You have written: "At the time this novel was first published, women were not allowed to attend school." What your readers hear: *I have no clue when this novel was first published, but it was a long time ago, before my mother was born.*) If you don't know when something happened—when the Normans invaded England, when the Declaration of Independence was signed, when Bobby Kennedy was shot—then find out. Evasive phrases will only make your readers think you are no true writer, but just an ignorant doofus doing a homework assignment.

1.3.4b. *When was it thought?*

When quoting authors or authorities unfamiliar to your readers, don't just say who's speaking, identify the historical moment in which they spoke. If you are writing about recent critical commentary on *Paradise Lost*, or about the influence of organized crime on the Russian economy, or about race relations in Mississippi, don't suddenly interject a quotation from a 19th century commentator without signaling the change in historical context. When writing about literature, don't slip back and forth between 21st century America and 14th or 17th century Britain. Give us a trip through history if you like, or a trip around the world, but don't give us whiplash. Transporting your reader instantaneously through time and space can be disconcerting, even if your text is science fiction.

1.3.4c. *Where did you get your information?*

Always attribute (1.3.2g). And be no less specific about where your authorities, or adversaries, or victims, truly said that which you have ascribed to them. In a news story or speech or op-ed piece, you may tell us who said what and let it go at that: if a question arises, or a libel suit, you have your reporter's notebook for documentation. For academic writing, always specify where you found the cited information or commentary. Protect your inside sources if you must, but do not mystify them, as when George W. Bush professes to obtain material for his political speeches by consulting with dead statesmen and living cows:

• *Sometimes there are a couple of cows waiting for me. You know, when I first got back from Washington, it seemed like the cows were talking back. But now that I've spent some time in Crawford, [Texas,] they're just cows. [...] We want those objections heard, of course—every citizen needs to hear a voice.* (George W. Bush.) [25]

• *Sometimes Churchill will talk back, sometimes he won't, depending upon the stress of the moment, but he is a constant reminder of what a great leader is like.* (George W. Bush.) [26]

In no academic discipline—neither in the social sciences, nor in the "hard" sciences, nor in the arts and humanities, not even in an essay for your phys. ed. class—are you exempt from the obligatory bibliography or "Works Cited" page in which every source is accurately identified.

1.3.5. *Why and how?*

> Costello: The left fielder's name?
> Abbott: Why.
> Costello: I don't know, I just thought I'd ask you.
> Abbott: Well, I just thought I'd tell you. [27]

1.3.5a. *How did it happen? What does it mean?*

Do you have a story to report? Unless you're a news correspondent, don't just say what happened; provide some insight, or a chewable thought. Let your reported details show how and why events fell out as they did. An elderly couple has died on the eve of their fiftieth wedding anniversary—was it from carbon monoxide poisoning? heatstroke? sleeping pills? If fumes killed them, was a defective furnace to blame? car exhaust? No need to editorialize. Just show how events happened to fall out as they did, without getting preachy about why everyone needs to install a carbon monoxide alarm.

1.3.5b. *Prove it.*

Have an argument to make? Don't just announce. Explain. Put some evidence on the table. "More research is necessary" and "Remains to be seen" are silly assertions. More research is always needed, and everything that has not yet happened remains to be seen:

• *We offer the [Republican] party as a big tent. How we do that, within the platform, the preamble to the platform, or whatnot, that remains to be seen. But that message will have to be articulated with great clarity.* (Dan Quayle.) [28]

When you are the speaker or writer, it is *your* job to articulate what ought to be seen, or thought, or done. Your audience cannot grasp a message that you are unwilling or unable to express.

   Another thing: don't expect us to take you at your word just because you consider yourself an expert, or because you hold a high office, or because you are *you*. "Because I'm the mother— that's why!" may work as a bumper sticker but it does not facilitate effective writing or persuasive public speaking:

• *I'm the commander. See, I don't need to explain. I do not need to explain why I say things. That's the interesting thing about being the president. Maybe somebody needs to explain to me why they say something, but I don't feel like I owe anybody an explanation.* (George W. Bush.) [29]

To win others to your side, state the facts, explain what they mean, and what we ought to do about it. Or at least be honest:

• *I'm also not very analytical. You know, I don't spend a lot of time thinking about myself, about why I do things.* (George W. Bush.) [30]

If you don't really know what you're talking about, some readers may be won over by simple candor. But the classroom instructor who grades your written work is probably not one of them.

1.4. BE CLEAR

1.4.1. Vision: *Think clearly.*

> *The world watches America. We're an influential nation, and*
> *everybody watches what we say. It's very important for the*
> *American president to mean what he says. That's why I*
> *understand that the enemy could misread what I say. That's*
> *why I try to be as clearly I can.*   —Pres. George W. Bush [1]

1.4.1a. *Clear the fog from your head.*

Whether your goal is to inform, explain, persuade, or merely entertain, clear thinking is the first step toward clear writing. Richard Nixon's signature phrase, "Let me make one thing perfectly clear," is a fine motto for the writer. This is not: "I hope you leave here and walk out and say, *What did he say?*" (George W. Bush).[2] Write as if your health, happiness, and eternal salvation all depend on the successful communication of one idea. If your mouth or printed page is full of mush, no one is obliged to pay attention. Before you speak, chew and swallow. Choose every word, construct every sentence, build every paragraph, in a manner that conveys exactly what you wish to say, without sludge. Writing without *specificity* will bore your readers. Writing without *clarity* will confuse them.

1.4.1b. *Consider the implications.*

A common source of audience confusion is that the speaker or writer has not made the words in his essay or script match the imprecise thought drifting about in his own brain. When Pat Brown, then governor of California, commented on the north coast flood, he described it as "the worst disaster in California since I was elected."[3] George W. Bush, recalling the 2000 election, observed: "There's no question that the minute I got elected, the storm clouds on the horizon were getting nearly directly overhead."[4] When our president announces that "The suicide bombings have increased. There are too many of them," and pledges to work "with both sides to bring the level of terror down to an acceptable level," he seems to imply that terrorist killings are fine so long as they do not get out of hand.[5] If he reports that a detained terror suspect, "a threat to the country," "is now off the streets, where he should be," the president seems to imply that the FBI should let the man get back to work as soon as possible.[6]

Confusing language indicates muddled thought:

• *For every fatal shooting, there were roughly three non-fatal shootings. And, folks, this is unacceptable in America. It's just unacceptable. And we're going to do something about it.* (George W. Bush.) [7]

• *We are concerned about AIDS inside our White House—make no mistake about it. [...] You know, hopefully, condoms will work, but it hasn't worked.* (George W. Bush.) [8]

• *My pro-life position is I believe there's life. It's not necessarily based in religion. I think there's a life there, therefore the notion of life, liberty and pursuit of happiness. [...] I would have said yes to abortion if only it was right. I mean, yeah, it's right. Well, no, it's not right. That's why I said no to it.* (George W. Bush) [9]

1.4.1c. *Be rational.*

Check and double-check your sentence logic. In the words of Richard Guindon, "Writing is nature's way of letting you know how sloppy your thinking is."[10] If your thinking is confused or tautological, fix it:

• *I have made good judgments in the past. I have made good judgments in the future.* (Dan Quayle.)[11]

• *The question is whether we're going forward to tomorrow or whether we're going to go past—to the back! The future will be better tomorrow. [...] We don't want to go back to tomorrow, we want to go forward.* (Dan Quayle.) [12]

• *It's important to think beyond the old days of when we had the concept that if we blew each other up, the world would be safe. [...W]e shouldn't be locked into a Cold War mentality that says we keep the peace by blowing each other up. In my attitude, that's old, that's tired, that's stale.* (George W. Bush.) [13]

• *[T]here's been tremendous death and destruction because killers kill.* (George W. Bush.) [14]

• *We are making the right decisions to bring the solution to an end. [...] I hope we get to the bottom of the answer. It's what I'm interested to know.* (George W. Bush.) [15]

• *I promise you I will listen to what has been said here, even though I wasn't here.* (George W. Bush.) [16]

Avoid imprecision when expressing cause and effect:

• *I believe we are on an irreversible trend toward more freedom and democracy—but that could change.* (Dan Quayle.) [17]

• *We are ready for any unforeseen event that may or may not occur.* (Dan Quayle.) [18]

1.4.1d. *Avoid absolute or sweeping statements.*

Be especially cautious with statements on the model, *A is not true; only B is true.* Such remarks usually reduce or falsify the complexity of a problem:

• *I am not part of the problem. I am a Republican.* (Dan Quayle.) [19]
• *There's no such thing as being too closely aligned with the oil industry in West Texas.* (George W. Bush.) [20]

Statements of the "Not A, but rather B" variety should usually be recast:

• Unclear: *Speaking as a man, it is not a women's issue. Us men are tired of losing our women.* (Dan Quayle, on whether breast cancer is an issue for men or women.) [21]
• More clear, but self-centered: *I speak as a man when I say that breast cancer is not a women's issue. We men have been losing our women to that disease and, frankly, we're tired of it.*
• Both clear and accurate: *Breast cancer is a concern for all thoughtful citizens.*

"*No doubt*" is a phrase to be used with caution: everything in life is subject to doubt except death and taxes. "Undoubtably" is not to be used at all: the word you're looking for is *undoubtedly.* But even on those rare occasions when there is truly no room for doubt, take care not to say the opposite of what you intend:

• George W. Bush, speaking of his War on Terror: *There's no doubt in my mind, not one doubt in my mind, that we will fail.*[22]

• George W. Bush, speaking of his War on Iraq: *There's no doubt in my mind that we should allow the world's worst leaders to hold America hostage, to threaten our peace, to threaten our friends and allies with the world's worst weapons.*[23]

1.4.1e. *Don't crisscross parallel structure.*

A sentence or set of ideas has *parallel structure* if the same pattern is used to show that two or more ideas have comparable importance or meaning:

•*Fourscore and seven years ago our fathers brought forth on this continent a new nation, [1a] conceived in liberty and [1b] dedicated to the proposition that all men are created equal. Now we are engaged in a great civil war, testing whether [2a] that nation or [2b] any nation [3a] so conceived and [3b] so dedicated can long endure.... The world will [4a] little note, nor [4b] long remember, [5a] what we say here, but it can never forget [5b] what they did here....* (Abraham Lincoln.)[24]

Parallel structure (both *A* and *B*; either *C* or *D;* neither *E* nor *F*) is a trap for the unwary:

• *I want to thank my friend, Senator Bill Frist, for joining us today. He married a Texas girl, I want you to know—Karen is with us—a west Texas girl, just like me.* (George W. Bush.) [25]

• *We must have the attitude that every child in America—regardless of where they're raised, or how they're born—can learn.* (George W. Bush.) [26]

• *[I]f you want to hurt people and help people in pain, the best way to do so is to call upon the great strength of the country.* (George W. Bush.) [27]

• *As governor of Texas, I have set high standards for our public schools, and I have met those standards.* (George W. Bush.) [28]

• *We're in for a long struggle. I think Texans understand that, and so do Americans.* (George W. Bush.) [29]

• *We live in a culture of moral indifference, where movies and videos glamorize violence, and tolerance is touted as a great virtue.* (George W. Bush.) [30]

• *If I'm the president, we're going to have emergency-room care, we're going to have gag orders.* (George W. Bush.) [31]

• *I am here to make an announcement that this Thursday, ticket counters and airplanes will fly out of Ronald Reagan Airport.* (George W. Bush.) [32]

• *We understand that there's been years of hatred and distrust, and we'll continue to keep the process moving forward.* (George W. Bush.)[33]

• *It's in our country's interests to find those who would do harm to us and get them out of harm's way. [...] They're hard-nosed killers, and we will work with the Iraqis to secure their future.* (George W. Bush.)[34]

• *Our enemies are innovative and resourceful, and so are we. They never stop thinking about new ways to harm our country and our people, and neither do we. [...] We will stand up for terror. We will stand up for freedom.* (George W. Bush.) [35]

Negative parallel structures (*neither-nor, not this nor that*) are a special source of trouble:

• *My friends, no matter how rough the road may be, we can and we will never, never surrender to what is right.* (Dan Quayle.) [36]

• *The most important job is not to be governor, or first lady in my case.* (George W. Bush.) [37]

• *First, we would not accept a treaty that would not have been ratified, nor a treaty that I thought made sense for the country.* (George W. Bush.) [38]

• *I can assure you we won't be putting money into a society which is not transparent and corrupt. And I suspect other countries won't, either.* (George W. Bush.) [39]

Be careful also with the logic of a parallel series, lest the sequence contain a discordant element: *With Dr. Bob's professional care you may expect a full periodontal evaluation; a brighter, healthier smile; and dental emergencies.* If one car in a series hops off the track, your intended meaning will miscarry:

• *I hope I stand for anti-bigotry, anti-Semitism, anti-racism. This is what drives me.* (George H. W. Bush.) [40]

• *If you're sick and tired of the politics of cynicism and polls and principles, come and join this campaign.* (George W. Bush, running for president.) [41]

• *It's amazing I won. I was running against peace, prosperity, and incumbency.* (George W. Bush, after the election.) [42]

• *Free nations are peaceful nations. Free nations don't attack each other. Free nations don't develop weapons of mass destruction.* (George W. Bush.) [43]

• *This is still a dangerous world. It's a world of madmen and uncertainty and potential mental losses.* (George W. Bush.) [44]

• *We will make sure our troops have all that is necessary to complete their mission. That's why I went to the Congress last September and proposed fundamental supplemental funding, which is money for armor, and body parts, and ammunition, and fuel.* (George W. Bush.)[45]

1.4.2. **Directness:** *Say it in plain English.*

> Everything should be made as simple as possible, but not simpler.
> —Albert Einstein[46]

1.4.2a. *Eschew obfuscation.*

Or rather: speak and write plainly. Complex ideas can demand difficult expression, but verbal fog will slow your readers down without letting them see where you are taking them. Your readers should not require four-wheel drive to push through the muck and rubble.

No matter whether you are writing a college essay, a letter of recommendation, or directions to your house, avoid high-sounding twaddle:

- Bad writing: *I have those hopes of her good that her education promises her dispositions she inherits, which makes fair gifts fairer. For where an unclean mind carries virtuous qualities, there commendations go with pity. They are virtues and traitors, too. In her they are the better for their simpleness. She derives her honesty, and achieves her goodness.* (William Shakespeare.) [47]
- Clear and direct: *Helena is a gifted young woman whose refined education highlights her natural goodness.*

1.4.2b. *Use familiar words.*

"Who is responsible," asked the attorney, "for having excavated this unnecessary subterranean conduit?"

"Don't look at us," said the workmen. "We only dug the ditch."

Some writers (not smart ones) think they will sound smart if they use fancy words. Resist the temptation to use an exotic word where a familiar one will do, or a long one where a short one will do. "Walk," don't *perambulate*. Never *osculate* if you can "kiss." "Spit" if you must, but do not *expectorate*. Don't tell your priest that you have *masticated* if you have only "chewed." It is best to write and speak without obscurity even if you consider yourself a German philosopher.

1.4.2c. *Explain unfamiliar abbreviations.*

Use acronyms, abbreviations, and clipped phrasing infrequently, and accurately. Your audience may otherwise be confused, as when George W. Bush alleged that a Democratic tax plan would "require numerous IRA agents," evidently intending the Internal Revenue Service (IRS) and not agents of the Irish Republican Army,[48] or when he spelled out "Ob-Gyns" to denote obstetricians and gynecologists faced with high insurance premiums for malpractice:

Too many good docs are getting out of the business. Too many O-B-G-Y-Ns aren't able to practice their love with women all across this country.[49]

The first time you mention an organization, spell it out, supplying the acronym in parenthesis; after which, it is okay to use the acronym:

- Bad: *FEMA really is the first voice oftentimes that someone whose lives have been turned upside down hears from.* (George W. Bush.) [50]

- Good: *The Federal Emergency Management Agency (FEMA) responds quickly to a disaster, to assist those whose lives have been disrupted by flood, fire, or storm.*

If there will be no second reference to the name, omit the acronym altogether. (If you don't know an *acronym* from an *abbreviation*, see 3.1, A Pretty Good Guide to Hard Words.)

1.4.2d. *He said, she said.*

"Said" is a good word, and one that bears repeating. Use it. Be cautious with such replacement words as *argued, asserted, claimed, commented, concluded, declared, disclosed, pointed out,* and *revealed.* Such verbs have subtly different meanings that must be respected. "She pointed out" implies that you agree with the speaker and are taking sides. So, too, for "she observed" or "noted that." "He claimed" or "he opined" implies that you are skeptical. "He concluded" may indicate that your source had nothing else to say on the subject.

Do not make any of your fictional characters or quoted sources "laugh" or "retort" or "intimate" or "frown" their words. "'Come back to bed,' she giggled"; "'Not right now,' he smoked," is bad writing.

1.4.2e. *Write straightforwardly.*

Convoluted: "Of government the properties to unfold would seem in me to affect speech and discourse." [51] Straightforward: "A political science lecture, coming from me, would seem pretentious." Unless you're a poet straining for a rhyme, the main idea of each main clause will appear in the usual order: 1. subject; 2. action verb; 3. object or descriptive phrase. "High above the Iraqi oilfields flew a U2 spy plane, as its crew of Halliburton engineers for weapons of mass destruction searched" is not poetry, it's mumbo-jumbo. Some people screw up their faces when sitting for a photograph. Others screw up their language when sitting to write. Relax. A plain, natural style is best.

1.4.3. Reception: *Broadcast a clear signal.*

> *The purpose of writing is to inflate weak ideas, obscure pure*
> *reasoning, and inhibit clarity. With a little practice, writing*
> *can be an intimidating and impenetrable fog.*
>
> —Bill Watterson, *Calvin and Hobbes*[52]

1.4.3a. *Be clear and consistent in your tone of voice.*

Your readers will be confused, or doubtful of your sincerity and good sense, if you mix gravity with levity, business with bedroom politics, anger with humor, eloquence and vulgarity, glibness with catastrophe: George W. Bush on the golf course, addressing the free world just before teeing off: "I call upon all nations to do everything they can to stop these terrorist killers. Thank you. Now watch this drive."[53]

1.4.3b. *Keep your tongue out of your cheek.*

If your writing is full of static, your audience will change channels. You may be the world's wittiest talker, but unless you have an unusually deft sense of irony, avoid sarcasm when sitting down to write. Irony is often lost on the young, as on dull-witted adults. Your sarcastic quips may get a laugh in face-to-face banter, but sarcasm on the printed page will look stupid to readers who don't catch your irony, and like smug condescension to those who do:

- Smug: *People do not deserve good writing, they are so pleased with bad.* (Ralph Waldo Emerson.) [54]

- Smug: *The fellow who thinks he knows it all is especially annoying to those of us who do.* (Harold Coffin.) [55]

- Smug: *I'm not really a good teacher because I don't really want to encourage young writers. Keep them down and out and silent is my motto.* (John Updike.) [56]

- Point unclear: *Business conventions are important because they demonstrate how many people a company can operate without.*

Sarcasm works best in fictional dialogue or comic writing, where the context clarifies the writer's satirical intent. My epigraph above, from the comic strip, *Calvin and Hobbes*, would be less clear if it were to appear in a textbook for Philosophy 101.

If you do not care at all about a problem, and could not possibly care less, then do not say that you could. In the latter twentieth century, somewhere in America, some sarcastic fellow must have said, "Like I could care less," meaning: "Frankly, I don't give a damn.

I could not care less." The sarcasm caught on, becoming proverbial across North America: "I could care less." Today, an entire generation of young people is confused about how to express their apathy or indifference. (I could care less, or I would not have mentioned it.)

1.4.4. *Completeness: Finish each thought.*

> How 'bout *them* transparent dangling carrots!
> —Alanis Morisette

1.4.4a. *Make your sticks and carrots visible.*

In 2002, when President George W. Bush issued his "clear statement of purpose" to Iraq, saying, "You disarm, or we will!" his intended meaning was: "Disarm voluntarily, or we shall invade your country," *not*: "The United States will disarm if you do not."[57] Some years ago, during a baseball game at Ebbets Field, New York, the fans began using the top of the outfield fence for their doffed shirts and jackets. The voice of the park announcer, Ted Rikards, came over the intercoms: "Would the fans along the outfield please remove their clothes!" The simple addition of one phrase—"from the outfield fence"— could have prevented the ensuing mayhem as fans along the outfield made a jolly effort to comply.

Omit no words whose absence may change or confuse your intended meaning:

• *It would be a mistake for the United States Senate to allow any kind of human cloning to come out of that chamber* [i.e., any kind of bill that permits human cloning]. (George W. Bush.) [58]

• *My administration has been calling upon all the leaders in the Middle East to do everything they can to stop the violence, to tell the different parties involved that peace will never happen* [i.e., that lasting peace will not happen without an immediate ceasefire]. (George W. Bush.) [59]

• *There's no cave deep enough for America, or dark enough to hide* [i.e., Osama bin Laden has no cave so deep and dark that American cannot find him]. (George W. Bush).[60]

1.4.4b. *Assist dangling comparisons.*

Incomplete comparisons are an even bigger problem. (That last was a bad sentence—"even bigger" than what?) Not without reason do advertisers love such statements as "Two more scoops" or "faster acting" or "gets clothes cleaner." Marketing research indicates that gullible consumers are disinclined to ask, More scoops than what or when? Faster than before? Faster than a competing product?

Cleaner than *Tide*? Cleaner than without ever washing my clothes at all? Say precisely what you mean:

- Vague: *Truck drivers kill more deer than hunters.*
- Better: *Truck drivers kill more deer than hunters do.*
- Or perhaps: *More deer than hunters are killed by truck drivers.*

- Vague: *The U.S. military has developed smarter weapons.*
- Better: *The U.S. military has developed "smarter" weapons than those used during the Second Iraq War.*

- Or perhaps: *The U.S. military has developed weapons smarter than the average American voter. At least the bombs can locate Iraq.*

1.4.4c. *Assist dangling verbs:*

No matter where your verbs appear in a sentence, make clear what subject performs the action:

- Unclear: *So as not to fall into the trash, I put your wallet on the dresser.*
- Clear: *I set your wallet on the dresser lest it fall into the trash.*

Dangling or inconsistent verb phrases will often pass unnoticed by the reader—but when spotted, they're funny, such as the bottle label, "SHAKE BEFORE USING," or the road sign, "STOP WHEN FLASHING."

The English *participle* is a versatile tool for writers, whether in present or past tense (*fighting, fought, loving, loved, finding, found*). Participial phrases can lend variety to your sentence structure, but therein lies a danger. If a sentence starts with a participle, then the subject of the sentence is also the subject of the participle. Neglect of this simple rule will lead to confusion about who's doing what to whom:

- *Playing ball in the backyard, Mary's rosebush caught Alfred's eye.*
- *Behaving indecently in a movie theater, a Sarasota police officer arrested Mr. Herman.*

In a sentence beginning with a participial phrase, the subject who performs the main action of the sentence is also responsible for the participle:

- Unclear: *Swimming up Oregon's Chetco River, Billy Bob caught four salmon in just twenty minutes.*
- Better: *Fishing last week in Oregon, Billy Bob pulled four salmon from the Chetco River in just twenty minutes.*

1.4.4d. *Clarify vague pronoun reference.*

Pronouns—especially *it/its, he/him/his, she/her/hers*, and *they/them/theirs*—are a frequent source of trouble:

- Unclear: *Before giving the baby its milk, heat it in the microwave oven.*
- Better: *Heat the milk in the microwave for thirty seconds before you give the baby her bottle.*

- Unclear: *The truth of that matter is, if you listen carefully, Saddam would still be in power if he were the president of the United States, and the world would be a lot better off.* (George W. Bush.) [61]
- Clear: *Saddam [Hussein] would still be in power [in Iraq] if he [my Democratic opponent, John Kerry] were the president of the United States, and the world would be a lot better off.*

They. Never use "they" as a vague, all-purpose term for those with whom you may disagree, such as your parents, teachers, government, senior management, art critics, terrorists, or the kids who egged your car:

- *When I was coming up, it was a dangerous world, and we knew exactly who 'they' were. It was us vs. them, and it was clear who them was. Today, we are not so sure who the 'they' are, but we know they're there.* (George W. Bush.) [62]

1.4.5. **Precision:** *Beware unwanted ambiguity.*

"Then you should say what you mean," the March Hare went on.

"I do," Alice hastily replied; "at least—at least I mean what I say—that's the same thing, you know."

"Not the same thing a bit!" said the Hatter. "You might just as well say that 'I see what I eat' is the same thing as 'I eat what I see'!"

"You might just as well say," added the Dormouse, who seemed to be talking in his sleep, "that 'I breathe when I sleep' is the same thing as 'I sleep when I breathe'!"   —Lewis Carroll, *Alice's Adventures in Wonderland*[63]

1.4.5a. *Put your words in order.*

As Groucho Marx observed, the meaning of an English sentence is conditioned by word order: "One morning I shot an elephant in my pajamas. How he got in my pajamas I don't know."[64] When the president says, "We hold dear what our Declaration of Independence says, that all have got *uninalienable rights endowed by a Creator*," his revision of the original text imagines that the Creator's endowment goes to "uninalienable rights," not to human beings.[65] When revising, look for careless word order and shuffle the phrases to improve clarity:

- Unclear (from a notice to visitors at a Russian Orthodox Monastery): *You are welcome to visit the cemetery where Russian composers, artists and writers are buried daily except Thursday.*
- Improved: *Every day but Thursday, you may visit the cemetery, where Russian composers, artists, and writers are buried.*

- Unclear: *A police officer has been shot in Brooklyn for the second time in less than a week.*
- Improved: *For the second time in less than a week, a Brooklyn police officer has been shot.*

- Unclear: *My wife had a frightening accident in the south parking lot, and she's pregnant.*
- Improved: *My pregnant wife had a frightening collision in the south parking lot.*

- Unclear: *Include your children when baking cookies.*
- Improved: *Have fun baking cookies with your children.*

1.4.5b. *Move or recast a misleading phrase.*

Sometimes a sentence whose grammar is perfectly correct may contain within it a distracting sequence of words that appears to mean something quite contrary until the reader has paused to re-read the sentence. The golf great, Arnold Palmer, tells the story of having a bad day on the green, years ago, when the television announcer made matters worse with a thoughtless remark: "Arnie, usually a great putter, seems to be having trouble with his long putt; he has had no trouble dropping his shorts."[66] "False scent" or "faulty telescoping" is the term that teachers and editors use for this phenomenon (i.e., for the misleading phrase, not for dropped shorts):

- Unclear: *Ms. Havisham asked her houseboy, Pip, to remove and clean her drawers in the kitchen.*
- Clear: *Ms. Havisham asked her houseboy, Pip, to remove and clean the kitchen drawers.*

- Unclear: *We have a customer by the balls in the toy department who needs help.*
- Clear: *By the balls in the toy department is a customer who needs help.*

A special caveat for reporters and poets: journalists and poets must take special care to weed out misleading phrases. The column-format of newsprint and of verse greatly multiplies the opportunity for unintended laugh lines to appear in the published text.

1.4.5c. *For words that have more than one meaning, think twice.*

Always signal, with an auxiliary verb if necessary, whether *read* is in the past or present tense (*Unclear:* "Homer and Bart read the chalkboard"). Will your "biannual" conference be held *every two years* or *twice a year*? Does your "MP" stand for a *Member of Parliament* or for *Military Police*? Make clear whether a "child killer" is a *killer of children* or a *juvenile delinquent.* Pause before describing Betsy Ross as a "sewer." The mistakes in your rough draft may indeed be obvious "boners" but you are well advised to find a different word for them before asking your secretary to take remedial action whenever she spots one.

Even little words can be mis-taken, as when George H. W. Bush's vice president, Dan Quayle, told the press that he and his wife Marilyn were asked to walk in front of the Reagans: "I'm not used to going in front of President Reagan," said the new vice president, "so we went out behind the Bushes."[67] Prepositions (*by, on, for*) are a frequent source of unwanted ambiguity: "Charles Wilson, 62, was thrown from the car on impact; his mangled body was found by a flock of sheep").

Your readers may be thrown off balance by something as trivial as a capital letter. Many ordinary words are also the proper names of people or places, but with a different pronunciation (*askew/Askew, begin/Begin, herb/Herb, job/Job, levy/Levy, mobile/Mobile, natal/ Natal, nice/Nice, polish/ Polish, ravel/Ravel*). When writing of a person or place whose name is a homonym, avoid starting a sentence ambiguously: "Begin endorsed the new peace plan." "Polish shoes generally cost less than Italian footwear."

1.4.5d. *When revising, disambiguate.*

Don't just say what you mean. Avoid saying what you don't mean. Innocent statements, poorly phrased, may carry unwelcome connotations. A church bulletin advises, "Don't let anxiety destroy you in a time of crisis—let Rev. Jimmy help." A hotel chain's Staff Handbook warns that "Kitchen-help must eat no more than two people at a time." A newspaper reports that "When the mating of pandas failed for the third time, veterinarians took over."

Titles and captions are especially vulnerable to unwanted ambiguity, as in these history-making and long-remembered newspaper headlines:

- MACARTHUR FLIES BACK TO FRONT
- HEAD OF IRAQ SEEKING ARMS
- UPTURNS MAY INDICATE SOME BOTTOMS TOUCHED

When phrase-tightening, take care that you do not introduce unwanted ambiguities:

- Clear: *The Testis Human Sperm Bank opened Monday. Semen samples were collected from a dozen men and then frozen in a stainless steel vault.*
- Unclear: *The Testis Human Sperm Bank opened Monday with semen samples from a dozen men frozen in a stainless steel vault.*

The second version, though shorter, raises the question, How does a guy who is frozen stiff donate semen? Nor will it work to write, "with semen samples in a stainless steel vault taken from a dozen men," because that would imply that the twelve men lost control of a vault containing their donated sperm.

Vice President Dan Quayle is perhaps best remembered for his comment on the motto of the United Negro College fund, "A mind is a terrible thing to waste." Mr. Quayle agreed: "What a waste it is to lose one's mind—or not to *have* a mind, is being very wasteful. How true that is!"—as if to say, *How wasteful it is to go insane! or not to have any mind at all—trust me!* [68] But the academic motto is itself badly phrased, for it denotes the mind of a college-bound African-American as "a terrible thing." The thought can be stated more clearly, *A human mind, uneducated, is a terrible loss.* George W. Bush expressed a similar thought, somewhat more eloquently though no less ambiguously, when addressing the Hispanic Scholarship Fund Institute: "If a person doesn't have the capacity that we all want that person to have, I suspect hope is in the far distant future, if at all"— which appears to mean, *If a Hispanic doesn't have the particular skills we're looking for, then the poor fellow is out of luck.* [69]

When revising, keep in mind that some readers, whether through incompetence or perversity, will take you the wrong way, no matter how hard you try to be clear. There exists a certain kind of driver who, when sees the road sign,

SLOW
CHILDREN

merely shakes his head, and exclaims "How sad!" without slowing down. A subway commuter, coming to the sign, "Pets must be carried on escalator," may turn around because she has left her cat at home. Titles, captions, and headlines are especially vulnerable to unintended ambiguity. Give your readers no opportunity to mistake your intended meaning.

1.5. BE CONCISE

1.5.1. Brevity: *Say it in few.*

> *"Brevity is the soul of wit."*
> —Garrulous Polonius

1.5.1a. *Don't just try to make it big.*

Confident writers concentrate on performance, not on length. If you are assigned an essay of 10,000 words, the worst possible strategy is to stretch it out with pointless repetition, or to add filler of no substance, like cotton bombast to a codpiece. Playing with your fonts is another poor strategy. By switching from 12-point Times to 12-point Geneva, you can expand an essay of nine pages to more than twelve pages without adding a single word. And in case you were wondering: your teacher will not be fooled. The best way to write an essay of 10,000 words is to write an essay of 20,000 words and then trim it by half, omitting every unneeded phrase.

1.5.1b. *Be short and to the point.*

Whether it's an email note, a sales manual, or an epic poem, use no more words than you need to complete the job. Strunk and White put it this way: "Vigorous writing is concise. A sentence should contain no unnecessary words, a paragraph no unnecessary sentences, for the same reason that a drawing should have no unnecessary lines and a machine no unnecessary parts." [1] Say only what needs to be said (less is more). "Smoking kills" is a fine, direct sentence; the statement is unimproved by the anti-smoking spokesperson, Brooke Shields, who has explained that "Smoking kills, and if you're killed, you've lost a very important part of your life." [2]

Your readers will be confused, not impressed, by convoluted clauses and branching syntax. Vary the length, but let most of your statements be sportscars, not stretch limos, or the traffic will suffer for it.

• Stringy: *With a stringy construction you may be understood well enough, and even when your prose is glutted with unnecessary ands and buts, but it is better just to begin a new sentence than to go on and on with the old one.*

• Improved: *Avoid stringy construction. Take out unneeded* and*s*. *Begin a new sentence.*

• Too long: *At times a writer may indulge himself with a long sentence, but he will make sure there are no folds in it, no vaguenesses, no parenthetical interruptions of its view as a whole; when he has done with it, it won't be a sea serpent with half of its arches under the water; it will be a torch-light procession.* (Mark Twain.)
• Improved: *When you indulge in a long sentence, let it have no folds, no vagueness, no distracting interruptions. Let it be a torchlight procession, not a sea serpent with half of its arches under water.*

As illustrated by the work of every great writer, long sentences can be clear and elegant, provided that each part snaps neatly into place, but that is easier said than done. Short is better.

1.5.1c. *Avoid excessive quotation.*

Say it in your own words. Inexperienced writers, or those without confidence, tend to glut their work with quotations. Excessive quotation will not make your writing more spicy, it will make your prose less digestible. Quote directly only when you need to reproduce another writer's exact words. Thoughtful paraphrase (with credit to your source) is concise and effective. Lengthy quotations will distract or bore your reader while taking up valuable space that you should use to develop your own material.

In news writing, quotation of sources and witnesses lends a personal touch, but quotes should be short, verbatim, and to the point: sound bites, not a pie-eating contest.

In expository writing as for a critical essay in a literature course, frequent quotation is necessary: you can't just talk *about* the text, you must *use* it, incorporating bits of the text (both quotes and paraphrases) within your discussion. Remember the English teacher's motto—"Stay close to the text" —but keep your quoted extracts brief and pointed, resorting to longer, block quotations only when you cannot find a convenient way to carve the quoted text into bite-sized chunks.

1.5.1d. *Know when to quit.*

Voltaire once remarked that "The best way to be boring is to leave nothing out."[3] Like Shakespeare's Polonius, Voltaire too often neglected his own advice. Follow a straight line from one part of your argument to the next. Waste no time moving from here to there. When we reach your conclusion we don't want to come out by the same door we went in unless we have something to show for it. Don't expect a merry band of loyal readers to keep you company as you go a-hunting all night through the dark woods. Just take aim, shoot the raccoon, and go home. Here's how:

1.5.2. **Compression: the <Delete> key is your friend**.

> *Verbosity leads to unclear, inarticulate things.*
> —Vice President Dan Quayle [4]

1.5.2a. *If it goes without saying, let it go without saying it.*

Statements like these cause schoolteachers and university professors to take early retirement, or an antidepressant, or both:

• *First, let me make it very clear, poor people aren't necessarily killers. Just because you happen to be not rich doesn't mean you're willing to kill.* (George W. Bush.) [5]

• *It's very important for folks to understand that when there's more trade, there's more commerce. [...] More and more of our imports come from overseas.* (George W. Bush). [6]

• *I think we agree, the past is over.* (George W. Bush.) [7]

Keep moving forward. Every statement, every phrase, should provide new information, or a fresh image or idea. Do not squander paper, ink, and the reader's goodwill on truisms: "War is violent." "People may disagree about abortion." "Men and women will never be the same." "Shakespeare's *Hamlet* can be interpreted in many ways." (As Horatio quips to Prince Hamlet, "There needs no ghost, my lord, come from the grave / To tell us this" [*Ham.* 1.5.124-5].) Do not insult your audience or waste their time by stating the obvious:

• *Hawaii is a unique state. It is a small state. It is a state that is by itself. It is different from the other forty-nine states. Well, all states are different, but it's got a particularly unique situation. [...] Hawaii has always been a very pivotal role in the Pacific. It is in the Pacific. It is a part of the United States that is an island, that is right here.* (Vice President Dan Quayle, addressing the people of Hawaii.) [8]

When revising your work, search for throwaway sentences, and throw them away. I cannot overemphasize this point. (That was a throwaway sentence.) It goes without saying that pointless writing is tedious. (So was that one.)

1.5.2b. *Stop drumming.*

Drumbeat repetition of the same few words not only violates the first commandment (*Be Interesting*), it also generates wordiness:

- Repetitious: *The California crunch really is the result of not enough power-generating plants and then not enough power to power the power of generating plants.* (George W. Bush.) [9]
- Better: *California had too few power-generating plants to forestall an energy crisis.*

- Repetitious: *It's important for all of us in Washington to stay in touch with the values of the heartland, because they're values that really are unique: it basically says that values, a values system of basic, inherent values, that override politics and different demographies and different religions.* (George W. Bush.) [10]
- Better: *Let those of us in Washington remember that our political and religious disputes must be informed by the values of the American heartland.*

- Repetitious: *There's nothing more deep than recognizing Israel's right to exist. That's the most deep thought of all. [...] I can't think of anything more deep than that right.* (George W. Bush.)[11]
- Better: *My administration is deeply committed to Israel's right to exist.*

1.5.2c. *Omit redundant meanings.*

If the president says that "People shouldn't read, into *venue locations*, someone's heart" (in defense of his decision to speak at a former slave plantation), he may mean, "Don't judge my heart by the places [venues] where I choose to speak." [12]

Verbose speakers and writers can turn any word or phrase into a pointless repetition, and often do: "first of all," "and also," "advance planning," "as a general rule," "close proximity," "personal beliefs," "consensus of opinion," "different alternative," "the reason why," "the reason is because," "the reason why is because," "true facts," "very unique," "single most," "yellow-colored," "end result," and a thousand more.

The English word, *tautology*, comes from the Greek words *tauto* (the same) and *logos* (saying) and it means, simply, a saying of the same thing. Learn to spot and line out needless repetition. To ask for a "PIN number" is to ask for a "Personal Identification Number number." To speak of the "HIV virus" is to speak of the "Human Immunodeficiency Virus virus." To write "Please R.S.V.P." is to say, *Please respond if you will, please.* An "ATM machine" is an "Automated Teller Machine machine." An "IRA account" is an Individual Retirement Account account."

Tautological repetitions in speech and writing indicate foggy thinking:

• *My viewpoint is that it's more of a choice than a biological situation. I think it is a wrong choice. It is a wrong. It is a wrong choice. I do believe in most cases it certainly is a choice.* (V.P. Dan Quayle on homosexuality.) [13]

• *I hope the ambitious realize that they are more likely to succeed with success as opposed to failure.* (George W. Bush.) [14]

• *I'm sure there is going to be moments when we don't agree 100% of the time [...] There's always a difference of opinion sometimes between the House and the Senate, whether it's at the state or federal level.* (George W. Bush.) [15]

• *Our nation must come together to unite.* (George W. Bush.) [16]

• *Now, by the way, "surplus" means a little money left over, otherwise it wouldn't be called a "surplus."* (George W. Bush.) [17]

If a novel or play has a theme, don't say that "the *theme continues throughout* the text" because that is what a theme *does*. For "State violence is a continuing theme throughout the entire film," try "State violence is a theme of the film"; or "State violence is a concern throughout the film"; or, better (because more active and direct), "The film explores state violence." Don't use the word *theme* just because it sounds academic. In fact, that may be a good reason not to use the word at all.

1.5.2d. *Sever conjoined twins.*

Do not salt and pepper, or rather, do not *pepper*, your work with familiar doublets where single words will do. Redundant doublets include such overworked phrases as *aid and abet, beck and call, bound and determined, clear and simple, each and every, fair and just, first and foremost, full and complete, hope and trust, intents and purposes, irrelevant and immaterial, null and void, safe and sound, sick and tired, sum and substance, why and wherefore.* If the president tells a liberated people, "Freedom is beautiful. And, you know, it'll take time to restore chaos and order," *order from chaos,* or *law and order,* may be the intended phrase.[18] (Incidentally: "Law and order," by legal convention, defies the laws of grammar and is treated as a singular noun: "Law and order was [not: *were*] Mussolini's top concern.")

1.5.2e. *Use few modifiers.*

Writing, when glutted with adjectives and adverbs, is boring or silly: "The tired brown basset hound rested his drooling jaw on the weathered porch, breathed a weary sigh, and fell sound asleep." "Flakes of dried spaghetti sauce clung to Santa's white beard as he bent over to give the sleeping Mrs. Claus a gentle, garlicky kiss." *Witness* and *audience* will often do for "eyewitness" and "live audience." "A member of the student body" is *a student.* For "the true facts," write *the facts*; for "comparatively few," try *few.* For "grave emergency," "real danger," and "terrible disaster," try *emergency, danger,* and *disaster.* For "I had a good, long talk bilaterally with Francois Mitterrand this morning," try simply, "This morning I spoke with Francois Mitterrand." [19] Nouns and verbs, well stitched together, need little or no embroidery.

1.5.2f. *Use few intensifiers.*

Avoid unnecessary intensifiers such as *a lot of, big, constantly, definite, definitely, frequently, often, particularly, quite, really,* and *serious.* The worst offender is "very," a word that had the life kicked out of it before you were even born. An interesting documentary is no better than a "very interesting" one, nor is good sex any less thrilling than "very good sex." It is no better compliment to say, "Ma'am, your crab cakes are very tasty," than to say, "Ma'am, your crab cakes are tasty." If emphasis is needed, exaggerate: "The sex was so good that even our neighbor had a cigarette afterward." Or: "Ma'am, I'd slay dragons for another one of your crab cakes."

Some writers, upon learning that *very* is a dead word, substitute "really" or "pretty" or "rather" or "extremely" or "extraordinarily." Others, in a vain attempt to sound erudite, omit "very" and "really" but saturate their language with such pompous intensifiers as *certainly, surely, indeed, to be sure* ("Surely, these intensifiers are overused, most especially in British prose. Such mannerisms are certainly unnecessary and, to be sure, tiresome indeed.")

Badly chosen nouns and verbs cannot be salvaged by using an intensifier as verbal duct tape. When you mean *very*, and need to say it, try *quite* (or, rarely, *notably* or *remarkably*). If an adjective is simply not strong enough to convey your meaning, choose another. For "very interesting," try *seductive*; for "very tempting," *irresistible;* for "very wrong," *naughty, sinful, wicked,* or *shamefully nice.*

Before you use an intensifier, search for a more specific or more colorful phrase:

- Fine: *It was cold yesterday in Chicago.*
- Unimproved: *It was very cold yesterday in Chicago.*

- Specific: *Chicagoans yesterday endured a wind chill factor of 60 degrees below zero.*
- Colorful: *It was so cold yesterday in Chicago that when a bicycle courier collided with a bus, he shattered into a thousand ice-splinters.*

- Fine: *Mike Kelly is a handsome lad.*
- Unimproved: *Mike Kelly is a very handsome lad.*
- Specific: *Mike Kelly is the handsomest lad in the parish.*
- Colorful: *Mike Kelly is so cute that a bishop would jump through a stained glass window just to get a second look.*

Avoid the use of *so* as an intensifier ("so sad") unless the thought is completed with a relative clause beginning in *that* ("so sad that I cried buckets"):

- Informal: *He's so fat!*
- Correct: *He's fat, and scant of breath.* (Queen Gertrude, on Prince Hamlet.) [20]
- More colorful: *He's so fat he won't go in the water unless Greenpeace protects him from the Danish whalers.*

1.5.2g. *Cut unneeded prepositions.*

Cut out, or rather *cut*, unneeded prepositions after verbs. Goods can be *bought* and *sold* without being "bought up" and "sold off." Committees and companies can be *headed* by the chair without being *headed up*. Regulations may be *loosened* or *tightened* without the "up." The kids can be *sent* to bed without being "sent off." Problems can be *faced*, and difficulties *met*, and opportunities *lost*, without being "faced up to" or "met up with" or "lost out on." Don't "continue on," just *continue*.

1.5.2h. *Cut the weasel words.*

Some qualifiers are weasel words that will allow you to C.Y.A. even if you are proved wrong: *it seems that, it appears that, arguably, basically, generally, mostly, possibly, probably, usually, various, a little.* When tempted to say, "somewhat of," bite your tongue. If "Old King Cole was somewhat of a merry old soul," just say that he "was a merry old soul" or "bipolar." Don't shilly-shally. State your position directly, and let your outraged readers write to say that they disagree.

The worst offenders, in speech and writing, are *kind of* and *sort of.* Such phrases can usually be omitted. Here below, the first "kind of" is correct; the others are not:

• *I love to bring people into the Oval Office, right around the corner from here, and say: "This is where I office, but I want you to know the office is always bigger than the person."* [...] *I always jest to people, the Oval Office is* the kind of *place where people stand outside. They're getting ready to come in and tell me what for, and they walk in and get overwhelmed in the atmosphere, and they say, "Man, you're looking pretty!"* [...] *In this job you've got a lot on your plate on a regular basis. You don't have much time to sit around and wander, lonely, in the Oval Office,* kind of *asking different portraits, "How do you think my standing will be?"* (George W. Bush, on his place in the White House, and in history.) [21]

• *I glance at the headlines just to* kind of *get a flavor for what's moving. I rarely read the stories, and get briefed by people who probably read the news themselves.* (George W. Bush, on his grasp of current events.) [22]

• *I* kind of *like ducking questions* [...] *just like my mother told me to do* (George W. Bush, on truthfulness.) [23]

Some writers love such terms as *adequate, enough, essentially, just, mere, only, pure, rather, relatively, sometimes, somewhat, exact, same,* popping out two or three limiters in the same breath where only one is desired, or none at all:

• Unclear: *[T]hat's* just *the nature of democracy. Sometimes* pure *politics enters into the rhetoric.* (George W. Bush.) [24]

• Better: *In any democracy, a leader's form of argument may be corrupted by unalloyed political scheming.*

• Or perhaps: *In a democracy, uncorrupted political idealism may sometimes invade the usual insincere, self-promotional speech-making.*

If a payment is "adequate enough," it is *adequate,* or *enough.* If your son-in-law is "just a mere caddy," he is *a mere caddy,* or *just a caddy.* In the sentence, "Unlike any other car, only the 1986 Yugo comes with a 10-week, one-thousand mile warranty," omit "only" or "Unlike any other car." If your sentence contains "on the same day that," try *on the day that.* For "at the same time that," try *when.* Never say or write, "the exact same." Try *the same,* or *identical,* or *an exact copy.* Do not say "same difference " for *no different* or "not hardly" when you mean either *no* or *hardly.*

If you must use qualifiers, use them correctly. If your reader is "absolutely breathless," and sits "literally glued to his seat," then your reader is a corpse in sticky underwear.

1.5.2i. *Don't just let it be: make it happen.*

When revising, you will find that almost every sentence in your first draft, even after the first round of cuts, can be condensed. You may easily improve a sentence on the model, *There is/are/was,* or *This is/are/was,* or *It is/was/has been* by deleting the lead phrase and recasting the sentence with an active verb:

- Wordy: *It has rarely been the case that a fired CEO has gone hungry.*
- Better: *Fired CEOs rarely go hungry.*

- Wordy: *There is one cookie-style, the mint chocolate, that accounts for 70% of the GSA's cookie sales.*
- Better: *Orders for mint chocolate account for 70% of GSA cookie sales.*

- Wordy: *There is a lot of speculation, and I guess there is going to continue to be a lot of speculation until the speculation ends.* (George W. Bush, on whether he would run for president.)[25]
- Better: *When I decide, I'll tell you.*

Such tedious phrases as these can be omitted altogether: *It has been found that, it has long been known that, it is evident that, it is interesting that, it has been noted that, it is well known that, it may be said that, it seems that, one thing is certain.*

Sentences on the model "It is X that does Y" or "X is a person who does Y" can be shortened to *X does Y:*

- Wordy: *Macbeth is a man who is very ambitious.*
- Better: *Macbeth desires to be king.*

- Wordy: *Dolly Parton, who was born in 1946, is a person who may be considered a baby-boomer.*
- Better: *Baby-boomer Dolly Parton was born in 1946.*

- Wordy: *Africa is a nation that suffers from incredible disease* (George W. Bush.) [26]
- Better: *AIDs has ravaged the continent of Africa.*

So, too, with verbs. "Make passive verbs, active." Does one really need to say that again? Yes: Quite apart from being more dull than the active voice (see 1.1.4b), the passive voice requires extra words. "Amber led the antiwar march" (active) is more concise than "The antiwar march was led by Amber" (passive).

1.5.2j. *Compress -ing verb phrases.*

Where possible, use the simple past, present, or future tense: "My son studies at Yale" (not "My son is studying at Yale"); "he drank" (not "he was drinking"); "Federal spending will bankrupt Social Security" (not "is going to bankrupt" or "will be bankrupting"). Unless followed by a destination ("I am going to Africa"), the verb phrase, *am [is, are] going to*, may be replaced by *will* or *shall*.

1.5.2k. *Recast wordy negatives.*

Positive assertions are more concise and forceful than negative ones:

* Wordy: *Do not put negative statements in the negative form.*
* Better: *Put even negative statements in a positive form.*

* Wordy: *Our students do not pay attention to the parking rules.*
* Better: *Our students ignore the parking rules.*

* Wordy: *One of the problems we have is that enough people can't find work in America.* (George W. Bush.) [27]
* Better: *Too many Americans are unable to find work.*

* Wordy: *"We got no better friends than Canada. They stand with us in this incredibly important Crusade to defend freedom"* (George W. Bush, at an Alaskan military base, on the way to South Korea, 16 Feb. 2002); *"We've not got no better friend than South Korea"* (17 Feb., in Seoul, addressing the South Korean press); *"We have had no better friend, and nobody provides such steadfast support, than the Japanese government"* (19 Feb., in Tokyo, Japan). [28]
* Better: *America's best friends, throughout my Iraq Crusade, have been Canada, South Korea, and Japan.*

It is rarely necessary to write *and also*, nor ever smart to say *also not*: "The kids are not going to church this morning and I'm also not going" should be recast: "Neither the kids nor I will attend church this morning," or, better yet, "The kids and I will skip church."

When you *must* use "not" in an English sentence, at least take care to straighten out your sentence logic. "Fluency in English," conceded President George H. W. Bush, "is not something that I'm often not accused of." [29] More clearly (and fluently): *Rarely am I praised for my fluency in English.* George Bush, Jr., has said: "I don't bring God into my life to, you know, kind of be a political person." [30] More clearly: *It is not for political expediency alone that I mention God in every speech.* For "This doesn't have nothing to do with reputation" (George W. Bush), write *This* [fill in the blank] *hurts no one's reputation.*[31] Virtually all negative statements can be expressed more succinctly without the use of *not*: for "are not able to" and "is not capable of," write *cannot*; for "do not like," *dislike*; for "not nice," *unkind;* for "do not have confidence in," *distrust*; for "does not work right, ever," *never works*; for "do not remember," *forget*.

1.5.21. *Suppress flatulent nouns.*

Avoid such overused and gaseous abstract terms as *problem, case, character, manner, nature, style, theme, parallel, position, factor, sector, purposes,* and *situation.* "The fact that" can usually be shortened to "That" (*That Alan Greenspan sneezed caused the markets to fall. That the Cubs are in first place comes as a happy surprise.*) For "Let me call your attention to the fact that we need—," try "We need—." For "The fact that I was absent," try "My absence."

- Wordy: *The fact that he relies on facts—says things that are not factual—are going to undermine his campaign.* (George W. Bush.) [32]
- Better: *My opponent's misreported facts will undermine his campaign.*

So, too, for "in terms of":

- Wordy: *Illegitimacy is something we should talk about in terms of not having it.* (V.P. Dan Quayle.) [33]
- Better: *Let's discuss how to reduce the number of babies born out of wedlock.*

For "agricultural and business sectors," write *agriculture and business.* An employee with "dependability problems" is *undependable.* A car with "reliability problems" *often breaks down.* A sponge "used for cleaning purposes" is one used *for cleaning,* or *to clean.* Men "of an ambitious character" are *ambitious.* An "oriental-style jacket" is an *oriental jacket.* For "in a careless manner," write *carelessly.* "Films of a violent nature" are *violent films.* A play having "the theme of adultery" is a play *about adultery.*

1.5.3. **Editorial zeal:** *Cut till it hurts.*

> *I have rewritten—often several times—every word I have ever published. My pencils outlast their erasers.*
> —Vladimir Nabokov [34]

After deleting every phrase you can do without, return to the top and cut another 10%. If your readers are interested in your story or argument, they will forgive your spotty punctuation and your spelling errors. But if your prose style is simply tedious—taking too many words to say what you've got to say— you risk losing our attention and sympathy. Abraham Lincoln once said of a lawyer, "That blower can compress the most words into the smallest ideas of any man I ever knew"—which is not high praise, but neither was the lawyer an unusual person. [35] For most serious writers, wordiness is the single toughest fault to overcome. Almost anyone can write a speech or essay of 10,000 words about nothing. It takes some discipline to write a seventeen-word haiku or the 265-word Gettysburg Address. During the "pre-writing" (brainstorming) phase, you can put almost anything you like on the paper, or onto your computer screen. When revising, make each draft tauter than the one before. Never let a long word or long phrase stand if you can find a short one to take its place. Inform, explain, persuade, scold, challenge, praise, cajole, or entertain. Just don't be a bore.

1.6. BE CHOOSY

1.6.1. *Circumvent sesquipedalians.*

Short words are best and the old words when short are best of all.
—Winston Churchill[1]

Le mot juste! Always use the right word, the aptest phrase. Don't settle for something close: "Never withhold a herpes infection from your partner" (better: "Never conceal..."). Do not write *feel* when you mean *believe, consider,* or *think.* Do not say "English" if you mean *British,* or "man" if you mean *humanity.* Do not call something that is *excellent,* "incredible," or something that is *frustrating,* "criminal." Do not tell your readers to "cut and paste" if you mean *copy and paste.* Do not say that you "understand how *tender* the free enterprise system can be" if you really mean *fragile* or *compassionate.*[2] Do not say that something is "literally" explosive or "really" nauseous if the thing cannot go boom and does not make you ill. Remember the Sixth Commandment: *Be choosy.* Make sure that your statements express your intended meaning.

Rarely is the best word a long one. The longest word in the English language, though patently contrived, is said to be *pneumonoultramicroscopicsilicovolcanoconiosis,* meaning "a lung disease caused by the inhalation of very fine silica dust"— to which the Anglican Church's long-established *antidisestablishmentarianism* and Shakespeare's *honorificabiltudinitatibus* are distant runner-ups. The longest place name in the English-speaking world is supplied by the town of Llanfairpwllgwyngyllgogerychwyrndrobwyllllantisiliogogogoc in North Wales. That you now "know" these words, and have seen them in print, is no reason to use them in your own writing.

So you scored a perfect 800 on the SAT Verbal? Congratulations! Now keep it to yourself because it bugs the rest of us when you wear your vocabulary on your chest like a scouting achievement pin. Don't make us slog through mire: use plain words to express even your most complex thought. Short words are easy to spell, easy to understand, and do not sound pretentious. Don't *endeavor,* just *try.* Don't *lend assistance* by *presenting* a *donation* to the *disadvantaged* and *underprivileged,* just help out by giving money to the poor. Use *among* and *amid,* not *amongst* and *amidst.* A *home* is better than a *residence,* and to *buy a car* better than *to purchase an automobile.* Find a *room while on the road,* not *accommodations whilst in transit.* If a presidential candidate says, "there is some *methodology* in my travels," he probably means only that there is a *method* to his campaign route, not that his itinerary follows a system of scientific principles and procedures. [3] If he is one who enjoys "interfacing" with his fellow citizens, he enjoys *meeting* them. [4] When he asks, "Why don't you *mentor* a child how to read?" he means *teach*.[5] Inflated diction makes for gaseous prose.

A feast of high-calorie words is easier to dish out than to swallow:

> *With the last gasp of Romanticism, the quelling of its florid uprising against the vapid formalism of one strain of the Enlightenment, the dimming of its yearning for the imagined grandeur of the archaic, and the dashing of its too sanguine hopes for a revitalized, fulfilled humanity, the horror of its more lasting, more Gothic legacy has settled in, distributed and diffused enough, to be sure, that lugubriousness is recognizable only as languor, or as a certain sardonic laconicism disguising itself in a new sanctification of the destructive instincts, a new genius for displacing cultural reifications in the interminable shell game of the analysis of the human psyche, where nothing remains sacred.* [6]

(The main thought in that gasping sentence: Romanticism gave way to Gothic horror. Indeed.)

1.6.2. Jargon: *Big 10-4, good buddy, now say it in English.*

> *Incomprehensible jargon is the hallmark of a profession.*
> —Kingman Brewster [7]

If your purpose in writing is to obscure meaning, as, say, during a war, jargon can be a useful device. To *reduce* or *neutralize* a nation's *assets* sounds better than to "kill most of the foot soldiers." To *pacify rural areas* sounds nicer than to "incinerate the villages with white phosphorus and napalm." A *robust* attack is one that devastates people and property. *Incident* is a useful all-purpose euphemism for those battles or skirmishes that went badly for the good guys or for innocent bystanders. A *degraded* target is one that has been *serviced* (bombed) but not yet *taken out* (wholly destroyed); in which case it must be *re-serviced*. *Collateral* damage denotes civilians or hospitals or schools that were serviced by accident.

Technical terms have their place, but jargon is used most often by those who don't really need it and inflicted upon those who do not understand it. [8] Use technical vocabulary sparingly and only when addressing those who already know the lingo. Readers are soon bored or confused, or at best amused, by gobbledygook. Simple words and a plain style will always get the job done better and quicker than specialized parlance, argot, patois, slang, cant, or technobabble. Leave jargon to money-lenders, advertisers, politicians, literary theorists, and the military. Your readers deserve better.

1.6.3. *Euphemisms.*

Euphemisms are a form of lying.
—George Carlin [9]

Most euphemisms are vague or wordy evasions, as when a doctor speaks of an "adverse patient outcome" (i.e., *death*). Do not substitute "sight impaired" for *blind,* or "that time of the month" for *menstruation,* or "dark-skinned" for *African American.* There is no shame in being blind, or female, or of African descent. When forced by social convention to use a euphemism, as for bodily functions, choose carefully. It is a little silly to call a public toilet a "bathroom" if it has no tub, or to describe what you did on a one-night stand with a stranger as "making love."

Be courteous to interest groups, denoting them as they wish to be called, but honor the language as well. To speak of handicaps in plain English is no sign of disrespect. Avoid coy and squeamish evasions, no matter how trendy. Such euphemisms as "visually impaired" for *blind* and "differently abled" or "wheelchair-assisted" for *crippled* are often unnecessary and sometimes inaccurate or even silly, inviting such parodies as "melanin-deprived" or "rhythm-impaired" for a white person.

Do not use the word, *community,* to impose, on a diverse population, a uniformity or fake harmony of values and beliefs ("The men up here represent a representative sample of what we call the faith community in America"—George W. Bush). [10] At the turn of the last century it became hugely popular to attach this chummy noun to every race, creed, color, and interest group—the "Hispanic community," "the homosexual community," "the academic community," "the law enforcement community," "the international community," "the community activists' community." *Community,* a wonderful thing to experience, is not a wonderful word. For "Hispanic community," write *Hispanics* (or "middle-class Hispanics," or "the largely Catholic Hispanic population of Miami" or "Latinos and Latinas"). For "business community," write *business people* or *entrepreneurs* or *corporate executives* (*not* "businessmen"). For "homosexual community," write *homosexuals* or *gay and lesbian.*

Malphemisms are worse. Keep pejorative epithets to yourself. A homosexual may call himself "queer." Some blacks may call themselves, or one another, "nigger." An Arab may call himself a "raghead." Some women may call themselves "bitches." But if you are a white heterosexual Anglo-Saxon male, you have no right to apply any of these epithets to another human being.

1.6.4. *Slang.*

> *Slang is a language that rolls up its sleeves, spits on its*
> *hands and goes to work.*   —Carl Sandburg [11]

Don't just sling slang: use it to good effect or not at all. Gilbert Chesterton once said that "All slang is metaphor, and all metaphor is poetry." [12] But even the most poetical slang may have a limited audience and a short shelf-life. What's *far out* or *fat* ("phat") or *funky* or *groovy* may be poetry one year and prosaic the next. A *dude* may be cool in California and a fool in Colorado. Grandpa may call his rusty Ford a *bomb* while his grandson reserves that term for a new Porsche. Then, too, slang words often carry unwelcome connotations —either obscene (*dork, frigging, sucks, blows, bites, experience below the belt*), misogynistic (*bitchy, on the rag, ragging, bloody*), homophobic (*gay* or *queer* used as a pejorative), scatological (*full of it, brown-noser, fudged data, reamed out*), or bigoted (*to gyp a consumer, to jew down the price*). If you must use slang, be attentive to the meaning of your words. Let Carl Sandburg do as he may. You will do better, after spitting on your hands in that first draft, to wash them before returning to work.

1.6.5. *Glossolalia.*

> *They have been at a great feast of languages, and stolen the scraps.*
> —Moth the clown, speaking of the scholars, Holofernes and
> Sir Nathaniel, in Shakespeare's *Love's Labor's Lost* [13]

Resist the temptation to show off. Use foreign words and phrases only when necessary to make your point clear. Otherwise, find an English equivalent. Examples include *ad infinitum* (endlessly), *bona fide* (authentic / in good faith), *carte blanche* (a free hand), *cause célèbre* (a famous case), *caveat emptor* (let the buyer beware), *chutzpah* (shameless audacity), *circa* (about, around [that year]), *coup d'état* (coup), *en bloc* (as a whole / together), *en masse* (in a group / all together), *en route* (along the way), *esprit de corps* (team spirit), *fait accompli* (a done deal [opposition is useless]), *hors d'oeuvres* (appetizers), *in toto* (as a whole), *modus operandi* (method of operation / M.O.), *mutatis mutandis* (with the necessary changes), *passim* (here and there, throughout the text), *per annum* (a year / per year); *per capita* (per person), *per diem* (a day / per day), *prima facie* (at first view), *pro tem* (for the time being), *quid pro quo* (exchange / given substitute), *raison d'être* (reason for living), *savoir-faire* (tact), *sine qua non* (prerequisite / essential condition), *tête-à-tête* (private conversation), *vis-à-vis* (in relation to), *viz.* or *videlicet* (namely). Each of these foreign words and Latin terms has its purpose, but to use them unnecessarily or incorrectly will impress no one, and will confuse many.

If you cannot stop yourself from using foreign words, at least be sure that your spelling is correct. Such words as *aficionado, braggadocio, cappuccino, chateau, chateaux, graffito, graffiti, hors d'oeuvres, impresario, mujahideen, obbligato, rococo,* and *sobriquet,* though often used, are often misspelled. For foreign words now accepted as English (*attaché, café, émigré, façade, résumé*), the original accent marks can usually be omitted, but retain those that will assist pronunciation or prevent confusion (cliché, exposé [n.], résumé).

1.6.6. *Counterfeit coinage.*

> *I've coined new words, like misunderstanding and Hispanically.*
> —President George W. Bush [14]

1.6.6a. *Nouns of agency require no inventees.*

The English language already has enough nouns ending in *-ee, -er,* and *-ist* to signify someone who acts, or is acted upon. Your contributions as a new-word imaginationer will be antinecessary. When President George H. W. Bush describes himself as "not the most articulate emotionalist," *I cannot well express my emotions* is the intended meaning. [15] When his son speaks of an "arbolist" or an "arbo-treeist," *arborist* or *tree-trimmer* is the intended word. [16] Teachers who are needlessly preoccupied with required federal paperwork cannot wholly devote themselves to the children—but the point is blunted by stating that excessive federal regulation turns a teacher into "a paperwork-filler-outer." [17] *Informant* or *source* is a better word than George W. Bush's "leakers." [18] It is more clear and less distracting to say of terrorist organizations that they support suicide-bombers than to say, with our president, that "They send *suiciders* out." [19]

Well-established words of the *-ee* type include *absentee, divorcee* (male or female), *employee, evacuee, referee,* and *refugee.* Don't invent new ones. Those unseated on a bus are *standers,* not "standees." Tutored students are *tutored students,* not "tutees." Most words of this sort, even if allowed by late-edition dictionaries, are silly. When possible, avoid calling *conscripts* "draftees," *an audience* "attendees," *prisoners* "detainees," or *test-takers* "testees."

1.6.6b. *Do not verb a noun.*

If our president says that that the war on terrorism has "*transfor-mationed*" our relationship with Russia, and that Russia's President Putin is "very forward-leaning as they say in *diplomatic-nuanced* circles," *transformed* and *diplomatic* are the intended words. [20] If he tells the British prime minister, "Look, my job isn't to try *to nuance*, my job is to tell people what I think," *make subtle distinctions* may be intended. [21] A *dialogue* is a conversation or discussion. It is not a verb. Don't "dialogue" with your boss or team or lover, just *talk*. Change the topic of discussion when convenient but do not "transition" to it. When you have studied a problem, do not "effort" or "brainstorm" a solution, just try to solve it.

Impact, a noun introduced to the English language by scientists in the latter 18th century, denotes the collision of two objects, as of a cannonball with your shin, or a speeding Corvette with a concrete bridge abutment. With a little tweaking it can do service as an adjective (an *impacted* bone is wedged together at the broken ends; an *impacted* tooth is driven into the gums). But it takes a deaf ear to employ *impact* as a verb meaning to *affect*. Following the 1989 Loma Prieta earthquake, Vice President Dan Quayle flew to Oakland to assess the damage. A section of Interstate 880 had collapsed, crushing dozens of cars below and killing 42 people. Asked for a comment, Mr. Quayle remarked, solemnly, "It looks like the top part fell on the bottom part. [...] The loss of life will be irreplaceable." He then added, "I would like to express my sympathy to all those impacted by this disaster." [22] The vice president was ridiculed for his thoughtless choice of words to denote the pancaked victims. But in 1986 and again in 2003, in televised commentary on the Space Shuttle disasters, NASA pundits used *impact* repeatedly in much the same way (e.g., "the loss of this vehicle will impact future planning"), forgetting what *impact* actually meant for those men and women who reached for the stars, and died.

1.6.6c. *Do not adjectivate, bureaucratize, ishify, or suffixate.*

Do not invent verbs by adding *–ed* to such *-ate* adjectives as *immaculate* or *proportionate*. No one wants to read your privated thoughts about chocolated milk. When George W. Bush says, "I've got a record, a record that is conservative, and a record that is compassionated," he probably means that his political record is both conservative and compassionate, not that he has two records, a conservative one plus one that has been dressed up to look compassionate. [23]

Big, brackish, bratty, and *British* are all fine words; *biggish, saltish, brattish,* and *Americanish* are not. Such newish adjectives are for weakish writers with a poorish vocabulary.

Bureaucrats and bad writers are fond of new words ending in *-ize*. It is better to set priorities or to rank your concerns than *to prioritize*, and more admirable to encourage your workers than to *incentivize* them. *Finish* your report, *complete* your negotiations, make your *final* offer, *close* the deal, and *end* the meeting, but do not "finalize" them or "nextize" them. Everyone likes *personal* attention but it is silly to call monogrammed letterhead and custom license plates "personalized." If the president offers to "help Russia *securitize*" dismantled nuclear warheads," *secure* is the desired word.[24] To *vulcanize* something improves its strength and resiliency, such as a vulcanized condom. To *Balkanize* means just the reverse: to Balkanize a land is to divide it into small, often hostile units, as happened on the Balkan Peninsula. When our president says that racial and sex quotas have "vulcanized society," he may mean that sex quotas attempted on the individual level have caused our whole society to use vulcanized latex. More probably, *Balkanize* is the word he has aimed for, and *divide* is the word he ought to have used. [25] Most English verbs and adjectives can do without your added prefix or suffix. Your readers will grimace, or should, when you offer them such unsavory fare as "interpretate" (*interpret*), "orientate" (for *orient*), or "effectuate" (for *effect*). Our president has praised the ability of the American people "to sort through what is fair and what is unfair, what is ugly and what is *unugly*," but "unugly" is hardly the same as *beautiful*.[26] Familiar words work best.

1.6.7. Malapropisms.

Words are innocent, neutral, precise, standing for this, describing that, meaning the other, so if you look after them you can build bridges across incomprehension and chaos. But when they get their corners knocked off, they're no good any more.
—Tom Stoppard [27]

A *malapropism*—so named after Mrs. Malaprop in Richard Sheridan's play, *The Rivals*—is a flagrant verbal error, spoken or written by someone blissfully unaware that he or she has just made fritters of the language, as when Shakespeare's Constable Elbow arrests "two notorious benefactors" (*malefactors*), villains who are "void [*devoid*] of all profanation [*veneration*] that all good Christians ought to have." "I resent your insinuendoes," said mayor Richard J. Daley of Chicago (having grown weary of innuendo and insinuation).[28] Malapropisms typically involve the use of a big word by way of confusion with another word that sounds similar but means something quite different, as when Vice President Dan Quayle announced that "Republicans understand the importance of *bondage* between a mother and child"—as if to imply that Democrats do not understand the value of incestuous sadomasochism; [29] or when the same vice president urged developing nations "to work towards the *elimination* of human rights in accordance with the pursuit of Justice." [30]

The Bush men—George H. W., George W., and Jeb—have so peppered their public statements with malapropisms that a new word entered the language, the *bushism*—"a big word whose sense is mangled by a public official or national leader," as when the younger Bush tried to say *obfuscate* and let loose with a word not ordinarily heard in polite society. Some memorable bushisms:

• *When I'm the president, we're not going to* obs-fuckat *when it comes to foreign policy.* [...] *I will have a* foreign-handed *foreign policy.* [31]

• *In 1994, there were sixty-seven schools in Texas that were rated* exemplorary, *according to our own tests. They said this issue wouldn't* resignate *with the people. They've been proved wrong, it does* resignate. [...] *My education message will* resignate *amongst all parents.* [32]

• *You know, the idea of idea of putting* subliminable *messages in ads is, it's ridiculous. You talk about* subliminable. [...] *This is a way to help* inoculate *me about what has come, and is coming.* [...] *I don't think we need to be* subliminable *about the differences between our views on prescription drugs.* [33]

• *The folks who* conducted *to act on our country on September 11 made a big mistake.* [...] *They* misunderestimated *the fact that we love a neighbor in need. They* misunderestimated *the compassion of our country. I think they* misunderestimated *the will and determination of the Commander-in-Chief, too.* [...] *I'm furious about innocent life lost. However, through my* furity, *even though I'm mad, I still believe peace is possible.* [34]

• *I think if you say you're going to do something and don't do it, that's* trustworthiness. [35]

Sometimes a word does not mean what you always thought it meant, or cannot be used as you've always used it. Such errors, while hilarious to your readers, may be hard for you to spot. Consult a thesaurus if you must to find a shorter word, or a dictionary to find the meaning of a longer one, but do not attempt fancy words that you don't really know. Let your readers laugh because you are witty, not because you slipped on a banana peel while trying to appear erudite.

1.7. BE ACCURATE

1.7.1. *Do your homework*

> *Accuracy is the twin brother of honesty.*
> —Charles Simmons [1]

1.7.1a. *Begin writing from what you already know.*

You can't write a good short story about life in Harlem if you've never been out of the suburbs. You cannot write a smart critical essay about *Much Ado about Nothing* if you know the primary text only from the summary at www.SparkNotes.com. Nor can you interpret the United States Constitution, for others, if you have not yet read it yourself:

> *You see, the Senate wants to take away some of the powers of the administrative* [i.e., executive] *branch. The legislature's job is to write law. It's the executive branch* [i.e., judicial branch's] *job to interpret law.* [...] *[W]e've had leaks out of the administrative* [i.e., executive] *branch, had leaks out of the legislative branch, and out of the executive* [i.e., judicial] *branch, and the legislative* [oops! already said that] *branch, and I've spoken out consistently against them* [i.e., against leaks, not against the three branches of government]. *We're moving on it, to protect the United Nations* [i.e., United States] *Constitution.* [...] *I am mindful of the difference between the executive branch and the legislative branch.* [...] *I know the difference, and that difference is, they pass the laws and I execute them* [i.e., my job is to sign and execute legislation, not to execute U.S. senators and representatives]. (George W. Bush.) [2]

The United States Constitution has established three separate but equal branches of government: the *executive*, the *legislative*, and the *judicial*. The three branches respectively *make*, *execute*, and *interpret* federal law. These basic facts—which must be learned by immigrants before they can become naturalized citizens of the United States, and by schoolchildren before graduating from the eighth grade—are readily available in any public library—or, for that matter, on the Internet. Better not to pontificate about the U.S. Constitution, or about any other subject or text, until you have done your homework.

1.7.1b. *Find accurate and up-to-date information.*

Trace all information, data, and quotations to original, or at least dependable, sources. Second-hand report is often mistaken, and quoted material, inaccurate. The Internet may be a convenient place to begin your research, but it's no place to stop. Much of what you find on the Web about your chosen subject, though stated as fact, may be out of date, plagiarized, misattributed, or wholly fabricated. Don't recycle bad information. Discover the truth.

1.7.1c. *Visit the library.*

Learn your way around. Library research, as you learn how to do it, can actually be fun. The information you need may be in a reference work, the back issue of a magazine, or a licensed databank. It may be on microfilm, or on the open shelves, or in special collections. A reference librarian will gladly coach you on how to find what you need, whether it's a science fact, an ancestor's biography, a poem, a quotation, a recipe, or an old film or photograph or map or piece of music. Librarians can even teach you how to find reliable information on the Internet.

If you need a book, article, film, or recording not owned by your local library, it can be ordered through interlibrary loan, usually at a small fraction of the purchase price; but the service takes a while, so plan ahead.

If your local library lacks a book or resource that you need, and you cannot get it through interlibrary loan, visit the library of the nearest college or university (Call first: special permission may be required.) You can find just about anything in a good college library if you are willing to look hard enough.

If, after studying your subject, you still don't know what you're talking about, don't fake it. Choose another subject for discussion, or another line of work.

1.7.2. *Stick to what you can prove (or at least, show).*

> *If a man writes a book, let him set down only what he knows.*
> *I have guesses enough of my own.*
> —Johann Wolfgang von Goethe [3]

1.7.2a. *No B.S.*

Politicians, corporate CEOs, capital lobbyists, and the defense attorneys for criminal suspects often publish disinformation to sway public opinion. To make their argument seem more convincing, the disseminators of bad information may supply or pass along bogus documentation, as when Ronald Reagan, in 1979, shrewdly alleged that "Eighty percent of air pollution comes not from chimneys and auto exhaust pipes, but from plants and trees." [4] To support this extraordinary claim, Reagan cited a nonexistent scientific study that he alleged was suppressed by the Environmental Protection Agency. Having identified trees as a health threat, the Reagan-Bush administration fought to relax exhaust-emissions standards and pushed for massive clear-cutting of old growth forests, before the killer trees could kill again—and succeeded.

Following suit, President George W. Bush in 2003 cited a "United Nations International Atomic Energy report" alleging that Iraq was "six months away" from developing a nuclear weapon (there was no such report); and claimed in his State of the Union address that "Saddam Hussein recently sought significant quantities of uranium from Africa" (citing a "Nigerian" document that he already knew to be a crude forgery circulated by his own administration).[5] The president then attacked his critics, saying, "Now, there are some who would like to rewrite history—revisionist historians is what I like to call them."[6]

Politicians may pull such stunts with impunity, even if whole forests of old-growth lumber, or troops of young people, die as a result. But in academia, fabricated documentation is treated as a serious offense, a breach of academic integrity akin to plagiarism: if you falsify information for a college essay, and are caught, you may expect to be expelled from the course, and perhaps from college. Milk your ideas for all they're worth but don't milk the bull. Save your inventive streak for writing fiction.

1.7.2b. *No hyperboles.*

Use superlatives sparingly and correctly. The *biggest, richest, oldest, worst,* etc., are a fruitful source of error. All such claims should be verified or qualified. "One of the longest" is more wordy and less pointed than "The longest," but also less likely to be wrong. Omit superlatives that are inaccurate or undocumented. Don't say "most" if you mean *several,* or "many" if you mean *a few.* Do not assert what happens "in most cases" unless you can back it up. Don't allege what "most experts believe" or what "most critics have argued" unless you have proof. A specific instance is usually more effective than a sweeping statement.

In *The Elements of Style,* E. B. White warns against the perils of exaggeration: "Overstatement is one of the commonest faults. A single overstatement, wherever or however it occurs, diminishes the whole, and a single carefree superlative has the power to destroy, for the reader, the object of the writer's enthusiasm."[7] But even the most cautious writer may sometimes be tempted to exaggerate. The master himself, E. B. White, slips into overstatement only a few pages later when stressing the need for clarity:

• Muddiness is not merely a disturber of prose. It is also a destroyer of life, of hope: death on the highway caused by a badly worded road sign, heartbreak among lovers caused by a misplaced phrase in a well-intentioned letter, anguish of a traveler expecting to be met at a railroad station and not being met because of a slipshod telegram ... think of the tragedies that are rooted in ambiguity; think of that side, and be clear![8]

Mr. White lays it on a little too thick when he puts vague writing up there with cigarettes, heart attacks, handguns, and drunk driving as a leading cause of domestic tragedy. Still, his point is clear enough: *Write clearly.* Just imagine a dear little child whose mother is killed in a car crash, and who thinks to himself, "It's *my* fault, because I wrote a muddy sentence." Think of that emotional calamity! Think of that side, and avoid overstatement!

1.7.2c. *No venom.*

Be fair to your opponents and precursors. If your argument is strong, and your information accurate, you have no need to misrepresent your adversaries, or to belittle those who have already written on your subject. It's unfair to misquote your opponents or to put words in their mouth. If you can score points with your reader only by distorting the views of those with whom you disagree, you are a lousy writer.

1.7.2d. *No cheap rhetorical tricks.*

When presenting your argument, speak for yourself. Don't tell us what Shakespeare really intended when writing *Hamlet,* or what God really meant when writing the Bible. Show us how the text works, or how it produces meaning, or how it challenges or perpetuates cultural assumptions, but don't ask us to believe that you can speak for the author.

Nor have you the right to speak for your readers. Avoid the imperial "We." It is arrogant to use "we" in a manner that presupposes sensible readers already agree with you, regardless of their race, creed, color, age, sex, values, or critical judgment:

• Arrogant: *We know that Jesus was born of a virgin and died for the sins of humanity.*
• Improved: *We who are Christians confidently believe,* etc.

- Presumptuous: *I confirmed to the prime minister that we appreciate our friendship.* (George W. Bush, speaking of Canada's prime minister, Jean Chrétien.) [9]
- Better: *I told Jean Chrétien that I consider him a friend.*

When President George W. Bush announces to the world that "We don't have a beef with Muslims," he seems to forget that many Americans are Muslims, and unmindful that his phrasing may not translate well to the Earth's estimated one billion Muslims whose native language is not English (*Okay, so you don't eat bacon, but don't expect us to have beef with you, either*).[10] Before you declare what "we" believe or think or feel or do or know, make sure that the rest of us know who's included: by "we," do you mean you and the rest of the world? you and the hamster in your pocket? or is it just you and others who already think exactly as you do and who therefore have no need to read your essay?

1.7.3. *Reality check.*

> *Facts are stupid things.*
> —Pres. Ronald Reagan, misquoting Pres. John Adams, who wrote that "Facts are stubborn things" [11]

> *I stand by all the misstatements that I've made.*
> —Vice President Dan Quayle[12]

1.7.3a. *Confirm every factual statement.*

Check your information against reliable sources. If your source is mistaken, prove it. Correct your own errors as well. If something you have said cannot be documented, cut it, or at least acknowledge that your report is unconfirmed.

1.7.3b. *Check your historical facts.*

Authors, scholars, and politicians are often remembered best, not for their eloquence, but for their mistakes. A case in point: In January 2002, President George W. Bush visited Tokyo, hoping to let bygones be bygones. A decade earlier, his father, President George H. W. Bush, inadvertently vomited into the lap of the Japanese prime minister while at a televised state dinner. The younger Bush, hoping to forget the bombs-over-Tokyo dinner mishap, rewrote history with an epoch-making speech notable only for its fuzziness about less-recent history: "For a century and a half now," he said, "America and Japan have formed one of the great and enduring alliances of modern times. From that alliance has come an era of peace in the Pacific."[13] In this revisionist history, George, Jr., seemed not only to forgive, but to forget, Pearl Harbor and World War II. A politician, left or right, can misstate the facts and still be elected if the voters are as clueless as he. But you are a writer: you cannot afford to be so fuzzy. Your goal as a writer is not just to get re-elected, but to convey accurate information or compelling opinion.

1.7.4c. *Check your geographical facts.*

Novelists and politicians not uncommonly place cities in the wrong nation, or even on the wrong continent. Such imprecision may be obvious to your readers even if the mistakes are not apparent to you—as when the playwright, Ben Jonson, ridiculed his recently deceased colleague, William Shakespeare, for having situated landlocked Bohemia on the seashore. Four centuries later, at a White House press conference, President George W. Bush followed Shakespeare's example, transporting Jordan and Egypt one thousand miles east to the shores of the Persian Gulf.[14]

When referencing cities, states, nations, continents, and planets, call them by their right name and spell them correctly. But you should also know where to find them on a map:

• *I love California, I practically grew up in Phoenix.* (Dan Quayle.) [15]

• *It is wonderful to be here in the great state of Chicago.* (Dan Quayle.) [16]

• *We have a firm commitment to Europe. We are a part of Europe.* (Dan Quayle.) [17]

• *For NASA, space is still a high priority. [...] It's time for the human race to enter the solar system!* (Dan Quayle.) [18]

• *We've got a big border in Texas—with Mexico, obviously. And we've got a big border with Canada—Arizona is affected.* (George W. Bush.)[19]

• *I was raised in the West. The west of Texas. It's pretty close to California. In more ways than Washington, D.C., is close to California [...] The people who care more about that land are the hard-working farmers and ranchers [...] of the state of Washington, D.C.* (George W. Bush.) [20]

If geography is not your strongest subject, conduct the necessary research or ask someone who knows—as when President Bush, always eager to learn, asked the 15-year-old Welsh singing sensation, Charlotte Church, what state Wales is in. Charlotte replied, "It's a separate country next to England," and the president replied, "Um, okay." [21] President Bush may never be called upon to write an essay or a speech on Welsh-American relations, but the question he put to Ms. Church was a fine way to begin his research.

1.7.4d. *Check all names.*

Call people, places, and things by their customary names. If you cannot accurately report familiar titles, personal names, and geographical locations, your readers will doubt your authority on more substantive matters. Do not, for example, confuse Theodore Roosevelt with Franklin D. Roosevelt, or George H. W. Bush (dad) with George W. Bush (son), or call Capitol Hill, "congressional hill."[22] Do not confuse the United Nations with the United States—

• *I look forward to working with* [...] *the United Nations Senate.* (George W. Bush, campaigning in South Dakota.) [23]

• *I'm not going to accept a lousy bill out of the United Nations Senate.* (George W. Bush, same day, in Indiana.) [24]

—or the White House "Rose Garden" with the U.S. National Park System—

• *This is our first event in this beautiful spot, and it's appropriate we talk about policy that will affect people's lives in a positive way in such a beautiful, beautiful part of our national—really, "our National Park System," my guess is you would want to call it.* (George W. Bush.) [25]

—or the president's State of the Union Address with a budget talk:

• *I suspect that had my dad not been president, he'd be asking the same questions: How'd your meeting go with so-and-so? ... How did you feel when you stood up in front of the people for the "State of the Union Address"?—"State of the Budget Address"—whatever you call it.* (George W. Bush, speaking of his 2001 State of the Union Address.) [26]

• *In my "State of the"—my "State of the Union," or "State"—my "Speech to the Nation," whatever you want to call it, "Speech to the Nation"—I asked Americans to give 4,000 years—4,000 hours over the next, the rest of your life.* (George W. Bush, speaking of his 2002 State of the Union Address.) [27]

(For additional help with names, see 3.5. Names.)

1.7.4e. *Check your dates.*

Check all dates in your book or essay or résumé against the historical record. Check all dates in your bibliography and notes against the publication record. Blunders can be embarrassing: "I have a record in office [...] and all Americans have seen that record: on September the fourth, 2001, I stood in the ruins of the Twin Towers. It's a day I will never forget" (George W. Bush).[28]

1.7.4f. *Check your numbers.*

Writers sometimes have more trouble with accurate numbers than mathematicians have with accurate words. Errors in the reporting or calculation of numbers will creep into your text when no one is looking. Double- and triple-check your numbers and tabulations, including those in your graphs and charts, before submitting your final draft.

1.7.4g. *Check your quotations.*

Quote from dependable sources. Here are four statements are widely ascribed on the Internet to former Vice President Dan Quayle:

• *"A low voter turnout is an indication of fewer people going to the polls."*
• *"Republicans have been accused of abandoning the poor. It's the other way around. They never vote for us."*
• *"If we don't succeed, we run the risk of failure."*
• *"It isn't pollution that's harming the environment. It's the impurities in our air and water that are doing it."*

The last of these Quayle quotations appears on more than 14,000 difference Web sites. But all four statements were invented in 1991 by the humorist, Al Jaffee, for a *Mad* Magazine parody headed, "Future Quayle Quotes We Can Expect to Hear."[29] The former vice president has had enough trouble already with the English language without your adding to his difficulties by reporting that he said dumb things he didn't actually say.

Once you have found an authoritative source, quote precisely, marking all omissions with a bracketed ellipsis (like so: [...]). Reproduce spelling, capitalization, and punctuation exactly as in the original. If you cannot confirm the exact words, cite your source for the paraphrase but do not use quotation marks. And don't quote without proper documentation.

1.8. PLAY BY THE RULES

1.8.1. *Grammar 101: The Parts of Speech and how to use them.*

> *If I don't practice, I am going to destroy this language.*
> —George W. Bush [1]

English is your language. Learn its rules: they are not as difficult as you may think. Children in grammar school who are no brighter than you, and adults whose native language is not English, have mastered the basic principles. You can, too.

The building blocks of language are the eight "parts of speech": *verb, noun adjective, adverb, pronoun, preposition, conjunction,* and *interjection.* Each has a conventional use.

1.8.1a. *Interjections.*

An *interjection* is a word, exclamation, or meaningless sound used to express emotion (**%#@!*), pain (*ouch*), surprise (*oh, hey*), or just to give yourself thinking time (*well, um, ah*). When writing, use interjections with restraint (and, where possible, use commas instead of exclamation points).

At those moments when you most a need colorful interjection, as during a fit of moral outrage, the rules of English grammar can usually be ignored.

1.8.1b. *Adjectives.*

An *adjective* is a word that describes, identifies, or qualifies a noun (person place, or thing): *able, big, cold, dark, easy, free, green, hot, zippy.* Use the adverbs, *more* and *most,* to express the comparative and superlative of an adjective that does not end in *–y* and that has two or more syllables: *hotter, hottest, sillier, silliest; more elegant, most elegant.* Shakespeare and George W. Bush often use such redundancies as "more worthier" and "most unkindest" where *more worthy* or *worthier, unkindest* or *most unkind,* will suffice.

1.8.1c. *Adverbs.*

An *adverb* is a word that describes either a verb ("Eat *right*, stay *fit*, die *anyway*"), an adjective ("*lightly* falling snow," "*hard*-lovin' woman"), or another adverb ("sing *most* sweetly). Many English adverbs end in *-ly*. Employ them only where necessary.

Keep related words together. Adverbs such as *all, almost, merely, nearly, only* should appear as close as possible to the word or phrase they describe. "Michael Jackson gave *almost one million dollars* to Unicef" means something different from "Michael Jackson *almost gave* one million dollars to Unicef." "Monica slept *only with Bill*" does not mean the same thing as "Monica *only slept* with Bill." To say that a commercial plane crash "only killed the pilot" implies that there are worse problems in life than getting killed: *killed only the pilot* is the intended phrase:

- Unclear: *[T]he* explorationists *are willing to only move equipment during the winter.* (George W. Bush, describing his plan for a staged thaw of the arctic tundra.) [2]
- Better: *The oil companies will move equipment only during the winter.*

Be careful with introductory adverbs:

- *Unfortunately, the people of Louisiana are not racists.* (Dan Quayle.)[3]

- *Unfairly but truthfully, our party has been tagged as being against things: anti-immigrant, for example.* (George W. Bush.)[4]

Cut illogical adverbs, such as "second-biggest" or "third most expensive." A thing is either "the biggest" (*brightest, hottest, weirdest*), or it's not.

- Illogical: *The John Hancock Building is the third-tallest building in Chicago.* (There is only one tallest building, not three.)
- Better: *The John Hancock Building (1969), briefly Chicago's tallest skyscraper, was surpassed by the Sears Tower (1973) and the Standard Oil Building (1974).*

Conjunctive adverbs such as *consequently, furthermore, hence, however, indeed, nevertheless, therefore,* and *thus,* are connectives that assert tight logical relations between the claims in question. However, remember that it is always a mistake to use conjunctive adverbs in successive clauses. Therefore, avoid doing what I'm doing here by way of example; otherwise, you will find that your writing sounds like a geometry textbook. Consequently, your reader will find you boring; thus, you should use such words sparingly and thoughtfully (and with correct punctuation), or not at all. *However* and *nevertheless* are stuffy and much overused substitutes for *but.* (For help with particular adverbs, see 3.1, A Pretty Good Guide to Hard Words.)

1.8.1d. *Conjunctions.*

"Coordinating conjunctions" (*and, but, or*) and "subordinating conjunctions" (*although, as, because, before, if, since, unless, until, when, while,* and many others) are used to connect two ideas in the same sentence. A subordinator makes one idea more important than the other ("X until Y." "Although A, B." "Unless P, Q.") Coordinated ideas are symmetrical ("X, or Y." "A, but B." "P, and Q"). Subordinating conjunctions can be used in place of *and, but, or, so,* to avoid the monotony of stringy construction:

- Stringy: *We're a peaceful nation and moving along just right and just kind of having a time, and all of a sudden we get attacked, and now we're at war, but we're at war to keep the peace.* (George W. Bush.) [5]
- Better: *Although we are a peaceful nation, we have been attacked and must now fight, in order to restore peace.*

1.8.1e. *Prepositions.*

Such words as *about, by, down, for, from, in, on, over, through,* and *upon* are called *prepositions.* People trying to master English as a second language are often bewildered by the rules for preposition usage, and for a good reason: there *are* no rules. Do you say you are afraid *about,* or *of,* flying? bored *of,* or *with,* television? angry *with,* or *at,* your mother? *Which preposition?* is rarely a question of logic, nor even of right or wrong: it's a question of *Normal or weird:* what's "right" is determined by what speakers and writers of English actually say and write. I am here advising you *on* prepositions, not *about* them. If you search *for* your keys, you are in search *of* them. Your boyfriend's dorm room stinks *of* dirty laundry, not *from* it. Vacationers embark *on* a journey, but *in* a ship. If you are certain *of* your answer, you will be definite *in* stating it. You may usually agree *with* your father but disagree *about* (not "on") politics: his political opinions are different *from* (similar or dissimilar *to*) your own. You may "charge a purchase"—or be "charged *with* shoplifting" (or face a "charge *of* shoplifting"), but to say that you were "charged *for* shoplifting" makes poor sense unless, perhaps, you were chased and tackled by a store security guard.

Reading someone who has preposition trouble is like dining with someone who has hiccups. The primary business still gets done, but the burplets are distracting, and if they come too often, comical. Unsure whether to write "different from" or "different than"? Unsure whether to "accede *with* your mother's wishes" or "accede *to*" them? There's an easy way to find answers: type the competing phrases in an Internet search, and see which one wins.

If you're feeling passive aggressive and wish to give your readers a sore brain, then go ahead and write such illogical phrases as "based off of," "centered around," "focused around," "absent in," "emigrate from," "immigrate to," "on a viewpoint," "get a perspective on" or "view about." Otherwise, don't. A moment's thought will prevent most such errors.

Prepositions are often used in English, not for a "prepositional phrase" (*in bed, under the table, over the hill and through the woods*), but for a "phrasal verb," in which the preposition changes the meaning of the verb (*catch on, fill in, put up with, play down, touch up*), sometimes with multiple definitions ("to *run up* a large hill" is not the same as "to *run up* a large bill." "Tom *went out*" means one thing, "The candle *went out*" means another).

Don't tack prepositions onto verbs without need. It is usually better to *buy, send,* or *meet,* than to *buy up, sell off,* and *meet with.* When a verb phrase is needed, always put the preposition next to the verb, or as close as you can get it. Don't wait till you get to the end of a sentence and then tack on a preposition. Your sentences have more punch if they close with a verb or a noun than with a lame preposition:

- Weak: *Whom is the bell is tolling for?*
- Better: *For whom does the bell toll?* (John Donne.) [6]

- Weak: *Sexism is the foundation all tyranny is built on.*
- Better: *Sexism is the foundation on which all tyranny is built.* (Andrea Dworkin.) [7]

- Wordy: *Apathy is the glove evil slips its hand into.*
- Better: *Apathy is the glove into which evil slips its hand.* (Bodie Thoene.) [8]

- Mild: *Please turn the damned television off.*
- Strong: *Please turn off the damned television.*

- Weak: *We need to put the money up in order to win this war* (George W. Bush).[9]
- Better: *We must put up enough money to win the war.*

- Weak: *A submarine could take this place out* (George W. Bush, to his tour guide at the William Clinton Presidential Center in Little Rock, Arkansas).[10]
- Better: *A submarine could take out this place!*

The rule is not inviolable:

Texan: *Where are you from?*

Harvard man: *I come from a school where we know better than to end
            our sentences with a preposition.*
Texan: *Okay—where are you from, jackass?*

Sending his reluctant child to bed one night, a father promised to
follow shortly with a book, and to read to her in bed. When dad came
upstairs with a tedious book about Australia, the girl (according to
the anecdote) replied with a remarkable sentence that set the world's
record for the most prepositions dumped at the end of an intelligible
sentence. "Daddy, what did you bring that book, that I don't want to
be read to from out of, about Down Under, up for?" (More succinctly:
Daddy, let's not read about Australia.)

1.8.1f. *Verbs.*

The most important word in a sentence is the *verb*, which
expresses action (*to fly, to crash, to complain*), or a state of being (*I
am, it was, they have been*). The verb indicates what happens, when
it happens (*past, present, future*), and how it happens (*passive or
active, imperatively or conditionally*). When writing and revising, be
sure that the verb and its context agree. You will confuse your
audience if you speak of the present as if it were already over ("Every
morning I come into the desk, and I would read the threat assess-
ments to America";[11] "She is a member of a labor union at one
point");[12] or if you write of the past as if it has just returned ("One
year ago today, the time for excuse-making has come to an end" (i.e.,
The time for excuses ended a year ago);[13] of if you mix past, present,
and future all together ("We're getting ready to have the first press
conference we had together in Slovenia" [George W. Bush]).[14]

In a sentence with multiple verbs, the verbs must stand in logical
agreement with one another. Not: "Iran would be dangerous if they
have a nuclear weapon" (George W. Bush); but: *The Iranian
government would be dangerous if it had a nuclear weapon.*[15]

"*Strong*" verbs do not conform to the dominant pattern of a preterit
(past tense) that ends in *-ed*: There is no shortcut to mastering the
many irregular English verbs except to memorize them.   The
standard preterits for *dive* and *sneak* are *dived* and *sneaked*, not *dove*
and *snuck*. The preterits of *shake* and *drag* are *shook* and *dragged*,
not "shaked" and "drug":

• *As the United States works to bring peace around the world, our
diplomats and/or soldiers can be drug into this court. And that's very
troubling to me.* (George W. Bush.) [16]

• *The important question is, How many hands have I shaked?*
(George W. Bush.) [17]

There is no rulebook for strong verbs. When unsure, consult a dictionary.

Subjunctive. A verb in the "subjunctive mood" expresses a wish, or a possibility, or a conditional state of affairs. The subjunctive is a source of many errors. Among the most frequent mistakes: "If I was" [condition or a person], for *If I were*; and "I wish I was" for *I wish I were*.

- Fine: *Jenny wishes Santa Claus were real* [not: "was" real].

- Fine: *If Janet had known how much trouble her uniform would cause at the Superbowl, she'd have kept it zipped* [not: "If Janet knew"; "Had Janet known" is also fine].

- Fine: *It looks as though Bubba may buy a new pickup. The Ford would have lasted longer, had he just kept oil in it.*

- Fine: *I ask only that you be careful with the handgun.* Should *you accidentally* shoot *someone, I* would want *to know right away.*

A common error arises with the use of "better" (*condition A would be better than an understood condition, B*): "I'd better hang up and you'd better get going" means *I had better hang up* (*than keep on talking*), and *you had better get going* (*than to keep listening to me*). In writing, the phrase, *had better*, may be contracted, as in everyday speech (*I'd, we'd, you'd*)—but do *not* say or write "I better," "We better," "You better," which makes no sense:

• *There are too many of our children who cannot read and write and add and subtract, and* we better *figure out how to not only figure out who can't read and write, but how to cure it, now, before it's too late!* (i.e., *we'd better* [George W. Bush]). [18]

Infinitives. In that last-quoted sentence, "to not only figure out" is what's called a "split infinitive." An infinitive (*to be, to die, to dream*) serves as one word though written as two. To write such phrases as "to *not* be" or "to *suddenly* die," or "to *perchance* dream" is to split the verb—which is, for the fastidious reader, a gruesome error because you're sticking your adverbial knife right between the ribs of the English infinitive. No one will arrest you: every British and American writer does it, now and then. These days, you can probably split infinitives all night long without getting caught. Times being what they are, you can be the worst serial infinitive-killer in the English-speaking world and still get published. Or, for that matter, elected. But *to unnecessarily split* your infinitives, as in this sentence, looks like ignorance and not like a stylistic choice. Here's the rule: the adverb, if you really need one, goes *before* the infinitive ("not to be," "perchance to dream"), or *after* the infinitive ("to die suddenly"), but not *inside* it. You are welcome to boldly break the rule whenever you please.

When using an infinitive with *too* ("too close to call," "too hot to work"), be careful not to say the opposite of what you mean:

• *We're too close, our relationship is too strong, to endure some of the sleights that come along.* (George W. Bush, speaking of his marriage to Laura Bush.) [19]

Participles. When leading off with a participial phrase (as I have just done), make it clear what subject performs the action. Each of these three sentences contains an error:

• *When dangling, supply a subject for your participles. Proof-reading carefully, mistakes will become apparent. Having fixed them, your readers may finally stop smirking.*

In the first sentence, you, the reader, are dangling. In the second, "mistakes" do the proofreading. In the third, "your readers" have corrected your mistakes. (See also 1.4.5, Disambiguate.)

Where possible, change *-ing* gerunds ("try doing") into infinitive form ("try to do") [see 1.4.3c.], or simple present tense ("try," "do"), even if it takes extra words to complete the sentence:

• Unclear: *It is time to set aside the old partisan bickering and finger-pointing and name-calling that comes from freeing parents to make different choices for their children.* (George W. Bush.) [20]

• Clear: *If we free parents to make choices for their own children, politicians need no longer bicker and point fingers and call one another cruel names.*

"Better to give than to receive" is a better sentence than "Receiving is better than giving." For "incapable of going," write "unable to go" or "cannot go."

Most *-ing* participles can be read as verbs (*She is reading*), as nouns (*Reading is more fun than TV*), or as adjectives (*I need a reading lamp*), which is a common source of confusion: *The counselors are discussing the problems of students' carrying guns, drinking alcohol, and suffering from eating disorders.* If your sentence already has a participle in it, and you add other common *ing* words to the mix, such as *during, something,* or *anything,* and *ing* nouns (*king, ring, wing*), the multiple *ing* words will get in one another's way (*I am planning on doing something really interesting* *during this morning's bookkeeping meeting).* Keep your essay, speech, or story unclogged with *ing* words. For "I am going to," *I will*; for "planning on selling," *plan to sell.* One *ing* participle per paragraph is plenty.

1.8.1g. *Nouns.*

A *noun* is a word that denotes a person, place, or thing. If it's a proper name, it's a proper noun, and takes a capital. Nouns do not give writers much trouble except in the possessive case (*child's play, children's bikes, the boss's car*; for which, see 1.8.3h. Punctuation 101: Apostrophes for possession).

Gerunds are nouns constructed from verbs: "I *run*" (verb). "*Running* is good for me" (noun). In the sentence, "I have been fishing all day," *fishing* is a verb that expresses the action. In the sentence, "Fishing is an art," *fishing* is a gerund. Gerunds may look like participles (*laughing, reading, working*), but they work like nouns and take the possessive.

- Bad: *Do you mind* me eating *lunch as we talk?*
- Good: *Do you mind* my eating *lunch as we talk?*

- Bad: *The kids were bothered* by Grandma snoring.
- Good: *The kids were bothered* by Grandma's snoring.

Where possible, make things active, changing gerunds into verbs (*Grandma snored all night, keeping the kids awake*).
- Unclear: *I reject any* labeling *me because I happened to go to the university.* (George W. Bush.) [21]
- Clear: *Don't call me a bigot for having visited Bob Jones University.*

1.8.1h. *Pronouns.*

A *pronoun* is a word used in place of a noun, whether demonstrative (*this, these, those, that*), relative (*which, who, that*), indefinite (*all, anybody, each, every, everyone, none, something*); or personal (*I, we, he, she, he, it, they, who*). The indefinite pronouns *anybody, anyone, everybody, everyone,* and *none* (="not one") all take singular verbs (everyone *is*, nobody *was*, none *has*, etc.).

Use the personal pronouns, *me, us, her, him, them, whom* for the object of a verb or preposition (*You and I do it,* but it happens *to, for, from you and me*). Some presidential blunders:

- George W. Bush on having dinner with the British prime minister: *Laura and I are looking forward to having a private dinner* with he and Mrs. Blair [i.e., *with the British prime minister and his wife, Cherie; or, with Tony and Cherie Blair*]. [22]

• George W. Bush, on his friendship with the president of Russia: It's *one thing* for he and me *to have a personal relationship* [i.e., *for him and me*].[23]

• George W. Bush, on the discourtesy of Osama bin Laden: We *do know that he has no sense of civility about who he kills* [i.e., *no sense of civility about* whom *he kills*]. [24]

When starting a new paragraph, don't use a personal pronoun until you have again identified the person or thing to which each pronoun refers. To begin a paragraph with *He, She,* or *They* is like leaving a memo by the telephone: "He called." You may know whom you mean, but no one else does.

Always supply one possible referent (*Ms. Monroe, Einstein, the twelve apostles, a BMW*) for each *she/her he/him, they/them,* and *it.* No one else in the paragraph should be competing for the pronoun. Here is President George W. Bush, speaking of al Qaeda terrorists:

• *They hate the thought of the fact that in this great country, we can worship* Almighty God *the way we see fit. And what probably makes* him *even angrier is we're not going to change.* (George W. Bush.) [25]

• *The best way to* fight evil *is to do some good. And the best way—let me qualify that. The best way to* fight evil *at home is to do some good. The best way to* fight them *abroad is to unleash the military.* (George W. Bush.) [26]

• *President Musharraf [of Pakistan] is still tight with us on the war against terror, and that's what I appreciate. He understands that we've got to keep al Qaeda on the run, and that by keeping* him *on the run, it's more likely we will bring* him *to justice.* (George W. Bush.) [27]

Sentences beginning with "It" tend to be both wordy and unclear:

• Lame: *It is a real pleasure to be back in Warsaw, this time by telecast.* (George W. Bush). [28]

• Better: *I am pleased to be seen again in Warsaw, if only on television.*

• Lame: *It is awfully hard to realize there can be peace in a place like the Middle East.* (George W. Bush.) [29]

• Better: *We must believe that peace can come even to the war-torn Middle East.*

• Lame: *Quotas are bad for America. It's not the way America is all about.* (George W. Bush.) [30]

`• Better: *If Yale had set affirmative action quotas back in 1964, a white guy with my skills would not have been admitted.*

- Lame: *It must be hard, to describe how to cause people to love one another.* (George W. Bush.) [31]
- Better: *If only we had a writer who could make people love one another!*
- Or perhaps: *No man can easily describe true love while suffering from erectile dysfunction.*

Him, her, and *them* must refer to a person, and not to a person's possession (a frequent source of error):

- Bad: *I returned* Tom's *manuscript and advised* him *to burn it.* ("Tom's manuscript is not a "he.")
- Good: *When I returned* his *manuscript, I advised* Tom *to burn it.*

For a singular noun, use a singular pronoun; and for a plural noun, a plural pronoun. Some presidential blunders:

- *Perhaps the biggest problem is that we have passed children from grade to grade, year after year, and* those child *hadn't learned the basics of reading and math.* (George W! Bush.) [32]

- *Drug therapies are replacing a lot of* medicines *as we used to know it.* (George W. Bush.) [33]

- *How can I help* somebody whose lives *have been adversely affected by the evil ones?* (George W. Bush.) [34]

Do not use "myself" for *me* ("Please kiss myself"), or "ourselves" for *us* ("Let the Iraqi people congratulate ourselves"). When President Bush explains that "The war on terror involves Saddam Hussein because of the nature of Saddam Hussein, the history of Saddam Hussein, and his willingness to terrorize himself," the intended phrase may be either *terrify himself,* or *terrorize others.*[35] When the president says he really likes it "when I'm talking about myself, and when he's talking about myself," the second "myself" should be read "me."[36] When he observes that "hostage nations" (i.e., *hostile ones*) think "they can bully *ourselves* and our allies,"[37] *us* is the intended word. And when he promises to do "whatever it took to help Taiwan defend theirself," a better phrase would be, *whatever it takes* [not "took"] *to help the Taiwanese people* [not "Taiwan"] *defend themselves* (or, better, *whatever it takes to help defend Taiwan*). [38]

Standard English has no such word as "hisself," "theirself," or "theirselves."

You will confuse your readers if you shift in mid-sentence from the third person (*he, she, they*) into the second person (*you*), or from the first (*I, we*) to the second (*you*), or from the first person plural (*we, our*) to the first person singular (*I, my*):

- Unclear: *Younger* workers *ought to be able to take some of* your *own money and invest it.* (George W. Bush.) [39]
- Better: *We must let younger workers invest some of their own money.*

- Unclear: *I want each and every American to know for certain that* I'm responsible *for the decisions I make, and* each of you *are as well.* (George W. Bush.) [40]
- Better: *Like any other American, I should take responsibility for my own decisions.*

- Unclear: Laura and I *will thank them from the bottom of* my heart. (George W. Bush.) [41]
- Better: *Laura and I will thank them from the bottom of our hearts.*

- Unclear: Let me put it to you *bluntly: in a changing world, we want* more people *to have control over* your *own life.* (George W. Bush.) [42]
- Better: *Let me tell you bluntly: in a changing world, we want more people to have control over their own lives.*

The pronouns, *anyone, no one, everyone, someone, each, anybody* and *everybody* each take a singular verb: *Anyone who wants tickets must hurry. No one loves me. Everybody gets restless in a stuffy room.*

1.8.2. Logic 101: *Just think it through.*

> *Like everything metaphysical, the harmony between thought and reality is to be found in the grammar of the language.*
> —Ludwig Wittgenstein[43]

Most of the remaining rules of grammar exist simply to ensure clarity and logical consistency, and are largely self-evident. For example:

- *We seemed totally invulnerable to, for example, the wars that took place here* [sic, mistaken adverb] *in Russia, or on the European continent.* [...] There was wars [*i.e.*, were wars] *on other continents, but we were safe."* "*America at one time was protected by two oceans* [sic, unneeded "at one time," with mistaken verb tense, since the oceans are still there] (George W. Bush).[44]

A singular subject (*it, boy, woman*) requires a singular verb (*goes, hurts, says*). A plural subject (*they, boys, women*) requires a plural verb (*go, hurt, say*):

• There is madmen *in the world,* and there are terror. [...] *I happen to believe missile* defenses is important *to keep the world more peaceful.* (George W. Bush.) [45]

Corrected: "There are madmen"; "there is terror" (or "there is terrorism"); "missile defenses are important." Such errors, in speech and writing, are more common than you may suppose:

• *Quite frankly,* teachers are *the only* profession *that teaches our children.* (Dan Quayle.) [46]

• Families is *where our nation finds hope, where wings take dream.* (George W. Bush.) [47]

• Babies *out of wedlock* is *a very difficult chore for mom and baby alike.* (George W. Bush.) [48]

• *What's not fine is, rarely is the questioned asked: 'Is our* children *learning?"* (George W. Bush.) [49]

• *Laura and I really don't realize how bright our* children *is sometimes until we get an objective analysis.* (George W. Bush.) [50]

• *Then you wake up at the high school level and find out that the illiteracy* level *of our children* are *appalling.* (George W. Bush.) [51]

• *Of all* states *that* understands *local control of schools, Iowa is such a state.* (George W. Bush.) [52]

• *I know there is a lot of young ladies who are growing up wondering* [...] *What is life choices about?* (George W. Bush.) [53]

• *If you don't have any ambitions, the minimum-wage job isn't going to get you to where you want to get, for example, in other words, what is your ambitions? And oh, by the way, if that is your ambition, here's what it is going to take to achieve it.* (George W. Bush.) [54]

• *The American* people wants *a president that appeals to the angels* (George W. Bush.) [55]

With a verb of being (*am, is, are, was, were*), take care not to say that one thing equals more than one thing, or vice versa:

• *Our* priorities is *our faith.* (George W. Bush.) [56]

• *Reading* is *the* basics *for all learning* [...] *Reading* is *the* beginnings *of the ability to be a good student.* [...] *So when your teachers say, read —you ought to listen to* her. (George W. Bush.) [57]

• *The* goals *for this country* are peace *in the world.* (George W. Bush.) [58]

• *The* goals *for this country* are a compassionate American *for every single citizen.* (George W. Bush.) [59]

• *I can't tell you what it's like to be in Europe, for example, to be talking about the greatness of America. But* the true greatness *of America* are the people. (George W. Bush.) [60]

• *Laura and I are proud to call John and Michelle Engler our friends. I know you're proud to call him governor. What a good* man the Englers are. (George W. Bush.) [61]

Such errors, when spotted, are easily corrected: *Reading is the basis for all learning* (or *Reading is a basic learning skill). Faith is our priority. Our nation's goals include peace in the world.*

• Unclear: [*Y*]*ou've got to make sure* every child *has the necessary foundation* to be *good* readers, *good* writers, *good* comprehenders (George W. Bush.) [62]
• Better: *Let us ensure that every child has the necessary foundation to be a good reader, a good writer, a good comprehender.*
• Better yet: *Let us ensure that all children learn to read, to write, and to understand.*

Especially susceptible are statements beginning with *there*:

• *There* needs *to be* debates, *like we're going through. There* needs *to be town-hall* meetings. *There needs to be travel. This is a huge country.* (George W. Bush.) [63]

(*There need to be debates, etc.; or, better, We should hold debates and town-hall meetings all across the country.*)

• *I mean, there needs to be a wholesale effort against racial profiling, which is illiterate children.* (George W. Bush.) [64]

(That sentence might be recast entirely for improved clarity, e.g.: *Illiterate children must protest against racial profiling.*)

"There's" means *there is,* not *there are*:

• Unclear: There's *no such thing as* legacies. *At least, there is a legacy, but I'll never see it.* (George W. Bush.) [65]
• Better: *Even if* legacy *is a real word, I shall never look it up in a dictionary.*

- Unclear: There's *not going to be enough* people *in the* [*Social Security*] *system to take advantage of people like me* (George W. Bush, on how he will avert a Social Security crisis.) [66]
- Better: *There will not be enough people,* etc.

- Unclear: *Washington is a town where* there's *all* kinds *of allegations. You've heard* much *of the* allegations (George W. Bush).[67] ("allegations," takes *There are,* not *There is*— and there are *many,* not "much," allegations.)
- Better: *Many of the allegations now circulating in Washington about my administration, you have already heard.*

Similarly, in statements on the model, "X is Y" ("War is hell," "Roses are red," "February is a long month"), the subject and the terms that describe it should indeed be comparable.   When our president says, "I think war is a dangerous place," a better phrase would be: *I think war is a dangerous activity,* or, more clearly: *I truly believe, if you are not careful, that war can kill you.*[68]

It is okay, figuratively speaking, to say "God is love" or "Microsoft is Bill Gates," but it is usually best not to identify a human being as an abstract noun:

- *I know something about being a government. And you've got a good one.* [Immigrant workers must] *get in line* [...] *to become a citizenship in a legal manner.* (George W. Bush.) [69]

- *I have a different vision of leadership. A leadership is someone who brings people together.* [...] *And I'm a proud man to be the nation based upon such wonderful values.* (George W. Bush.) [70]

1.8.3. *Punctuation 101.*

> *This fellow doth not stand upon points... His speech was like a tangled chain—nothing impaired, but all disordered.*
> —Theseus, on the mispunctuated speech of Peter Quince (*MND* 5.1.118-26)

1.8.3a. *Punctuate thoughtfully.*

The only really important rule of punctuation is to think about what you're doing.   Most errors arise not from ignorance but from laziness.   Careless pointing makes a text ambiguous, confusing, or unintelligible.   When writing your high school essay, or a consumer complaint, or the personal statement for your college application, or your résumé, or an office memo, you may have been thinking: *If I don't punctuate correctly, who will notice?*   But the readers of your badly proofread work will be thinking: *What a dimwit.*

Punctuation not only helps the reader understand what you have to say without distraction; it also shapes the meaning of what you have written:

Dear John,

I want a man who knows what love is all about. You are generous, kind, thoughtful. People who are not like you admit to being loveless and cold.

You have ruined me for other men. I yearn for you! I have no feelings whatsoever when we're apart. I look to be forever happy—will you let me be yours?

Gloria

Here is the identical text, differently pointed: [71]

Dear John,
I want a man who knows what love is. All about you are generous, kind, thoughtful people, who are not like you. Admit to being loveless and cold!

You have ruined me. For other men, I yearn; for you, I have no feelings whatsoever. When we're apart, I look to be forever happy. Will you let me be?

Yours,
Gloria

1.8.3b. *End punctuation.*

The *period* is a friendly mark of punctuation. Use periods to keep sentences short. Your readers will love you for it. Do not, however, break sentences into fragments:

- Bad: *A challenger is somebody who, you know, generally comes from the pack and wins. If you're going to win. And that's where I'm coming from.* (George W. Bush.) [72]
- Better: *I may be following the pack right now, but as the challenger I expect to come from behind, and win.*

- Bad: *We had a good Cabinet meeting. Talked a lot of issues. The Secretary of State and Defense brought us up to date about our desires to spread freedom and peace around the world.* (George W. Bush.) [73]
- Better: *At the Cabinet meeting, we talked about key issues. The Secretary of State and Secretary of Defense brought me up to date on our mutual desire to spread freedom and peace throughout the world.*

Fragments are not always "wrong." If you know what you're doing, and if your fragment will not confuse readers, it is perfectly okay to make an emphatic word or expression serve the purpose of a sentence, and to punctuate it accordingly, even though it is not a complete thought. (As in dialogue? Yes.)

A comma splice is a mistake, fix it [sic]. Do not join two or more complete thoughts ("independent clauses") with a comma, it is a distracting error, don't annoy your readers with a sentence like this one, learn when to stop:

- Bad: *The cure for boredom is curiosity, there is no cure for curiosity, in fact, if you're a cat it can kill you.*

- Good: *The cure for boredom is curiosity. There is no cure for curiosity. In fact, if you're a cat it can kill you.*

A full stop is usually better even for short sentences like these:

- *It's your money. You paid for it.* (George W. Bush, on his tax cuts.)[74]
- *It's clearly a budget. It's got a lot of numbers in it.* (George W. Bush, on the 2001 Federal budget.) [75]
- *Good things come to those who wait. Bad things also come.*

Exception: If a compound sentence is comprised of short, sequential clauses, commas will usually do the trick, even without an *and* or *but*:

- *She slipped, she fell, she sued the shopping mall.*
- *It's not that life is too short, it's that death is too long.*
- *Join the army, meet interesting people, kill them.*

In such cases, the order of the ideas may dictate which punctuation works best. It is okay to write: "Save a tree. Eat a beaver." Or: "Save a tree; eat a beaver." Or: "Eat a beaver, save a tree." Each has a slightly different emphasis. Suit yourself.

1.8.3c. *Question marks.*

All direct questions should end with a question mark, even short ones. (*Is that right? Yes. Always? Yes.*) The question mark goes at the end, even if the question ends with a phrase that is not itself a question:

- *Why can cookware not be made from human hair, if, as scientists tell us, healthy hair is stronger than aluminum?*

Indirect questions end in a period:

• *To be or not to be, that is the question.*
• *The editors asked Hemingway if he could write another one of his great stories about catching fish.*

1.8.3d. *Exclamation marks.*

Save exclamation marks for necessary exclamations, usually in dialogue (*Look out! No! Ouch!*). Extra pointing does not increase urgency!!!! It only looks as if you're trying to be cute!!!! And it's annoying!!!! If you are the sort of person who falls in love with people who pepper their love letters with multiple exclamation marks where a less impassioned lover would use just one ("I love you!") or none at all ("Goodbye—"), then by all means reciprocate in kind. But when writing for any other audience, use exclamation marks sparingly or not at all.

1.8.3e. *Semicolons.*

The semicolon is a pretentious and overused mark of punctuation:

• Okay: *Change your semicolons to periods; begin anew.*
• Better: *Change your semicolons to periods. Begin anew.*

• Okay: *Women do not like timid men; cats do not like prudent mice.*
• Better: *Women do not like timid men. Cats do not like prudent mice.*

Most of the semicolons that you see in student papers, office documents, personal correspondence, and legal contracts, should be periods. Most of the rest should be commas. A few should be dashes. Many others are mistaken colons.

To indicate a strong rhetorical break or pause between ideas, a dash before the conjunction is generally preferable to a semicolon (use sparingly):

• *The early bird gets the worm—but it's the second mouse that gets the cheese.*

It is never good to write, "Dear Mom; Happy birthday," not even if your mom is thrilled to hear from you. A semicolon may, however, be used in those rare instances when a comma seems too feeble, and a full stop, too much—as when two short but complete thoughts are so closely interrelated as to form a single compound thought:

• *Some women do not admit their age; some men do not act it.*

• *Love is grand; divorce is a hundred grand.*

• *I'm not a vegetarian because I love animals; I'm a vegetarian because I hate plants.*

• *My husband has never suffered from alcoholism; in fact, he enjoys it.*

• *Fred is not a complete idiot; some parts are missing.*

• *George Washington was the first U.S. president to grow pot; John F. Kennedy was the first president to smoke it.*

• *The first bomb dropped by the Allies on Berlin during World War II killed the only elephant in the Berlin Zoo; the first bomb dropped by America in the 2003 Iraq war killed a family of seven who were at home eating breakfast.*

Difficulty often arises with "conjunctive adverbs" (such connectors as *after all, consequently, however, nevertheless, therefore*). If the connecting adverb appears in the middle of a phrase or clause, wrap it in commas:

• *Only two things are inevitable: death and taxes. Death,* however, *does not get worse each year.*

• *But even more efficient,* however, *is the transference of heat and cool as a result of circulating water below the (it's called "thermal heating and cooling") okay.* (George W. Bush.) [76]

If your "however" is linked to an adjective, then a semicolon, *however useful,* must not be used; the two-word phrase is bracketed by commas:

• *When you have eliminated the impossible, whatever remains,* however improbable, *must be the truth.* (A. Conan Doyle.)

Trouble arises when the "however" (or other connecting adverb) introduces the second complete thought in a compound sentence; in such instances, a semicolon marks the end of the first thought (as in this very sentence).

• Bad: *A man with a healthy liver can drink a pint of beer an hour indefinitely without getting drunk, however, the man who persists may no longer have a healthy liver.* (Here, a semicolon is needed after "drunk" to mark the end of the first complete idea, and to fix the comma splice.)

If in doubt, separate all complete thoughts from one another with a full stop. No one but the most curmudgeonly semicolon-lovers will object:

• *A man with a healthy liver can drink a pint of beer an hour indefinitely without getting drunk. However, the man who persists may no longer have a healthy liver.*

A semicolon may also be used as a kind of reinforced comma in a list or series, to provide clarity when the individual phrases have internal commas:

• *If a park-statue is of a hero on a horse that has both front legs in the air, the hero died in battle; if the horse has one front leg in the air, the hero died as a result of wounds received in battle; if the horse has all four legs on the ground, the hero died of natural causes. If a dog in the same park has one rear leg in the air, he is relieving himself.*

• *If this is coffee, please bring me some tea; but if this is tea, please bring me some coffee.* (Abraham Lincoln, attrib.)

• H. L. Mencken, who died before either Bush was elected president, said that President Warren Harding *"writes the worst English I have ever encountered. It reminds me of a string of wet sponges; it reminds me of tattered washing on the line; it reminds me of stale bean-soup, of college yells, of dogs barking idiotically through endless nights.* [77]

1.8.3f. *Colons.*

Most frequently, a colon is used to separate minutes from hours in the time of day (6:45 am, 4:30 pm).

In bibliographic citation, a colon separates the main title from subtitle, and the city from the publisher:

English, Angelique. *How to Write: Not Your Usual User's Guide to the English Language.* New York: Wicked Good Books, 2015.
Strunk, William, and E. B. White. *The Elements of Style.* New York: Macmillan, 2d ed., 1972).

A colon distinguishes between the chapter and verse of a Biblical citation (Deut. 23:13, Psalms 137:9, Acts 19:19-20).

Use colons for the speech tags in dramatic dialogue or an interview transcript:

David Fink: When you're talking about politics, what do you and him [your father, George H. W. Bush] talk about?
George W. Bush: Pussy. [78]

Similarly, a colon, used informally, may set off deliberate sentence fragments, as for a résumé, a directory of names, or a glossary:

- *Budget*:   A method for going broke methodically.
- *Campers*:   Nature's way of feeding mosquitoes.
- *Lottery*:   A tax on people who are bad at math.
- *Shin*:   A device for finding furniture in the dark.

Block quotations may be introduced by a colon (as I have done here):

- The LORD was with the men of Judah. They took possession of the hill country, but they were unable to drive the people from the plains, because they had iron chariots (Judges 1:19, *New International Version*).

Resist the temptation to introduce quotations, or a list, with such usually unnecessary phrases as *for example*: or *as follows*: or *the following*: The colon alone can usually do the work.

Colons may be used to introduce virtually any quotation that represents a complete thought. Block form is unnecessary with shorter quotes:

- *It was Patrick Henry, an American patriot, who said: "Give me liberty, or give me death!" But when he said it, he was the owner of sixty-five slaves.*

- *President George H. W. Bush, during his 1987 visit to Auschwitz, expressed historical interest in Nazi methodology: "They're big on crematoriums," he observed, "there's one over here, one over there." After leaving the memorial, he remained puzzled: "Boy, they were big on crematoriums, weren't they!"* [79]

To introduce a fragment or partial quotation, omit the colon:

- Fragmented: *The president has said that the American economy is:* "*ooching along.*"[80] (Omit the colon, add no comma, and it's fine.)
- Fine: *As our president always says: "Let me put it to you this way."* [81]

As used within an English sentence, the colon implies a logical relation (*as follows, namely, thus, like so*): the words after the colon will explain or complete what has just been said. For conciseness, you may also wish to use a colon in place of "because":

- *If you toss a penny 10,000 times, it will "come up heads" only about 4,950 times: the "heads" picture weighs slightly more than the lettering on the other side.*

Do not place a colon after a preposition (*from, to, on*, etc.):

• *Marathon runners are advised to: load up on carbohydrates, drink plenty of water, and grease their feet.* (Omit the colon, add no comma, and it's fine.)

Most editors prefer that the first word after a colon be kept in lower-case, even if what follows constitutes a complete thought:

• *Birds cannot survive in space: they need gravity to swallow.*

• *Praise God: he's insecure.*

• *Support the rich: vote Republican.*

• *Ms. Parker requires only three things of a suitor: he must be handsome, ruthless, and stupid.*

• *Borrow money from pessimists: they don't expect you to pay them back.*

• *As you know, these are open forums: you're able to come and listen to what I have to say.* (George W. Bush.) [82]

The rule is flexible. If the complete sentence following the colon is closely related to others that follow, a capital letter may assist clarity.

1.8.3g. *Quotation marks.*

Titles. Use quotation marks for poems under 500 lines. Use italics (or underlining if you don't have an italic function) for poems of more than 500 lines. Titles of chapters, magazine articles, or episodes should be in quotation marks. Titles of books, magazines, films and television shows should be italicized (except in journalism, where quotation marks may be used instead).

Quotations. When quotation marks are used for actual quotations, everything between the opening and closing quotation marks should be a verbatim quote:

• *"A friend in need," said Maxine, "is a friend I can do without."*

• *When Amber became a popular name for girls, Crayola Corp. stopped making crayons in the color called "raw amber."*

Imagined quotations may also be set in quotes: To attract a man, women should wear a perfume called "New Car Interior."

Any changes you introduce within the quotation marks must be signaled by square brackets:

• *"After all, this [Saddam Hussein] is the guy that tried to kill my dad at one time"* (George W. Bush). [83]

• *"America needs a military," said President Bush, "where our breast [sic] and brightest are proud to serve, and proud to stay."* [84]

• *President Bush stated today that diseases "such as arthritis and osteoporosis can be less be-a-be-a-dilatating* [i.e., debilitating] *than they once were."* [85]

When quoting poetry, insert a slash to indicate the break between lines of verse, and retain the capital letters: Prince Hamlet in his first soliloquy wishes that his "too too sallied flesh would melt, / Thaw and resolve itself into a dew" (*Ham.* 1.2.129-30).

A bracketed word in a literary text from which you are quoting indicates that the editors have corrected what they take to be a mistake in their copytext. When quoting, retain the square brackets, making no changes of your own except, perhaps, an omission, which is indicated by a bracketed ellipsis: The Bevington edition of *Hamlet* emends "sallied" (London, 1623) to *sullied*: "Oh, that this too too [sullied] flesh would [...] resolve itself into a dew" (*Ham.* 1.2.133-34).[86]

For a quote within a quote, use single quotes ('like so'):

• When he was Governor of Texas, George W. Bush issued a proclamation to celebrate Jesus Day: "I urge all Texans to [...] follow Christ's message of love and service in thought and deed. Therefore, I, George W. Bush, Governor of Texas, do hereby proclaim June 10, 2000, 'Jesus Day' in Texas, and urge the appropriate recognition whereof; in official recognition whereof, I hereby affix my signature this 17th day of April, 2000." [87]

Quoted questions. If a question contains a quoted phrase that is not itself a question, the question mark goes at the end of the sentence, after the quoted phrase:

• *While in Brazil, president Bush asked the Brazilian president, "Do you have blacks, too?"*[88] (Here, the question mark *belongs* to the quotation.)

• *Have you read Philip Roth's short story, "The Conversion of the Jews"?* (Here, the brief quotation is contained *within* the question.)

For a quotation within a quotation, use single quotes:

• *President Bush spoke Tuesday of how he likes to tease radical Islamist groups such as al Qaeda. "You know," he said, "the enemy hit us, and they said, 'Oh, this great country is going to wilt. They're not great. They're weak.' I like to needle them by saying they must have been watching too much daytime TV!"* [89]

• *The president praised Americans for their compassion: "People from all walks of life, all politics [sic] parties, some of who [sic] probably have never been to New York City before, have said [...], 'How can I help somebody whose lives [sic] have been adversely affected by the evil ones?'"* [90]

• *The president edits the text of his speeches:* "People make suggestions on what to say all the time," he said. "I'll give you an example: I don't read what's handed to me. People say: 'Here, here's your speech.' Or: 'Here's an idea for a speech.' They're changed. Trust me." [91]

If (as in many academic essays), each quotation is followed by a citation, then closing quotation marks go at the end of the quoted line(s), but *before* the citation; and the period goes at the end of the sentence, *after* the citation, like so: "The economy is moving in the right direction" (President George H. W. Bush, 4 Oct. 1991). "I don't want to buy into the predicate [i.e., *premise*] about [the U.S. being in] another recession. I don't feel that way" (25 Oct. 1991). "The economy has turned the corner, headed for recovery" (31 Oct. 1991). "I'm not prepared to say we are in a recession" (8 Nov. 1991). "It will not be a deep recession" (4 Jan. 1992). "The economy is in free-fall" (15 Jan. 1992).

Enclose square brackets as needed to identify speakers not clearly identified in the quotation: "This president [George H. W. Bush] is going to lead us out of this recovery" [i.e., this recession] (Vice president Dan Quayle, 17 Jan. 1992).[92] "[Vice president] Dick Cheney and I do not want this nation to be in a recession. We want anybody who can find work to be able to find work" (George W. Bush, 5 Dec. 2000).[93]

1.8.3h. *Apostrophes for possession.*

You may think apostrophes a silly nuisance. You may consider it a trivial offense to insert superfluous apostrophes or to omit the apostrophe where it is needed. Well, go ahead: *sin*. But most of your readers will notice your mistakes, and they will feel quietly superior to you. Make too many mistakes of that sort, and your readers will take you for a dolt. The rules for the humble apostrophe are not really so difficult: you can master them if you try.

No apostrophe for simple plurals: The one rule of apostrophes that almost everyone understands is that you do not use an apostrophe with a simple plural (*two six-seater lifeboats, fourteen passengers, two swimmers*). But pluraled surnames are a frequent source of confusion. If a sign in the front yard reads *The Smiths* (or *The Joneses*), it means that members of the Smith (or the Jones) family live here. If the sign reads *The Smiths'* (or *The Joneses'*), the apostrophe implies an omitted word: this is *the Smiths' house* (*the Joneses' home*). If the sign reads *The Smith's* (or *The Jones'*), it means that the sign painter found apostrophes confusing.

Form the plural of regular nouns by adding an *s* (or, sometimes, *es*) with *no apostrophe* (*boys, boxes, the Andersons*). The same rule obtains for denoting plural numbers:

• *Your manuscript 3s and 5s look the same.*
• *In the 50s, the Rev. Billy Graham was as big as Elvis.*
• *If you can remember the Sixties, you weren't there.*

Acceptable exception: It is permissible but unnecessary, when forming the plural of a single letter, to use an apostrophe. The letter itself (but not the *s*) is italic:

• Historically, to "Mind your own *P*'s and *Q*'s" meant to focus on your own pints and quarts (of beer), not on your neighbor's.
• Please try to learn your *ABC*'s [*or: ABC*s].
• Lisa gets mostly *A*'s while Bart gets *D*'s and *F*'s [*or: A*s...*D*s and *F*s].

Singular possessive. Form the possessive of singular nouns by adding an apostrophe and an *s*:

• The *orangutan's* warning signal is a loud belch.
• The *Administration's* "Nigergate" warnings were known forgeries.
• A *pig's* orgasm lasts for about thirty minutes.
• *James's* attention span in bed is about five minutes.
• An *ostrich's* eye is bigger than its brain.
• *Charles's* ears are too large for his head.

Ancient names, abstract nouns. An exception is usually made for Moses ("Moses' magic rod"), Jesus ("Jesus' disciples"), and for classical names that end in -*s* ("Isis' temple"). So, too, for abstractions ("for goodness' sake"). Write "Achilles' heel" (if the heel belongs to Achilles' foot), but "an Achilles heel" (as a figure of speech meaning a *vulnerable area*). If a possessive noun sounds infelicitous ("Jesus' wrath"), change it to the form "A of B" (*the wrath of Jesus, the compassion of Moses, for the cause of justice*).

Plural possessive. Most plural nouns take an apostrophe-plus-*s* (or -*es*) to denote possessive (*the girls' soccer league, the Smiths' Volvo, the Joneses' sailboat*).

Exceptions: Plural nouns that do not end in -*s* (*children, people*) need an apostrophe-plus-*s* to signify the plural possessive (*children's literature, people's opinion*).

Singular possessor	**Plural possessor**
• a *man's job*	• *men's rest room*
• a *woman's paycheck*	• *women's rights*
• an *ox's eyes*	• *oxen's pasture*

The plural of *child* is *children*; the toys of the *children* are therefore *children's* toys, not *childrens'* toys. (There is no such word as *childs, child's, childrens'* or *childrens*.)

Avoid double possessive constructions: Rephrase such awkward constructions as "Bob Jones's Jehovah's Witness neighbor's house" (*the house of Bob Jones's neighbor, a Jehovah's Witness*).

Possessive pronouns. Learn the difference between *its* (possessive) and *it's* (=*it is* or *it has*); between *whose* (possessive) and *who's* (=*who is* or *who has*); between *his* (possessive) and *he's* (= *he is* or *he has*); between *hers, theirs, yours* (possessive) and *her's, their's, your's* (no such words). Confusion of *it's* and *its* is a common but distracting error. Like "his," both "its" and "whose" always denote possessive:

- Correct: He's *sending us his resumé.* It's *on its way.*
- Correct: It's *a bad film, but I never judge a book by* its *movie.*
- Correct: It's *not hard to tell* whose *car is illegally parked, but* who's *fool enough to ticket the mayor's wife?*

Never write "it's self" or "its self" for *itself,* or "one's self" for *oneself*:

- Incorrect: *The first aircraft to shoot* its self *down was an American F14 fighter in Vietnam, using a Sparrow air-to-air missile.* (Write: *itself*)

1.8.3i. *Apostrophes for contraction.*

Use contractions sparingly, especially in academic papers. For informal writing (and for fictional dialogue), contractions may be used freely, including such formations as "could've" (for *could have*), "would've," "should've." (It makes no sense to write "could of," "would of," "should of," which will look to your educated readers like ignorance even if you are only trying to be cute).

For formal or technical writing, always spell out *it is, there is,* rather than use the common contractions, *it's, there's.* Never use "there's" to mean *there are.*

A few contractions begin with an apostrophe: *the class of '06, 'Twas the night before Christmas, 'tis the season to be jolly.* If your word processor has its "preferences" set to so-called "smart quotes" ("like so" and 'like so'), you will have trouble with apostrophe-first contractions. Instead of getting a smart single-quote, you'll get a stupid backwards apostrophe, every time:

- Dumb "smart" quotes: *'Tis the season to be jolly for the class of '06.*
- Correct: *'Tis the season to be jolly for the class of '06.*

1.8.3j. *Commas.*

The comma is a wonderfully versatile unit of punctuation. It may be used to indicate a brief pause in the flow of a sentence, or to separate the items in a series, or to distinguish parenthetical phrases from the main idea. To omit necessary commas will confuse the sense:

• *Fear of impurity prevented Medieval nuns from removing their clothes to wash, until a divine vision revealed to St. Bridgette that the Lord would not object to her taking a bath once every two weeks.*

To remove the comma from that otherwise accurate sentence would imply that nuns of St. Bridgette demanded she have a vision as a *prerequisite* to their bathing, when in fact the saint's vision provided a corrective to those nuns who had been afraid to bathe in the first place. Don't drive your readers crazy with omitted, or misplaced, or superfluous commas. The rules are not hard to master. You just need to pay attention to what you're doing.

Use commas to separate items in a series. The American convention is to use a comma after the next-to-last element even when it is followed by a conjunction:

• *"My formula for success is rise early, work late, and strike oil"* (Paul Getty).
• *"Honest criticism is hard to take, particularly from a relative, a friend, an acquaintance, or a stranger"* (Franklin P. Jones).
• *Jocasta was a tall, beautiful, well-built, but neurotic mother.*

If a series contains one or more doublets (*a* and *b, x* and *y*) do not break up the doublet with a comma:

• *Mary had a little lamb, some salad, two beers, a gin and tonic, a martini, a whiskey and soda, and a glass of milk before passing out.*

If a parenthetical phrase and a series appear in the same sentence, place commas accordingly so as not to confuse your reader:

• *The national tick collection, housed in the Smithsonian Institution, contains 120,000 ticks, as well as 7,996 fleas, 1,272 lice, more than 14,000 neotropical mosquitoes, and 8,000 marine nematodes.*

Parenthetical material. Use commas to bracket a parenthetical number, word, phrase, or clause:

• *Rebecca Ann Chase, 8, of The Dalles, Oregon, scored a hole-in-one on the first hole she ever played—the 125-yard, par-3, fifth hole at the Oak Knoll golf course.*
• *The buttock muscle, or gluteus maximus, is the largest muscle in the human body.*
• *An uncovered swimming pool in Phoenix, Arizona, will collect about twenty pounds of dust a year.*
• *Napoleon's sister, Pauline Bonaparte, was a notorious nymphomaniac.*
• *The last passenger pigeon, named Martha, died of old age in the Cincinnati Zoo on September 1, 1914.*

The abbreviations *inc., sr.,* and *jr.,* take a comma before and after (except, of course, at the end of a sentence):

• *Sammy Davis, Jr., only had one eye.*
• *Geraldo Rivera is the junior son-in-law of Kurt Vonnegut, Jr.*

Et al. and *etc.,* like any other parenthetical remark, are set off by commas, but it is best to avoid using *et al.* and *etc.* altogether.

Introductory phrasing. Use a comma to separate an introductory phrase or incomplete thought from the main idea that follows:

• *In the time it takes a man to swim 130 meters, a shark can swim a mile.*
• *Though both men were slave-owners, Robert E. Lee during the Civil War freed his slaves before Ulysses S. Grant.*
• *If this were a dictatorship, it would be a heck of a lot easier, so long as I'm the dictator.* (George W. Bush, 19 Dec. 2000.) [94]

Use commas to set off a quoted statement or phrase if there is a syntactical break, such as he said *or* she said:

• *Asked about the northwest salmon population, the president replied, "We don't need to be breaching no dams that are producing electricity."* (One comma is needed after the introductory phrase, a second one after *replied* [George W. Bush].) [95]

Omit the comma when the quoted phrase is a seamless part of your sentence:

• *Asked about the northwest salmon population, the president replied that we should breach "no dams that are producing electricity."* (sic, no comma after *breach*).

Compound sentences. A "compound sentence" contains two or more complete thoughts ("independent clauses") joined by a "coordinating conjunction" (*and, but, or, nor, for, so,* or *yet*). Place a comma before the conjunction:

• *One word sums up probably the responsibility of any vice president, and that one word is "to be prepared."* (V.P. Dan Quayle.) [96]
• *Always go to other people's funerals, or they may not go to yours.*
• *The lion and the lamb shall lie down together, but the lamb shall get no sleep.*
• *The weasel cannot soar like the eagle, but neither does he get sucked into jet engines.*

Omission of the comma may cause confusion:

• *Fred shot the deer and his wife Mary, an excellent cook, made venison.* (There should be a comma after "deer.")

Exceptions: If the two independent clauses in a compound sentence are rather short, and so closely related as to form one complete thought, the comma can sometimes be omitted without loss of clarity:

• *Make your machine idiot-proof and someone will make a better idiot.*
• *It's not a dictatorship in Washington but I tried to make it one in that instance.* (George W. Bush, as president, Jan. 2004.) [97]

When the reverse is true, and you wish to emphasize a rhetorical break between ideas, or to indicate a pause, it is sometimes okay to place a dash instead of a comma before the conjunction (*The early bird gets the worm—but it's the second mouse who gets the cheese*); or to remove the conjunction and replace it with a semicolon:

• *The Nubian wild ass is extinct; my brother is not a Nubian.* (The semicolon takes the place of comma-*but*.)
• *Bubba has used up all of his sick days; he's calling in dead.* (The semicolon takes the place of comma-*so*.)
• *"You don't get everything you want; a dictatorship would be a lot easier."* (George W. Bush, as governor of Texas, July 1998.) [98]

Break up or compress a stringy compound sentence:

• Stringy: *I appreciate people's opinions, but I'm more interested in news, and the best way to get the news is from objective sources, and the most objective sources I have are people on my staff who tell me what's happening in the world.* (George W. Bush.) [99]

• Better: *I can appreciate opinions, but I need news from objective sources. I have people on my staff who tell me, with complete objectivity, what's happening in the world.*
• More concise: *Although I do not read the news, trusted advisors keep me abreast of current events.*

In compressing a compound sentence, remove unneeded words but use a comma to assist clarity:

• Wordy: *Attila the Hun died while he was having sex, and Elvis Presley died while he was sitting on a toilet.*
• Concise: *Attila the Hun died while having sex, and Elvis, while sitting on a toilet.*
• *The pen is mightier than the sword, and the computer keyboard, bigger than the bomb.*

It is okay to use a comma to set off a parenthetical clause such as "I know" or "you know" or "that's for sure!" without beginning a new sentence:

• *"A dictatorship would be a heck of a lot easier, there's no question about it."* (George W. Bush, 30 July 2001.) [100]

Some places to omit the comma:

Omit the comma before coordinating conjunctions (*and, but, or*, etc.) when there are not two complete thoughts (*a* and *b; c* or *d; e* but *f*):

• *Hermia is little but fierce.*
• *Grandpa evidently stopped to think and then forgot to start again.*
• *In 1922 Harry Truman joined the Ku Klux Klan but resigned his membership a few months later.*

Omit commas from a series joined by prepositions (*a* of *b* of *c* of *d*):

• *The armistice ending World War I was signed on the 11th hour of the 11th day of the 11th month of 1918.*

Do not put comma after a question mark or point of exclamation:

• *"Will you please leave me alone?" asked Heather.*
• *"Please leave me alone," she said. "You're not my type."*
• *At last she said, "Piss off!"*

A quotation or quoted fragment involving no syntactical break front or rear requires no comma to set it off from the surrounding text—

• *At a White House reception, when Senator Paul Wellstone said he opposed the Gulf War, President George H. W. Bush called him a "chicken shit."*[101]

Nor is a comma required when a complete quoted thought is introduced by *that*:

• *Speaking of violence in Iraq, President George W. Bush conceded that "This is historic times. This has been tough weeks in that country. I pray every day there's less casualty."*[102]

1.8.3k. *Marks of parenthesis.*

Parentheses are handy little devices. Use them sparingly.

There is *always* a space (like so) before a parenthesis. To do otherwise(like so) will distract your readers.

Put no space between a closing parenthesis and punctuation. To do otherwise (like so) , is a mistake (wrong again) .

(If your parentheses enclose a complete sentence, put the period inside the closing bracket.)

Citations. If the opera is not over until the fat lady has sung, neither is a sentence over until the end-punctuation. When providing a citation for quoted material, the page number (or line reference) goes at the end of your sentence, enclosed by parenthesis. The citation is part of your sentence; it's just not part of the quotation. Put your quotation marks at the end of the quote, *before* the citation, and your period at the end of the sentence, *after* the citation:

• Wrong: *In the gospels, Jesus says, "Think not that I am come to send peace on earth: I came not to send peace, but a sword (Mat. 10.34)." He promises to cause division on the earth...* (Here, the citation is not being quoted. Do not put it inside the end-quotation marks.)

• Wrong: *Stabbing his stepfather, Hamlet exclaims, "The point envenom'd too? / Then, venom, to thy work!"* (Ham. 5.2.321-2) *Hamlet then pours poisoned wine down the dying man's throat...* (The citation belongs with the first sentence, not with the second. Put a period after the closing parenthesis.)

• Right: *Mae West said, "The curve is more powerful than the sword" (Leider, 127). She knew that the female bosom...*

1.8.3-*l.* *Hyphens.*

In general, it is best to do without hyphens, even for such long words as *coeducation, noncommittal* or *noncompetitive*. But the omission of a necessary hyphen can confuse the sense of your sentence:

• *The sisters of St. Bridgette's convent have cast off coats and clothing. They can be seen by the homeless, and tried on for size, every weekday from 9 till noon.*

Here, the omission of a hyphen in *cast-off* implies that the nuns of St. Bridgette have been exposing themselves in order to entertain the city's poor, Monday through Friday.

Hyphenate compound numbers when they are spelled out (*twenty-three*); spelled-out fractions used as adjectives or nouns (a *two-thirds majority*); or to link two words into a compound word (*African-American, best-educated, slam-dunk*).

Do not put a hyphen between an *-ly* adverb and the word it modifies (a *fully loaded gun*), or between an adverb-plus-adjective phrase that follows the verb (*A dog will not bite if well groomed* [correct]; cf. *A well-groomed dog will not bite* [correct]).

As a suffix, *like* is not hyphenated unless the word that precedes it is a proper noun, ends in a double *l*, or has three or more syllables (*fishlike, godlike, manlike, shell-like, wall-like, hippopotamus-like*).

If you are unsure whether to spell compounds as one word or two (*airfield, wheat field, anticlimax, anti-inflammatory, faint-hearted, halfhearted, chalkboard, pine board*), try typing the compound as a single word without a hyphen and see if your electronic spellchecker accepts it without prompting a correction. Then double-check your spellchecker's wisdom.

A moment's thought will clear up most ambiguities: A *high-school girl* is one who attends high school; a *high schoolgirl* is student on a mountain, or on LSD. A *fine-tooth comb* is one with thin teeth; a *fine tooth-comb* is a good device for combing your mouth. A *little-used car* may have a high resale value; a *little used-car* is both used, and little. Do not depend on hyphens to resolve ambiguities: for "a little used car," try calling it "a small used car" or "a car rarely used."

• Unclear: *My corns have been examined by four foot doctors.*
• Untrue: *Physicians four feet tall have examined my corns.*
• Clear: *Four foot-doctors have examined my corns.*
• Better yet: *Four podiatrists have examined my corns.*

Be careful with phrases that may be one word or two:

• *Darling, please* come back *to bed.*
• *I'm too worn out to make a* comeback.
• *Exercise a little* common sense.
• *A* commonsense *answer is often wrong.*

• *The workers are hoping for a* bailout, *and the executives, for a government* handout.
• *It's time to* hand out *pink slips to the workers and to* bail out *the executives.*

Don't confuse a hyphen (-) with an en dash (–) or an em dash (—).

1.8.3m. *The em dash* (–).

To mark a strong rhetorical break, or a pause, try using the em dash—like so—but get it right, it's not a hyphen. Don't overdo it: the em dash—like marks of parenthesis—should be used sparingly—not as in this dash-glutted sentence. Where possible, use commas instead of dashes or parentheses.

The em dash is used most often to set off a parenthetical comment more boldly than commas would do:

• *The great question—which I have not been able to answer—is,* "What does a woman want? (Sigmund Freud.)
• *I didn't—I swear I didn't—get into politics to feather my nest or feather my friends' nests.* (George W. Bush.)

Make an em dash with two hyphens--as here--and not with a single hyphen; or you may produce an em dash by using your word-processor's function keys (option+shift+hyphen on Microsoft Word). An em dash takes no space before or after.

1.8.3n. *The en dash* (–).

The en dash is half the length of an M (that is, the width of an uppercase N) and slightly longer than a hyphen. It is used primarily to connect words or numbers (3–6, 223–27). Write: *Sybil lived in Salem 1664–1692*, or *Sybil lived in Salem from 1664 to 1692* (but not: *Sybil lived in Salem from 1664–1692*).

1.8.4. *Capitalization.*

Capitalize the proper names of people, places, organizations, and things. Capitalize the first and last word, and every important word, in a title. Capitalize the Sun, Earth and the Moon only when used as names for our star, our home planet, and its satellite. Don't worry too much about all of the other rules for capitalization. Your problem with capitalization is the least of your worries. (*Exception:* When sending an email note to your English teacher, don't be such a knucklehead as to write entirely in lower-case.)

1.8.5. *Numbers and dates.*

All numbers must be accurate and clearly expressed. In formal prose, write out numbers requiring fewer than three words:

• *The octopus has three hearts.*
• *Cuckoo birds go "cuckoo!" forty-two times a minute during the mating season, which lasts about twenty-eight days.*
• *One hundred grams of peanut butter contain an average of thirty-four insect fragments and one or two rodent hairs.*
• *Of the 4.4 billion people in developing countries, nearly three-fifths lack access to safe sewers, and a third have no access to clean water.*

Use numerals for decimals (1.54), fractions ($7^1/_3$), and numbers requiring three or more words (386). Decimals must have a zero if less than 1 (*0.36*) except when referring to gun calibers (*.22* rifle, *Colt .45 Magnum*, etc.).

Use numerals with units of measure (except time), no matter how small.

Do not start your sentence with a numeral. If you must begin with a number (rarely a good idea), spell it out. If you are a mathematician writing for mathematicians, you may ignore this rule.

On a sign displaying a cost of eighty-nine cents for a Snickers bar, the price can be written as "$0.89," or as "89¢," but should not combine the two forms: ".89¢" is less than one cent, and "$.89¢" is nonsense.

To denote a sequence of pages, be economical but clear: *For Wednesday's assignment, read* The Riverside Shakespeare, *pages 1921-3, 1936, and 1945-52.* Use commas to assist the reader in expressing large numbers:

• *111,111,111 x 111,111,111 = 12,345,678,987,654,231.*
• *One may twist a Rubik's Cube into exactly 43,252,003,274,489,856, 000 different positions.*

In journalistic writing, write out the ordinals one through nine; use numerals for *10* and above; use a numeral plus the word for round numbers of *1 million* or more: *India has 50 million monkeys.*

Roman numerals are best reserved for royalty (*Richard III*), Popes (*Pius IX*), World War I and World War II. Do not confuse "Queen Elizabeth II" (a queen of England) with the *Queen Elizabeth 2* (a cruise ship). Some teachers (and journal editors) still require upper and lower case Roman numerals to denote the act and scene of a play, as in the good old days. The use of Arabic numerals (*Ham.* 2.2.191-2, not *Ham.* II.ii.191-2) is today widely preferred.

Dates should be written so: *May 10, 2005* (*month, day, year,* with a comma between the day and the year); or like so: *10 May 2005* (day, month, year, with no comma between the day and the month). Writing the date numerically (5/10/05) may cause confusion, since the American convention of writing the month first differs from the practice of most other countries.

For the day's number, omit the abbreviated forms "1st," "2nd," "3rd," etc. Abbreviate the centuries thus (the 19th century, a 20th-century composer) in news writing.

Abbreviate the year only if the meaning is clear (30 June '06 - 1 July '07). In formal prose it is better to write out the year in full, especially in phrases involving two or more dates:

• First Lady Nancy Reagan legally changed the year of her birth from 1921 to 1923.

• Though she was officially not yet born, or even conceived, Nancy Reagan wore diapers from 1921 to 1923.

In news writing, the year may be omitted altogether when referring to dates in the same year in which the news article appears.

1.8.6. *Document formatting.*

1.8.6a. *Materials.*

Use good paper, a good printer, good ink.

1.8.6b. *Margins.*

Ensure a comfortable and consistent margin on your printed typescript, typically 1.25 inches right and left, one inch at top and bottom. Do not justify the righthand side. Some genres, such as a screenplay or a PowerPoint presentation, require special margins.

1.8.6c. *Front matter.*

Use a title page only for major projects, not for classroom essays, résumés, or short stories. Your name and other necessary information (e.g., course title, return address, date) will appear in the upper left corner of page one. Your title, centered on the first page, requires no quotation marks, italics, or underlining unless it contains quoted material or another title. (See inset, "How to Privatize Social Security").

1.8.6d. *Numbering*.

Number your pages, preferably at top right, with a continuous header that will identify the document, should one or more pages become separated.

1.8.6e. *Get your act together.*

For classroom essays, though not for magazine submissions, staple or clip all pages together at the top left corner. Most classroom teachers prefer stapled essays, so that pages do not get lost.

1.8.6f. *Font fun.*

Some writers, especially high school students, like to toy with their computer typeface, changing the font or font size half a dozen times in the same paper. Large or small or bold type may, sometimes, aid the reader but don't tinker with your fonts just because you can. Let us take interest in your writing, not in your fascination with changeable computer fonts.

1.8.6g. *Italics.*

Italicize titles of books, magazines, newspapers, films, television shows, music albums, and poems of more than 500 lines. Use quotation marks for titles of chapters, articles, television episodes, songs, and short poems. (Editors typically capitalize and italicize *The* for the title their own periodical, e.g., *The Wall Street Journal*); you are not obliged to do so unless applying there for a job.)

Italicize foreign words and phrases unless they have already been adopted as English words. Some other common uses of italic print.

• Italicize the Latin names of a species (*Equus asinus*).
• Italicize any word being discussed as an object of discussion:
The Sanskrit word for *war* means "desire for more cows."
• Italicize lawsuits (*Brown v Board of Education, Roe v Wade*).
• Italicize the names of ships, aircraft and spacecraft.
• Italicize any word you wish to stress, but don't overdo it. A well-constructed sentence creates its own natural emphasis.

Some teachers and editors may require you to use underlining throughout, instead of italic print. If it's your call, choose whichever mode seems best-suited to your project. Just be consistent. Don't mix underlining and italics in the same document

1.8.7. *Notes and bibliography.*

Every academic discipline, every magazine or journal, every book publisher, will expect you to follow its standard form for documentation. Conventions and requirements may differ widely from one writing assignment to another, or from one college course to another. The two most widely used style manuals ("style" in the sense, document-styling) are the *Chicago Manual of Style* (preferred by most book publishers) and the Modern Language Association's *Handbook for Writers of Research Papers* (preferred by most college teachers in the arts and humanities). Each system has its advantages.

Before you begin writing, inquire which style guide will be required for the assignment: it can be a tedious labor to reformat an entire essay from one form of documentation to another just because you "forgot" the formatting requirements.

Don't wait until you are done writing to supply documentation for your quotations and borrowed material. Supply the references as you go, double-checking each citation for accuracy, both in the quotation itself and in the bibliographic reference.

1.8.8. *Always proofread one more time.*

Before venturing out of doors this morning, did you look in the mirror and fix yourself up? Thank you. We'd rather not see your hair uncombed, your face unwashed, your teeth unbrushed, your shirt unbuttoned, your socks mismatched, your shoes untied, and your fly unzipped. So what makes you think any of us wants to look at your writing before it's been tidied up?

Proofreading is an endless labor, but it should become more intensive as the project draws to a close. Better it is to proofread your final draft five times, than each of five early drafts once. Your eye will tend to see what you think you wrote rather than what's actually on the page. Your readers, of course, will have no trouble spotting the howlers:

• *Congratulations to Joe and Mary Lambe on the girth of little Joshua, their second sin. Mrs. Lambe, who remains in bed with gramps, will be hel in the hospital a while longer; but only for testes.*

• *As a senior sales associate on the second floor, I was responsible for ruining Lingerie.*

• *Vulgarity should be treated with good taste and proper regard for the sensibilities of the audience. There is a thin line between defensible onscreen nudity and outright immortality.*

The time to check your spelling, and to correct your capitalization, fonts, and document-format, and to tinker with punctuation, will come at the very end of your project, just hours before your paper is due.

1.8.9. *Save for a rainy day.*

Retain a digital or a machine copy of every draft, including your final one. Accidents happen. If you couldn't be bothered to ensure against possible disaster, don't blame the oversight on your dog (or intended reader, or computer). It's your own damned fault.

George W. Bush
Economics 101
Yale University
[DATE]

How to Privatize Social Security

I'm going to spend a lot of time on Social Security. I enjoy it. I enjoy taking on the issue. I guess it's the Mother in me.[1] The all which is on the table begins to address the big cost drivers, for example, how benefits are calculate, for example, is on the table, whether or not benefits rise based upon wage increases or price increases. There is a series of parts of the formula that are being considered, and when you couple that, those different cost drivers, affecting those changing those with personal accounts, the idea is to get what has been promised more likely to be, or closer delivered to, what has been promised. Does that make any sense to you?

It's kind of muddled. Look, there is a series of things that cause the like, for example, benefits are calculated based upon the increase of wages as opposed to the increase of prices. Some have suggested that we calculate the benefits will rise based upon inflation as opposed to wage increases; there is a reform that would help solve the red if that were put into effect. In other words, how fast benefits grow, how fast the promised benefits grow, if those, if that growth, is affected, it will help on the red. Okay, better? Yes.[1] Your own money would grow better than that which the Government can make it grow.[2] If they pre-decease or die early, there's an asset base to be able to pass on to a loved one, to help that loved one transition.[3]

We got people working all their life at hard work, contributing by payroll taxes into a Social Security system.[4] They want the federal government controlling Social Security like it's some kind of federal program.[5] But there's not going to be enough people in the system to take advantage of people like me.[6]

1.9. DO NOT STEAL MUCH

What a good thing Adam had. When he said a good thing, he knew nobody had said it before.
—Mark Twain [1]

Oscar Wilde: I wish I had said that.
J. M. Whistler: You will, Oscar, you will.
—Flying Circus TV Show [2]

1.9.1. *Speak with your own voice.*

Let us suppose that you have just completed an essay on "Puritanism and the Rise of American Capitalism." Your final draft seems, to you, to be both good and original. Your teacher says she agrees. You're thrilled. But just as you begin to smile and to stand a little taller, she stabs you through the heart by remarking icily that the good parts are not original, and the original parts are not good. [3]

It's small wonder that so many student-writers find themselves panicked when faced with a research paper or an expository essay, preferring rather to write fiction. We English teachers will demand something "original" one moment, and in the next ask why on earth you seem to have done so little research. On Monday, we'll tell you to look to other writers for ideas and inspiration, and on Tuesday tell you to exhibit "a strong and authentic sense of your own voice." We require you to consult authorities, and to disagree with authorities; to quote other writers, but to make the argument your own. Caught "between a rock and a hard place," you may find it hard to be original when even the metaphor itself is as old as the hills, used by millions of thieving writers before you, including quite a few who didn't get the idea straight out of Homer.

It's often hard to know, especially early on, when to quote, when to paraphrase, and when to do without another's input. Rule of thumb: Speak authoritatively, from your own voice, based on the information you have gathered; cite other authorities only as needed, to make your argument stronger, not longer; and acknowledge those whose insight or information helped you to build your case.

1.9.2. *Plagiarism is bad.*

Plagiarism is the art of taking something from another writer, without credit, and making it worse. To plagiarize is not a crime. Men have died from time to time, and worms have eaten them, but not for plagiarism. No one ever went to prison for literary theft. Some big names have tried it, and got caught, and lived to steal again—Shakespeare, Corneille, Stendahl, Coleridge, Martin Luther King, Alex Haley, to name a few. Moses (in the Old Testament), Matthew, Mark, Luke, and John (in the New), Mohammed (in the Quran), and Joseph Smith (in the Book of Mormon), all borrow material from earlier texts without acknowledging their sources.

But here I must adopt a more admonitory posture, lest angry parents write me to say that I am to blame for authorizing their child to do something that led to academic disgrace.

Thieves and sluggards, beware: even if you are not embarrassed to steal the words or information or ideas of another writer, it is certainly an embarrassment to get caught—and as academic offenses go, it's one of the worst. Wholesale plagiarism—such as the submission, under your own name, of a paper or paragraph written by someone else with only slight alternation—is grounds for censure, failure, suspension, and/or expulsion from school. It doesn't matter whose property you have lifted—whether from a friend who took the same course last year, or from an online "paper mill," or from a book at the library—if you put your name to substantial blocks of text that represent the work of someone else, you don't belong in an institution of higher learning and may be asked to leave. The breach of academic integrity may also become a permanent mark on your academic transcript. Acts of juvenile plagiarism have a way of popping up years later, in the news media, just when your career seems at last to be taking off.

The best way to avoid trouble is to document the works you have consulted, and to acknowledge those from which you have borrowed. Your paper will appear stronger, not weaker, if you credit your intellectual forebears and your documentary sources. Citing the works of others will not imply that you're an idiot with nothing to say; it will indicate that you are aware of others who have addressed the same problem, though perhaps less artfully, or less persuasively, than you have done.

If your borrowings are so audacious, and your documentation so spotty, that you find yourself standing before a faculty tribunal, charged with intellectual dishonesty, be prepared to defend yourself with a full set of drafts and notes. All great writers, all popular writers, all original thinkers, are accused, sooner or later, of plagiarism. The accused are often not guilty. You may be one of the great innocent writers of all time.

1.9.3. *Originality can be bad, too.*

"Originality," in academic writing, is hardly a singular virtue. If you have discovered something that has never been noted before by other readers, nor ever discussed in published scholarship—if you have something uniquely new to say about Homer, or about *Paradise Lost*, or about stem-cell research— then it may be time for you to knock off and take a nap.

Don't try so hard to go where no one before you has gone, or to share a divine revelation never before disclosed to earthly mortals. Say what you've got to say with as much authority as you can muster, based on the information you have gathered.

The kind of originality that matters is that which takes something old or familiar and turns it into a source of fresh knowledge, or entertainment, or insight. In between the thievish and the quirky is the inventive borrowing of the "bricoleur"—the writer who cobbles together a commentary or story with just a little of this and a little of that—ideas, examples, turns of phrase—that he or she has picked up from other writers, but deftly rearranged. The first rule of good writing is not to be "original," but to be interesting.

1.9.4. *Works Cited.*

Give due credit for anything that is not commonplace—most especially, facts, figures, tables and graphics, paraphrased ideas, insights, and quotations that your readers may be seeing for the first time. Common knowledge requires no footnote. Cite someone who has challenged "common knowledge."

Make sure that your quotations, paraphrases, attributions, citations, and "Works Cited" page are complete and accurate. Don't pad the W.C. with works not cited in your paper. No one will be impressed with your ability to compile a bibliography of works that have not contributed to your own.

1.10. JUST GET IT RIGHT

> *The first draft of everything is shit.*
> —Ernest Hemingway, attrib.

> *Blot out, correct, insert, refine*
> *Enlarge, diminish, interline;*
> *Be mindful, when invention fails,*
> *To scratch your head, and bite your nails.*
> —Jonathan Swift

1.10.1. *Revise early and often.*

Finished with your first draft? Good! You have said what you needed to say! Now it's almost time to start writing what you will need to write. Here's an excellent plan that you probably won't follow:

Step 1. Finish your essay or article, to your entire satisfaction, at least three days before the due-date.

Step 2. Don't look at the piece for twenty-four hours.

Step 3. Print a hard copy and re-read your most recent draft it as if it were the work of someone who's not quite as smart as you, nor as eloquent. (Sadly, when you pick up your "final" draft after a day's rest, the essay will suddenly feel like a load of crap.)

Step 4. Scribble all over the printed draft.

Step 5. Turn on your computer and begin the real work of writing, which is to revise, cut, revise, cut, and revise. This time, get it right, or at least make it better.

(If you neglect step 1, you may need to skip step 2 and proceed directly to step 3.)

1.10.2. *After each revision, print a hard copy and read it.*

Infelicities that do not show up on your computer screen will become glaringly obvious when you peruse a hard copy of the identical text. Every few hours, print up what you've got, inspect every scrap, and scrape out what's unfit for readers' consumption. The recycled paper bin is a writer's best friend. Don't let him go hungry.

1.10.3. *Editing helps: the search-and-replace function.*

When using on a word processor, use the *Find* and *Search/Replace* functions as an aid in revision. Conduct a search-and-destroy mission for such bland and over-used words as *a lot, very, different, people, situation, society, theme, there, this, it.* Cut or replace each offender with a specific substitute. A search for *to* will turn up instances of split infinitives (*to accidentally split*). A search for *all, only* and *always* will locate misplaced adverbs: "Goethe could *only* write if he had an apple rotting in his desk" should read, "Goethe could write only if he had an apple rotting in his desk.") A search for conjunctive adverbs (*however, therefore, thus*) will pinpoint those places where you have used hot glue to connect your ideas. A search for *not* will turn up wordy negative constructions that can be recast in a direct positive form.

1.10.4. *Double-chock your electronic spill-chucker.*

It may hard to find certain words in the dictionary, such as *hors d'oeuvres* or *fiery,* if you don't already know how to spell them. You have an electronic spellchecker. Use it. Electronic grammar- and style-checkers can also be helpful if used with thoughtful discrimination. But never will there be a satisfactory substitute for the human eye. Spellcheckers are particularly unreliable with proper nouns. Do not allow your word processor to change Antony and Cleopatra to "Anonym and Clipart," or Shylock to "Skylark," or Jocasta to "Jokester." If you cannot tell Venice from Venus—like the student at the State University of New York who described the Rialto as "the business end of Venus"—your computer cannot help you.

Beware homophones and near-misses. A spellchecker will overlook errors of usage, in which you have misused a word spelled correctly, or have mistaken one word for another. That's why you still need an old-fashioned dictionary: an electronic spellchecker cannot be trusted to choose your words. Unless you're trying to be funny, don't inform your classics or drama professor that "The clowns in Greek comedy wore large fallacies." *Busing* is a way to get your kids to school; *bussing* is a way to excite your lover. If your lips cannot tell the difference, neither can your laptop. Nor can your computer tell an *egress* from an *ogress, Emily* from *email,* or *omissions* from *emissions.* Microsoft Word finds in this poem no spelling errors:

My New Microsoft Spellchecker

I have a spelling checker,
Disk cover don my PC:
It plane lee marks four my revue

Miss steaks aye kin knot sea.
Each frays come post up on mice screen
Eye trussed too bee a joule.
The checker pours oar every word
To chick sum spelling gruel.
Ice strike a quay and Taipei word,
And weight four it two say
Weather rye yam rung oar write—
Itch hoes me strait a weigh.
Ass soon as uh missed ache is maid
It nose bee fore two lung
And icon putt the air-or rite:
Its hard lea ever rung.
Iran this poem threw wit,
Ewe law be glad tune owe:
It's vary polished, in its weigh—
Microsoft tolled me sew.
Bee fore wee rote with checkers
Hour spelling was inn deck line,
Butt now when wee dew have a laps,
Wee halve no cost 2 wine.
And now, bee cause my spelling
Was red with such grate flare,
There are know faults in awl this peace,
Of nun eye yam a wear.
A checker is a two-ell,
Witch freeze yew lodes of thyme.
It help shoe right awl stiles two reed,
And aides U when ewe rime.
To rite with care is quite a feet
Of witch won Canby proud,
And you mussed dew the best Yukon,
Sew flaws are knot aloud.
That's why eye brake in two averse,
Cause eye sew wont too pleas.
How graded is, that aye did bye
This soft wear four pea seas!

To avoid embarrassing mistakes, use the words you know, and use
them correctly. (For help with difficult words, and with similar words
often mistaken for one another Part 3, Write or Wrong: "A Pretty
Good Guide to Hard Words.")

1.10.5. *Read your work aloud.*

Kick everyone out of the house or lock yourself in the bathroom. Now read your story or essay out loud, once through from start to finish; then again, one sentence at a time, pausing to circle the rough spots. The ear catches wrong notes, or monotony, or needless repetition, that the eye misses. Listen to yourself: Do your sentences flow smoothly? Is each assertion both necessary and interesting? Do you sound confident, sincere, intelligent, and well-informed? Or do you sound more like a bored student just doing his homework?

1.10.6. *Find a trusted associate editor.*

Your primary reader—the teacher, editor, or supervisor who will judge your performance—should not be the first person to read your work. Give your early drafts instead to someone both capable and plainspoken—your mother, boyfriend, roommate, Internet chum, whoever. Ask her to find fault with what you have written and with the way you have written it. Invite him to scribble all over your paper or, if it's a digital copy, to type all over it. You shouldn't have much trouble finding someone willing to make suggestions: as H.G. Wells once remarked, "No passion in the world is equal to the passion to alter someone else's draft."[1] In your next ensuing draft, take those suggestions seriously.

Unless you're an incurable basket case, don't waste your trusted reader's time by asking him or her to read your earliest draft. (Remember the immortal word of Ernest Hemingway for the first draft of anything.) Even after you think you've finally got it right, read it yourself, in a hard copy, before you foist it on someone else.

If you are a beginning writer whose work needs more than just cosmetics, you may need to develop a whole team of associate editors: a cheerleader to get you pumped up, a physician to treat your sickest sentences, a dietician to put some meat into them, a beautician to make your phrasing less ugly. Over time, you will need less help. If you take their advice, and if you exercise a little self-discipline, those trusted associates can help move your prose out of the intensive care ward and into the outpatient clinic where it belongs.

1.10.7. *Trouble-shooting: run the gamut.*

"A writer," said the Nobel Prize winner, Thomas Mann, "is someone for whom writing is more difficult than it is for other people."[2] The labor seems Sisyphean, the goal unreachable. Most writers, when the time comes to begin revising in earnest, hardly know where to start. You, however, do not have that problem because you have *How to Write*. The Index and Ready Reference at the rear of this wonderful little book provides the handiest checklist ever compiled in the entire history of writing instruction.

Take your tasks one at a time. Don't try to revise everything all at once, or you'll end up with a revised mess.

1.10.7a. *First read-through*: Get interesting.

Which paragraphs, sentences, and phrases are interesting? Which are dull? Begin with the first imperative: Make it interesting! Turn to Ready reference 1.1.1a–1.1.6b. Run through the checklist: Review your *Angle* (1.1.1: "Begin with a bang," "It's not really about you," etc.). Consider your *Tone* (1.1.2: "Be confident," "Don't lecture..."). Improve your *Variety* (1.1.3: "No gimmicks," "Vary your sentence structure"...) and *Vitality* ("Choose lively verbs...")/ Check for *Freshness* (1.1.5) and *Image-ination* (1.1.6). Cut or improve every boring paragraph, every dull phrase.

1.10.7b. *Second read-through*. Get organized.

Improve your structure, paragraph development, and sentence logic. (Ready reference 1.2.1a–1.2.6.)

1.10.7c. *Third read-through*. Get specific.

Make sure every statement is specific, or followed by something particular, informative, visual. Sharpen your points. (Ready ref. 1.3.1a– 1.3.4b.)

1.10.7d. *Fourth read-through*. Make it clear.

Just because you know what that sentence is supposed to mean doesn't mean that your readers will understand it. (Ready ref. 1.4.1a– 1.4.5d.)

1.10.7e. *Fifth read-through*. Make it concise.

Be tough-minded. First, leave out the parts that impatient readers will skip. Then keep cutting, until it hurts to cut another word. (Ready ref. 1.5.1a–1.5.3).

1.10f. *Sixth read-through*. Get choosy.

Line out jargon and inflated diction; check for incorrect usage. An almost-right word is no good. Find the right one. (Ready ref. 1.6.1– 1.6.7.)

1.10.7g. *Seventh read-through*. Make it accurate.

If you've ever written for publication, you know that rigorous fact-checking takes time, but it's a necessary labor. Writers who don't check their facts *deserve* to get sued, or to fail the course, or to lose their job. (Ready ref. 1.7.1a–1.7.4g.)

1.10.7h. *Eighth read-through.* **Play by the rules.**

Now it's time to pay attention to the boring stuff: *grammar, logic, punctuation.* (Ready ref. 1.8.1a–1.8.9.)

1.10.7i. *Ninth read-through.* **Don't steal.**

Is every borrowed fact, every borrowed phrase, duly noted? Have you cited the source for every quotation? (Ready ref. 1.9).

1.10.7j. *Tenth read-through.* **Just get it right.**

Back to the beginning: revise, revise, revise, until you have run out of time.

1.10.8. *Know when to stop fiddling.*

Meet your deadline. No matter how hard you try, you will never get it "right" until your essay or story has been graded or published— at which point it's simply too late to do anything further by way of improvement. Submit your work for publication or a grade. Move on to a new project.

1.10.9. *Hygiene.*

If you have drooled or wept or bled or dripped coffee on your paper, or if your printer has had an apoplexy, reprint your document before submitting it to your significant readers. No teacher or editor wants to read a typescript that looks as if it has been used on the floor of a parakeet cage.

If you don't do at least ten revisions of your own work before foisting it on the public or your English teacher, youa re not a serious writer.

Part 2: *How do they do that?*

2.1. *How to Write Gender-Neutral Prose*

2.2. *How to Write a Report*

2.3. *How to Write Email*

2.4. *How to Write a Letter*

2.5. *How to Write a Résumé*

2.6. *How to Write Persuasively*

2.7. *How to Write an Expository Essay*

2.8. *How to Write a Novel*

2.9. *How to Write Poetry*

2.10. *How to Write a Screenplay*

2.1. *How to Write Gender Neutral Prose.*

*You teach a child to read, and he or her will be able to pass
a literacy test!* —George W. Bush [1]

*If you see a train-wreck coming, you ought to be saying,
"What are you going to do about it, Mr. Congressman," or
"Madam Congressman"?* —George W. Bush [2]

2.1.1. *The problem.*

Once upon a time, it was widely believed—by as much as half of
the English-speaking world—that male writers and readers were the
only ones who mattered. The all-inclusive "man" or "mankind" came
therefore to signify *person* or *humanity* while "he" signified *any
human being*, including women, as in these unrevised first drafts:

• *And God said, "Let us make* man *in our image, after our
likeness..."*
• *That's one small step for* a man, *one great leap for* mankind.

Such poorly phrased statements as these are easily remedied   by
plugging in "humankind" or *humanity* for "man" and "mankind," and
person or *human being* for "a man."

Gender-neutral prose, though a great leap forward for humanity,
is a small and usually easy step for the individual writer. But *person,
people, humanity,* and *humankind* are not always the best substitutes
for "man" and "mankind." It is often uninteresting to speak of so
vague an entity as "a person," and hard to speak truthfully about so
diverse a class as "humanity." You shall do better, when revising, to
be more specific:

• First draft: *The Pap test, which has greatly reduced mortality from
uterine cancer, is a boon to* mankind.[3]
• Final draft: *The Pap test has been a boon to women's health, greatly
reducing mortality from uterine cancer.*

Difficulties sometimes arise with a generic singular subject. It is no
improvement to change "The man in the street wants a tax cut" to
"Street people want a tax cut," or to commit such presidential boners
as this one: "When your teachers say 'read,' you ought to listen to
her." [4]

Solution: be more specific: "The voters want a tax cut." "Complete
your reading assignments."

2.1.2. *Subject-verb trouble.*

When perplexed by gender trouble, some writers use the plural pronouns *they, them, their, themselves,* with reference to the singular subject. This strategy, though adopted by such thoughtful rebels as Jane Austen, is not the best solution, for it substitutes a disagreement in *number* for the original inconsistency in *gender,* as in these poorly revised statements, where both versions are inconsistent:

· *A physician* should write clearly when issuing *his* prescriptions.
· *A physician* should write clearly when issuing *their* prescriptions.

· *The nurse must assess* each *patient. She must take* his *weight, temperature, and pulse.*
· *Assess* each *patient. Take* their *weight, temperature, and pulse.*

· *If* a member *registers after April 1,* he *must pay an additional fee.*
· *If* a member *registers after April 1,* they *must pay an additional fee.*

· *Some*one has *parked* his *car on my lawn.*
· *Some*one has *parked* their *car on my lawn.*

· *Every*one *bought* his Taylor Swift *tickets on the Internet*
· *Every*one *bought* their Taylor Swift *tickets on the Internet.*

· *To* each his *own.*
· *To* each their *own.*

Another, usually poor, choice for revision is to substitute "he or she," "his or her," "him or her" for the universal male:

· *Some*one *has parked* his or her *car on my lawn.*

In a moment of exasperation you may even be tempted to become a Mad Slasher or Dasher:

· S/he *has parked* his-her *car on my lawn.*

The use of *he or she* is often unavoidable. But there is nothing to be said for such hermaphroditic distractions as *s/he* and *him-her.* Resist the urge to slash personal pronouns.

2.1.3. *A gender-neutral cavalry to the rescue.*

Most gender inconsistencies are easily corrected. In many instances you may simply delete the exclusive masculine pronoun:

· *A physician should write clearly when issuing prescriptions.*
· *A nurse must take the weight, temperature, and pulse of each patient.*

• *Someone has parked on my lawn.*
• *Everyone bought* Shrew *tickets on the Internet.*

Or you may adopt a plural subject, retaining a plural pronoun:

• *Physicians should write their prescriptions clearly.*
• *All of the students bought their* Shrew *tickets on the Internet.*

Where appropriate, you may change the frame of reference:

• *We all bought our* Shrew *tickets on the Internet.*

Or you may adopt a plural subject followed by *who*:
• *Members who register later than April 1 must pay an additional fee.*

Or you may simply make the sentence more specific:

• *Someone with a Yugo station wagon bearing New Jersey plates has parked on my front lawn.*

It is also okay to alternate male and female pronouns if care is taken not to confuse the reader:

• *It's easy to lose money, even in a bull market. One investor may put all of his eggs in one basket. Another may invest too much of her money in high-flying tech stocks.*

A familiar phrase or cliché such as "To each his own" may resist correction. If you cannot find a suitable equivalent from proverbial lore (e.g., "Different strokes for different folks," "You go your way, I'll go mine"), then simply invent a fresh turn of phrase.

There is, of course, no problem with using "he" when you are actually writing of the generic male, nor with using "she" for the generic female—

• *The modern man typically worries more about his hairline than about his waistline.*
• *Everyone intending to use the women's locker room should bring her own towel.*

2.1.4. *Neutralizing professional bias.*

There was a time when *freshmen, policemen, firemen, clergymen, chairmen,* were assumed to be male for the simple reason that they always *were*—and our very language helped to perpetuate that inequitable state of affairs by conditioning our beliefs, values, and expectations. Today, substitute diction is readily available, such as *first-year students, police officers, firefighters, clergy,* and *department*

chair.   Except as required by context, do not write "male nurse,"
"male secretary," "female lawyer," "woman doctor," "career woman,"
as if these were surprising or inappropriate career choices. Do not
call a female student a "co-ed," nor a professional assistant a "girl,"
nor an unmarried woman a "spinster." Avoid the archaic suffix, *-ess.*
Though *goddess* may never fall out of fashion, either as a word or as a
cultural role, "actor," "poet" and "author" are preferable to *actress,*
poetess, and *authoress.* For *steward* or *stewardess,* try "flight
attendant." For *waiter* or *waitress,* write "server."

It's not that tough to write gender-neutral prose. You just have to
tinker a bit with your sentences, which is something you ought to be
doing anyway.

2.2. *How to Write a Report.*

2.2.1. *Know your audience.*

Choose the most effective mode of presentation, the right pitch,
and appropriate graphics to accomplish your purpose—a classroom
report, a news story, a business report. Don't waste time telling your
readers what they don't need to hear or won't bother to read.

2.2.2. *Stay focused on the five Ws.*

From your collar-grabbing lead until the final word, don't lose ever
sight of the five Ws: *Who, What, When, Where,* and *Why.* If you don't
have all of the pertinent facts, do your homework. Be ready to
answer questions or to field replies.

Especially in news reporting, resist the temptation to editorialize.
Keep your opinions and witticisms, and most of your adjectives, to
yourself.

2.2.3. *Be specific.*

Choose your details carefully. One police detective, in his incident
report, states vaguely that "The suspect resisted arrest." At trial, the
defense attorney says, "An innocent, unarmed man smirked at you
just before *you* slammed his face into the hood of a car and
handcuffed him, and you call that *resisting arrest?*"—at which point
the officer may have lost his opportunity for his version of the story to
be fully considered.

A police detective in another city files an incident report providing
a few salient facts and a verbatim quotation:

• *When I attempted to subdue Sven Karlsson, he whispered, "Go to
hell, you fascist son of a Chihuahua bitch." He then shouted to three
other big drunken Swedes, "Hey, guys, it's a [expletive] piñata." He*

struck me in the chest with a bottle of tequila, bruising three ribs. He then jumped into the swimming pool with his clothes on and dared me to dive in after him....

That Mr. Karlsson resisted arrest will be clear to the ladies and gentlemen of the jury, not only from the policeman's courtroom recollection, but from the detailed police report, drafted within hours of the officer's bruising encounter with the defendant.

A third detective, reporting on a police raid at a suburban house of prostitution, omits nothing—tediously recording even such details as the dish of stewed prunes that sat on the table, and the number of prunes, and the approximate cost of the dish—until his audience simply loses interest.

2.2.4. *Be brief.*

If you want to get creative, write a novel. For a report, it's *Just the facts!*—but include all facts that are essential to the story. Let us see, hear, smell, feel what happened. What caused the train wreck? What is needed for the public schools in Afghanistan? Are migrant workers in your community being paid a living wage? Are Ken and Barbie losing market share to Tickle Me Elmo? Hook our interest. Tell your story. Sign off.

2.3. *How to Write Email.*

2.3.1. *Write it, don't just type it.*

Email is less formal than paper-mail but that is no reason, when communicating electronically, to forget everything you know about effective writing. Begin with a personal greeting (by *name*, not: "Hi, Professor"). Construct coherent paragraphs, and close with a personal signoff. Be interesting, be organized, specific, clear, concise, and accurate. In short, try to write well even when corresponding by email.

2.3.2. *Edit your message.*

Use the subject line, if only as a matter of self-interest. Given the quantities of spam that have already glutted your addressee's *In* mailbox, your messages are more likely to be read if you identify both yourself and your subject.

Observe the conventions of spelling, capitalization, and punctuation so that readers are not distracted by errors and idiosyncrasies.

writing in lower case will not make your message sound like the free verse of e. e. cummings. it will only make you look lazy.

BUT WRITING IN ALL CAPS IS PERCEIVED AS SHOUTING, AND MAKES YOUR MESSAGE HARDER TO READ.

Some email programs include editing and spelling aids. Use them. Manually proofread every message at least twice before you hit the "send" button.

Never forward personal email to other readers without the writer's permission, not even if someone has done it to you.

2.3.3. *Be civil.*

If you're angry or annoyed, sleep on it for a night and proofread your message in the morning—you may want to change a few things.

Don't be sarcastic. A horizontal smiley face may indicate that you were only trying to be funny, but a :-) is no substitute for saying what you really mean.

The ease and easy anonymity of electronic communication have made it possible for anyone to publish anything about anybody at any time for any reason—and for that very reason cyberspace has become clogged with foul-smelling sludge from resentniks whose idea of a good time is to spew verbal abuse at or about others. "Flaming" usually says more about the flamer than about the flamed. If it makes you crazy that the world contains people whose opinion, skin color, religion, diet, or sexual orientation differs from your own, then that's your problem, not theirs. Lay off.

When attacked—as, say, in a Usenet discussion group—resist the temptation to respond in kind. If you need to argue online, your thoughtful, pointed prose will score more points than smug vituperation. Let your adversary be defeated by his own inferior ideas and poor writing, not by your own over-the-top nastiness.

2.3.4. *Identity and privacy issues.*

Identify yourself in every email communication just as you do in your everyday telephone conversations. If you're a conscientious whistle blower, or if you have any defensible reason whatsoever to conceal your identity, then exercise your right to remain anonymous, but don't suppose your email musings are really secure from unintended readers, or your identity secure from disclosure.

Nor do Internet communications simply vanish into the Ethernet. Thanks to the ease of forwarding—which is not something that anyone should do to you, but it happens—the message you send to a friend, colleague, or stranger may eventually be read without your permission by hundreds, perhaps thousands of readers, including your professor, boss, neighbors, and your own children. If you have written well, courageously, and discreetly, that's nothing to worry about.

2.4. *How to Write a Letter.*

2.4.1. *Your life in letters.*

The letters you have written to friends and loved ones over the years may, one day, be the only surviving written record of your life. Toward that end, make every letter worth reading, not just for the moment but for generations to come. Be observant, be creative, be witty and charming. Your correspondence may end up in your great-grandchild's attic or in the County Historical Society Library. By that time, of course, you won't care what people think of your writing, so care now.

If you have something to say (to your mother, lover, or boss) that you would never, ever, want anyone else to read, fine: put away your paper and pen, turn off the computer, and place a telephone call.

2.4.2. *Your education and career.*

When writing about yourself—as when you apply for a job, or for admission to a school or program—let your field of expertise, your zeal for excellence, your passion for the work, shine through in every sentence. Take care to present yourself in the best possible light without puffing your abilities or unique genius.

Keep your object squarely in view. If you are asked to submit a "Personal Statement," do not take the phrase too literally. Do not assume that the admissions or hiring committee will want to know about your parents' messy divorce, or about your Hummel collection, or your pet poodle named Bob. They want to know who you are, what you have accomplished, and where your life is going—and they want to know how well you can write about all of that.

Focus on the interests and needs of your reader, not on your own needs or desires. Applicants for admission or employment commonly, but foolishly, say how much the organization can do to fulfill their hopes and dreams. But those readers at the college or company already know that their organization has much to offer. The question for them is rather, what can *you*, the applicant, bring to them? How are you more likely than other candidates to bring lasting credit to the institution, or value to the corporation?

Give your reader reason to stay tuned. Instead of the hackneyed close, *I look forward to meeting you*, you might say, *It would be convenient for me to meet with the Admissions Committee in the first week of January, since I will be in New York anyway that week, to perform at the Metropolitan Opera House.* Or: *When I meet with you for the interview I will be bringing along the syllabuses for two of the most successful courses I've ever taught.* Or: *When we meet, I will show you some extraordinary photographs of the landscaping work I have done for other homeowners.* Be truthful, be modest, but be interesting.

In signing off, don't spend ink on such trite statements as "*I thank you in advance.*" (This may be taken to mean, "I expect you to do as I have asked, so hop to it!" or perhaps, "At the price these days of a first-class postage stamp, I certainly don't feel like writing you people *twice!*") A provider of consumer goods, or a college registrar, may be impressed if you present payment in advance of a due date—but "I thank you in advance" cuts no onions for anyone. Just say "Thank you" or "Thank you for your consideration." If you are granted the requested job interview, or refund, or foundation grant, it won't kill you to send another thank you note after the favor has been granted.

2.4.3. *Writing about issues and people.*

Even today, when so much correspondence is conducted electronically, "snailmail" can still be the surest and quickest and most effective way to make your voice heard, whether in academia, the marketplace, or the political process. When writing about a problem (e.g., a consumer complaint), or issues (a letter to your congresswoman), or in behalf of another person (such as a letter of reference), seize the opportunity to change the world for the better. Be lively, specific, and persuasive. If your letter is comprised of boilerplate that might be attached to a hundred different letters about the same person or topic, you're wasting time and paper.

No matter whether your letter is designed to inform, persuade, sell, request, recommend, reprimand, or cajole, its purpose will fail if the document goes unread or is disregarded. Before writing, take the trouble to identify the particular individual, within the organization, who is best able to respond to your concerns. Address both the envelope and your letter to that individual.

As always, find an effective hook: motivate your addressee to read beyond your first sentence. Cut all extraneous chat: let your main points be inescapably obvious. What Winston Churchill said of public speaking applies as well to letter writing: "If you have an important point to make, don't try to be subtle or clever. Use a pile driver. Hit the point once. Then come back and hit it again. Then hit it a third time—a tremendous whack."

In a letter of two or more pages, internal headings may help to clarify and emphasize your main points, thereby to expedite attention to your letter.

Sign off with a complimentary close that is suited to the purpose at hand. If you are sending copies of your letter to other persons than the addressee, identify the additional recipients in a cc: line below your signature. Be sure to make a note of any attachments or enclosures. To ensure that enclosures do not become separated from your letter, staple them together in the upper lefthand corner.

Take steps to facilitate a response. Be sure to include your return address not only on the mailing envelope but on your stationery. This is especially important when writing to someone who may otherwise lack contact information for you—a former teacher, your congressional representative, a corporation. Don't assume that your mailing envelope will be kept with the letter.

Never put a letter into an envelope until you have proofread it, several times, for errors and infelicities.

Don't forget to sign your letter before sticking it in the envelope.

A self-addressed stamped envelope, folded neatly and enclosed with your letter, may help to ensure a speedy response.

Look twice, lick once. Make double sure, when sending out multiple letters at the same time, that you have placed each letter in the corresponding envelope. It could prove embarrassing if Yale receives your letter addressed to Princeton; or MacDonald's, your letter to Burger King; or your dear mother, a letter intended for Dearest Heather.

2.5. *How to Write a Résumé or "CV" (Curriculum Vitae).*

Q. *What executive experience do you have to be vice president of the United States?*

Dan Quayle: *What executive experience do I have? I have worked, when I was going to law school, in the Governor's office, as administrative assistant! I worked in the Attorney General's office. And I also worked as the director of the Inheritance Tax Division of Indiana—I was known as the chief grave-robber of my state. I also was the associate publisher of the* Huntington Herald Press *and I've met a payroll before.* [5]

2.5.1. *Your self-presentation matters.*

Your résumé may be one of hundreds reviewed for the same position. Find those points of interest in your past experience that will help the personnel managers or hiring committee to remember your résumé as one of the best they have seen. If you submit a CV (*curriculum vitae,* or "course of life") with no cover letter, you may wish to include, near the top, a short introductory paragraph that highlights your educational and work history, your areas of interest and expertise, your recent research or other accomplishments. No matter whether you hope to be a plumber, musician, or astrophysicist, make clear that you are a purposeful, self-motivated person, with a zeal for excellence in your work.

Describe your experience using active verbs.

* Boring: *I was involved in a community literacy program.*
* Better: *As a Project Literacy volunteer for the past six years, I have taught dozens of poor children in my community how to read and write.*

Supply dates and locations for your work and education. Use past tense to describe completed activities: *In my fifteen years as a driver for Coors Inc., I never had an accident or a traffic citation.* List no more than one or two unfinished projects, and use the present tense: "My work in progress includes a screenplay, commissioned by Miramax" (if true), but not: "I hope someday to write a screenplay."

Omit or explain jargon, abbreviations, and acronyms that your audience may not understand.

2.5.2. *Be organized and be specific.*

There is no "correct" format for a résumé, bio, or curriculum vitae, but since one CV may change the direction of your entire life hereafter, make the most of the opportunity. Most such documents consist of the same basic parts:

* *Your name (top center) and contact information*
* *Your educational background (colleges or universities attended, years of attendance, degrees earned)*
* *Your professional experience (employers, job title, years of service)*
* *Professional references, with contact information*

It is a good idea—though not many people actually do it—to include a small color photograph of yourself on page 1, so that recipients of your CV will associate the name with a face.

Use an eye-pleasing layout, presenting the facts of your life in a plainly legible and consistent format. A list of bulleted sentences (or intelligible fragments), with subheadings, may include such matters as the following:

* *Academic degrees*
* *Awards, honors, directory listings*
* *Professional associations and affiliations*
* *Offices held*
* *Publications*
* *Conference presentations*
* *Interviews with the news media*
* *Professional service to the government, or to academic institutions*
* *Service to charitable organizations*
* *Involvement in your local community*

List your publications, conference presentations, or other achievements in reverse chronological order. If your bibliography is a long one, as for senior scholars or research scientists, you may wish to group publications by type, again with subheadings (e.g., books, journal articles, technical reports, conference papers, reviews).

2.5.3. *Know what to leave out.*

No one—not even your future soulmate, much less a busy admissions or hiring committee—wants to read your entire autobiography. Resist the impulse to include every impressive deed you ever performed. To reach your target audience, select the information that will register most forcibly. The National Endowment for the Humanities does not need to know that you once won an award for cheerleading or that you caught a prize-winning catfish. But if you are a high school student applying for your first full-time job, it is perfectly appropriate to list your experience delivering newspapers or selling Girl Scout Cookies.

Avoid saying things in your CV, cover letter, or job interview that you would not want quoted later on in life, after you have become president of Microsoft, or president of the United States: "You know, I could run for governor, but I'm basically a media creation. I've never done anything. I've worked for my dad. I worked in the oil business. But that's not the kind of profile you have to have to get elected to public office" (George W. Bush in 1989).[6] Much better to emphasize your strengths: "I was a pitbull on the pantleg of opportunity" (George W. Bush in 1999). [7]

Highlight those qualities in yourself that your audience will value:

• Too general: *I'm gonna talk about the ideal world. I understand reality. If you're asking me, as the president, would I understand reality? I do. [...] I don't know whether I'm going to win or not. I think I am. I do know I'm ready for the job, and if not, that's just the way it goes. [...] The fundamental question is, "Will I be a successful president when it comes to foreign policy?" I will be, but until I'm the president, it's going to be hard for me to verify that I think I'll be more effective. [...] So I think anybody who doesn't think I'm smart enough to handle the job is underestimating. [...] The important question is, "How many hands have I shaked?"* (George W. Bush.) [8]

• Specific but ineffective: *As your next president, I may invade and occupy Iraq, and destroy its infrastructure, and kill some 200,000 of its people without provocation, plus some few hundred of our own. I may oppose global efforts to save the earth's ozone layer, ice cap, and rain forests. I may alienate the entire world against the United States.*

My reckless spending may turn a record treasury surplus into a record deficit. But I promise to cut taxes and to oppose gay marriage.

• Pointed and effective: *As your next president, I promise to cut your taxes and to oppose gay marriage.*

Tell the truth, but include only such facts as will help you to get the job. Do your best to put setbacks in a sympathetic light. If you spent three years in San Quentin, you may want to list that period in your life as "A break from full-time employment, during which I devoted myself to study and self-improvement."

Your CV need not contain such personal information as your age, ethnic or racial identity, religion, marital status, or sexual preference—nor do potential employers have the right to ask—but neither is there any harm in sharing such data if you think it may help you to get the particular job or assignment or grant for which you are applying. Include nothing in your bio— especially not in a Web bio— that would put your company's or clients' or family's security or privacy at risk. Never include your social security number on a résumé, most especially not in documents posted on the Internet.

2.5.4. *Choose your references carefully.*

When listing personal or professional references on your bio, make sure that you have chosen individuals who seem genuinely confident of your abilities and who admire your accomplishments. If you took an economics course from a famous professor who gave you a C- for a final grade, it may be risky to name her as a professional reference.

Before naming your personal or professional references, ask their permission to use their name and contact information. If you are unsure whether your referee of choice will give you a strong recommendation, try testing the waters. Ask for advice before asking for a reference: "Professor Hernandez, I'm toying with the idea of applying to Princeton for graduate school. How do you think I would stand up against other candidates?" If he says that Princeton is not for you, believe him. Or apply anyway, but without listing him as a reference. (Prof. Hernandez does not owe your future any favors. He is obliged to give Princeton his frank opinion.)

2.5.5. *Be accurate.*

Make sure that your contact information, bibliography, names of referees, and dates are precisely correct. Present yourself in the best possible light but do not puff the record. Do not give yourself inaccurate job titles or lend yourself honors that you never received. Self-praise matters far less than the praise of your confidential letters of reference. Falsified résumés often turn up years letter to embarrass—and, often, to destroy the careers—of the liars who submitted them in hopes of taking a shortcut to success.

2.5.6. *Prepare a flawless document.*

Proofread, make corrections, and print out a fresh copy.

Repeat.

Repeat again. Never deliver a résumé or job application until you have proofread it, several times, for errors and infelicities.

Use good quality cotton paper and leave ample margins (at least one inch on all sides).

A justified right margin will make your résumé more difficult to read than if you let the right margin float.

Use a single side of the paper to facilitate photocopying: if your CV is an impressive one, someone on the other end may wish to make copies of it.

2.6. *How to write persuasively.*

If you don't stand for anything, you don't stand for anything. If you don't stand for something, you don't stand for anything. [...] I know what I believe. I will continue to articulate what I believe and what I believe—I believe what I believe is right. [...] I think if you know what you believe, it makes it a lot easier to answer questions: I can't answer your question. [...] I don't care what the polls say. I don't! I'm doing what I think what's wrong. [...] The great thing about America is, everybody should vote. —George W. Bush (2000) [9]

[More concisely:] *We stand for things.*
—George W. Bush (2004)[10]

2.6.1. *Know what you want to say.*

Many writing tasks—a letter to the editor, a campaign speech, a classroom essay, a consumer complaint—have the common goal of persuading others to change their policy, behavior, or belief. Your object may be to sell a product, or to sell yourself, or to close a deal, or to communicate your vision for the future. Or you may wish only to provide a fresh perspective of familiar material. Whatever the occasion, don't just tell readers what you think, or what they ought to think and do. Be cleverly persuasive.

Until you complete a first draft you may be unsure about the precise form that your argument will take but you should be able from the outset to state your position clearly and succinctly, if only to yourself. Do not feel obliged, as commonly taught in high school, to state your thesis baldly in the first paragraph. It may work best to hook your reader's interest before introducing your point of view. But do not leave us groping in the dark, trying to figure out where you stand. Identify, early on, the problem that you will address and the angle from which you will approach it.

Let us hear your voice. Take a stand. Be earnest. Be inventive. Be lively. An essay that sounds as if it was churned out for teacher will not be worth writing, because it will not be worth reading. If you care deeply enough about the stand you are taking, maybe we will care, too.

2.6.2. *Know your audience.*

Don't preach to the choir. Imagine the kind of person who most needs to read your work: over-stressed business managers, Green Party voters, troubled adolescents, gay senior citizens, whoever. Pitch your remarks to reach those ideal readers. Don't imagine yourself writing for someone who thinks exactly as you do, or there is no point in writing the essay at all.

2.6.3. *Design your argument.*

Construct and present an orderly discussion, without digression or pointless repetition. We should be able to follow your train of thought without the aid of caffeine or a second read-through.

Support each main point with examples that illustrate, explain, or clarify your thesis. There is no need to be exhaustive. It is a mistake to suppose that your case will be stronger if you mention every possible argument in favor of your position, or refute every possible argument that might be levied against it. Your object is to win readers over to your side, not to build a fortress. The inclusion of weak points implies that you cannot tell the difference between good evidence and bad.

2.6.4. *Anticipate objections.*

Start from the premise that your readers will be thoughtful adults who know your subject but who disagree with you. Take care not to overestimate the strength of your position. Instead, consider the strongest objections that might be raised to your argument, and raise them. Then demonstrate how the objections can be overcome. Do your homework. If you base your argument, not on facts, but on what "just seems logical" to your own possibly fallible mind, your argument is likely collapse like a house of cards in a high wind.

Vice president Dan Quayle, head of President Bush's Space Council, once made the following argument for a manned mission to the red planet:

• *Mars is essentially in the same orbit [as the Earth]. Mars is somewhat the same distance from the sun, which is very important. We have seen pictures where there are canals, we believe, and water. If there is water, that means there is oxygen. If oxygen, that means we can breathe!* [11]

Mr. Quayle's argument, which was subject to a number of reasonable objections on scientific grounds, failed to persuade NASA that Mars was ready for colonization.

2.6.5. *Marshal the evidence.*

To demand that your audience believe you for your own sake, without argument or evidence, is another poor strategy. Vice President Quayle, again:

A. *Let me say it one more time. Maybe you don't understand. It is ill-relevant.*
Q. *Why?*
A. *Because. Because I said so.* [12]

To claim immunity to criticism and objections is no way to run an argument. Demonstrate that you are right without seeming to presuppose that your position is the correct one.

Another bogus strategy is to set up a straw man, or woman, and then blast the phony bastard full of holes. During campaign season, the television airwaves are noisy with such arguments, as embattled candidates deliberately misrepresent their opponents: "He never saw a take hike he didn't like." "She wants to commute the life sentence of serial killers and child molesters." "He wants to abolish marriage and the nuclear family." "If he doesn't support my Iraq policy, he's a racist."

Nothing useful is accomplished by such arguments, whether in politics, business, academia, or in your own home. If you offer to disprove or discredit what others have said or believed, first show that someone of interest or authority has indeed said or believed it. Do not waste your time and ours by disproving what does not need to be disproved.

Didacticism, too, is a turnoff. Go easy on the *oughts* and *shoulds*.

If you are overpleased with yourself, don't let it show. To claim that you are the first person ever to understand the true mystery of Prince Hamlet, or to allege that the Harry Potter books are full of castration anxiety, or to assert that global warming is nothing to worry about, or that God is on your side, are theses that will persuade no one unless you can prove it. If you are a scholar's scholar, a leader of men, and the cat's very meow, let your readers figure that out for themselves. A writer's self-congratulation can be irritating: "God loves you, and I love you, and you can count on both of us—as a powerful message that people who wonder about their future can hear, it's a powerful message! And it's a message that a lot of people can spread" (George W. Bush).[13]

Above all, do not be arrogant. Those who disagree with you are not necessarily stupid, criminal, or mentally ill.

2.6.6. *Don't knock rhetoric until you've tried it.*

Somewhere in our recent cultural history, *rhetoric*—the skillful use of language—became a dirty word. A quick search of the Internet indicates that hundreds of ordinary citizens, perhaps thousands, think we have "too much rhetoric" in public discourse; and yet no lonely voice has suggested that perhaps we have too little. Whether you are a high school student, a college professor, an attorney, or the president of the United States, it is no crime to have mastered the English language, and to use it subtly to good effect.

Thoughtful rhetoric can strengthen the evidence presented in a persuasive or expository argument. Any lawyer worth his fee can tell you, for example, that the same fact stated in two different ways may convey a different impression:

• *Freddy Knox met Dr. Clark and sold him a weapon. Knox took $300 for it.*
• *Jim Clark found Mr. Knox and bought an illegal handgun. He paid Mr. Knox $300 for it.*

Often it is not what you say, but how you say it, that will shape the reader's perception. Consider this listing for a popular Hollywood film:

• *Transported to a surreal landscape, a young girl kills the first woman she meets and then teams up with three complete strangers to kill again.*

That not-untruthful blurb is a satirical TV listing, from the *Marin County Independent Journal*, for the 1939 classic, *The Wizard of Oz*.[14]

Fine tune your argument so as to keep readers on your side without falsifying either or your own position or your opponent's. Be especially cautious with the construction, *not X, but Y.* Such remarks are usually inaccurate. When possible, line out such words as *always, never, all, no, none, most, every, only,* and find a more modest term.

Sweeping generalizations about your topic, or about your opponent's position, will only make your audience want to argue with you: A distinguished linguistics professor was lecturing on the phenomenon of double negatives. As the class session drew to a close, he drew himself up and declared solemnly: "In conclusion, let me remind you that while there are numerous instances in which a double negative may convey a positive, there is no instance in which a double positive conveys a negative." Whereupon, from the black of the room, one student muttered: "Yeah, yeah—".

2.6.7. *Reach a conclusion.*

A conclusion is not the same thing as a summary. Be decisive. Give your readers a fresh insight they can take home with them even if it is only to show that the text or question at hand is radically indeterminate, resistant to closure. But do not drag us through ten pages of argument only to say in the end that you cannot make up your mind. Better to dance gracefully out on a limb than to sit upon the fence, or upon a couch of flaccid relativism.

2.7. *How to Write an Expository Essay.*

I am returning this otherwise good typing paper to you because someone has printed gibberish all over it and put your name at the top.
—English Professor, Ohio State University

2.7.1. *Make the assignment mean something important.*

An expository essay—such as a philosophical or historical argument, or a critical discussion of a literary work—is neither a research paper nor an exercise in creative self-expression. It is not a report on what scholars have had to say on your chosen topic. It does not present your personal feelings. Like any other kind of persuasive writing, the expository essay is a reasoned defense of a thesis, one whose purpose is to analyze the meanings or cultural values that may be generated or challenged by the primary text.

2.7.2. *Preserve good form.*

Academic writing has certain rules that must be observed. Every discipline has conventions for style, form, and documentation. Learn them. Follow them. Learn to love them. Let your informed readers attend to your argument without being distracted by your own quirky notions of good form.

2.7.3. *Know your audience.*

When writing an academic paper, pitch your essay, not to the instructor, but to the brightest students in the class, who (if they should have the opportunity to read your paper) will say, "Gee, I wish *I* had written that."

2.7.4. *Know your medium; observe established conventions.*

The best way to master any kind of writing is to study what others have done. You cannot write a first-rate history or philosophy paper without having read some history and philosophy. You cannot write a critical essay without have read some literary criticism, or a Women's Studies paper without knowing some feminist theory. The more you read in a particular genre—whether it's fiction, advertising, journalism, office memos, a film review, or academic writing—the sooner you will master the discourse.

2.7.4a. *No rehash.* When explicating a literary text discussed in class (or, for that matter, any story already known to your target audience), avoid retelling the plot.

2.7.4b. *Stay close to the text.* What English teachers mean, when they remind their you to "stay close to the text," is that you cannot just talk *about* the text, you are expected to use it, embedding in your discussion savory bits of the primary literature, both quotes and paraphrases: Hamlet finds his father-uncle "More than kin and less than kind"—more that just a relative, but neither gracious, natural, or similar (*Ham.* 1.1.65). Keep the quotations short, choosing gems that will highlight or strengthen your critical point. If you rely on long quotations, without integrating the original language into your own commentary, your essay is likely to bore your target auidence.

2.7.4c. *Observe standard form for quotations.* When quoting poetry, reproduce the text exactly as in your source, capital letters and all, but insert a slash to mark the beginning of each new line of verse: "There once was a fellow named Lou, / Whose limericks stopped at line two" (Anon.). For direct quotations of more than four lines, use block form, indented two tabs over (left-justified, not centered); omit the quotation marks (since the block form itself indicates that the material is a quotation); and quote the text exactly as it appears in your source:

> I admit my last effort was bent,
> But my poetic powers are spent
>   On an ode to a gusset
>   Who has made so much fuss, it
> Must be that my grammar is went. [15]

But block quotations take up space, break the flow of your writing, and allow the reader's mind to wander. Most quotations should be brief, each one woven seamlessly into your own prose.

2.7.4d. **Stick to the text we've got.** Don't suggest what could have, should have, or might have happened in some other version of the story that the author did not, in fact, *write*. It is okay to analyze Othello's reasons for strangling Desdemona. It is not okay to say that he should not have done it, or to speculate what he would have done, had he not misplaced his handkerchief. Othello is a fictional character who can say and do only what's found in the fictional text.

2.7.4e. **Use present tense for exposition.** Reserve past tense for historical events, *i.e.*, when recounting what actually happened in the past. Use the present tense when discussing what *happens* (not what *happened*) in a narrative. Prince Hamlet never really existed. Neither did Pinocchio. When you comment on what characters "said" or "did" in a work of fiction, you seem naively to believe that the characters were once real people who spoke and acted as they do in the novel or play. Shakespeare's King Richard III has little in common with the historical King Richard III. The Samuel Johnson of Boswell's *Life* is not identical with the Samuel Johnson of history. Take care to distinguish one from the other by sticking to the appropriate verb tense. When writing about the Bible as literature, and not as the infallible Word of God, use present tense even to denote what Adam does, where Moses goes, what Jesus says, and how God feels about sin.

2.7.4f. **Don't conflate the author's viewpoint with that of the narrator, or with any of the author's fictional characters.** It is a mistake to presume that the author of a novel or play or poem "voices his opinion" somewhere in the fiction. None of the characters in literature, not even the narrator, can be assumed to speak for their respective authors. It is best to preserve this distinction even when explicating an autobiographical text, since the "I" who wrote the book is never identical to the constructed "I" of the autobiography.

2.7.4g. **You cannot speak for the author.** When you expound on what "the writer was trying to say," you are presuming to know the author's intention. Your discussion should focus on meanings found on the written page, not on meanings you think were in the author's head when he or she wrote it.

2.7.4h. **Don't confuse fiction with life outside the text.** A novel or film may represent the real world, but it "shows" little, and "proves' nothing, about what happens in real life. Here is former Vice President Dan Quayle (as the director of President George H. W.

Bush's Space Council), calling for a Star Wars Missile Defense System: "We should develop anti-satellite weapons, because we could not have prevailed without them in *Red Storm Rising*." [16]

Mr. Quayle was mistaken: the plot and special effects of a Hollywood fiction can prove nothing about real-world military technology. The same mistake is made by student writers who argue that Shakespeare's *Taming of the Shrew* (1594) "shows" that Elizabethan women were shrewish and in need of taming, or that Conrad's *Heart of Darkness* (1899) "demonstrates" that much good came from the British colonial presence in Africa, or that the hit film, *Independence Day* (1996), "proves" that the world can be saved by a Jewish intellectual and a married black soldier backed by the American military. A culture's values, beliefs, and anxieties may be apparent in a fictional text—and that's fair game for critical discussion—but do not write as if you have mistaken the fictional narrative for an accurate assessment or illustration of the real world.

2.7.4i. ***Know the secondary literature, but do not depend on it as a crutch.*** Refer to published expository essays or other academic literature as needed, consulting a balanced range of sources; but when you finally sit down to write, foreground your own critical engagement with the primary material. When characterizing the view of another commentator, say precisely whom you have in mind, and list the work in your "Works Cited" page. Never speak glibly or vaguely of what "the critics" or "scholars" or "most readers" or "most directors" have said about the text, or we'll know you're just bluffing: if you haven't conducted any research, it will not work to create, from the top of your own lazy head, a host of stupid adversaries. Cite one representative example and move on.

2.7.4j. ***Acknowledge those whose ideas or information have proved helpful.*** It is no shame, in academic work, not to have been the first person to think what you have thought. It is a great shame, however, to borrow someone else's work or ideas or suggestions and to give no credit where credit is due.

2.7.4k. ***Eloquence and a compelling argument are more important than originality.*** Do not try to write something about Shakespeare or Milton or Austen or Woolf that has never been said before. Just say what you've got to say as well as you can say it, giving due credit to those who got there first.

2.7.4-l. **The *MLA Guide for Writers of Research Papers*** is an essential resource for students majoring in language or literature. Buy a copy. Study it. Learn to love it.

2.8. *Advice for Writing a novel.*

Somerset Maugham advised: "There are three rules for writing a novel. Unfortunately, no one knows what they are."[17]

2.9. *Advice for Writing Poetry.*

Don't.

2.10. *Advice for Writing a Screenplay.*

See 2.9, *Advice for Writing Poetry.*

Part 3:

Write or Wrong

3.1. *A Pretty Good Guide to Hard Words*

3.2. *The Queen's English*

3.3. *Names*

3.4. *Latin Abbreviations*

Note: College-bound students will score significantly higher on the Verbal SAT exam if they have studied 3.1, "A Pretty Good Guide to Hard Words."

Part 3: WRITE OR WRONG

3.1. *A Pretty Good Guide to Hard Words*

I don't think writers are sacred, but words are. They deserve respect. If you get the right ones in the right order, you can nudge the world a little or make a poem which children will speak for you when you're dead.
            —Tom Stoppard [1]

• **a, an.** Use *an* before a vowel-sound or a silent *h-* (an *honorary* degree, *an hour* ago, *an NBA* player, *an eighty*-year-old man; and, in Oxbridge English, *an historical* event). Use *a* before a pronounced *h-* (*a hospital* bed, *a hotel*, *a horrible* person, *a history* lesson), and before a consonant sound even if it is spelled with a vowel (*a one*-year lease, *a united* front, *a eulogy*).

• An **academe**, by the definition of Ambrose Bierce, is "an ancient school where morality and philosophy were taught," while an **academy** (from *academe*) is "a modern school where football is taught."[2] But *academe, academia,* and *the academy* have lately come to be used interchangeably as general terms for the entire system of higher learning.

• To **accede** is to give assent, or to come into an office or dignity. To **exceed** is to go beyond. The fair maid *accedes* to her princely suitor's wishes by accepting his hand in marriage. She *exceeds* his wishes by living happily ever after while teaching him aspects of marital bliss that he never dreamed of.

• To **accept** is to receive what is offered, or to take a statement or opinion as true. To **except** is to exclude. *Except* may also be used as a conjunction meaning *but* (marking exclusion). The sentence, "All accept that reindeer can fly" means that *Everyone believes they can fly.* The sentence, "All except that reindeer can fly" means, *All of the reindeer can fly except that one.*

• **Accurate** means errorless. **Precise** means exact or clearly delineated. The respective nouns are **accuracy** and **precision.** A statement may be *accurate* but not *precise*, or vice versa: "Bubba used to drink about a liter of whiskey a day" (accurate but not precise). "Bubba said he could drink two and a half liters and still drive" (precise but not accurate). "Bubba's corpse registered a blood alcohol level of 0.31 percent" (accurate and precise).

• An **acronym** is a word formed from the initials or other parts of several words, such as ATM, CIA, NASCAR, NATO, NOW, radar, RAM, or snafu. An **abbreviation** is a shortened form of a word or phrase. "FBI" is an acronym, "F.B.I." an abbreviation, and "the Feds," slang. Acronyms do not require periods.

• An **acute** illness or problem is nasty but brief. Those which drag on are **chronic**.

• An **admissions** office or committee is responsible for deciding which applicants will be *admitted*. An **admission** may also be an instance of *admitting* a statement to be true, as when President Bill Clinton made the admission that he may have received a necktie from Monica Lewinsky. **Omission** denotes things, ideas, statements, or words deliberately or accidentally left out or undone. A "sin of commission," according to the Church, is something you ought *not* to have done but did *anyway*, such as the priest's molestation of a child. A "sin of omission," is something you did *not* do but *ought* to have done, such as a bishop's failure to intervene. An **emission** is something released from something else, such as pollutants erupting from a smokestack. If the president reports that "Some of the biggest sources of air pollution are the power plants, which send tons of *admissions* into our air," *emissions* is the intended word.[3] Only rarely do energy companies or ecclesiastical authorities make "admissions," and never at all except when caught, so to speak, with their pants down.

• If you heard the report in **advance**, you had **advance** notice or information. Your BMW benefits from **advanced** technology. To receive an *advance* is either to be paid before you did the work, or to receive a sexual proposition before you did anything to encourage it. "Becoming advanced in age" is a wordy euphemism for *growing old*, at which point the word's other meanings rarely come into play.

• **Adverse** means unfavorable or antagonistic. In a legal action, the **adverse** party is the other side. An **aversion** is a strong dislike for something. To be **averse** is to feel disinclined, or to wish to avoid. If our president says, "I'm not adverse to a camera," he means that he is willing to be photographed, but seems to say that his face won't harm the equipment.[4]

• **Advice** is a noun. **Advise** is verb. Give nice mice *advice* about lice. *Advise* wise guys about flies.

• To **affect** something is to have an **effect**: "The blackout *affected* [had an *effect* upon] the entire metropolitan area." Used as a verb, to *effect* is to bring about a result ("The blackout *effected* a shutdown of the city center"), but its use as a verb is best avoided, to prevent confusion (use *cause* instead). To complicate matters still further, *affect* when used as a noun (AF-fect) means emotional response: "The autistic child showed no *affect* even when frightened."

• To **aggravate** is to make worse. To **annoy** is to bother, provoke, or exasperate. To confuse the two words may *annoy* some purists, but it will not *aggravate* them.

• **Aggression** denotes the act or practice of initiating hostilities or of launching an invasion, an organized **assault**. On a personal level, both *aggression* and *assault* may signify hostile speech or destructive behavior. An **affront** is an open insult, deliberately offensive. These terms are always negative. If the president opines that "we need a full affront on an energy crisis that is real in California and looms for other parts of our country," his intended meaning may be, "We need to resolve California's energy crisis before it spreads."[5] CEOs may like the sound of "an aggressive" sales rep or advertising campaign, but for the rest of the English-speaking world the word implies *belligerent, obnoxious*, and *pushy*. *Assault* the enemy if you must, but do not "assault" a problem, your colleagues, or your dinner.

• An **alibi** is not a lie or an excuse. It is one's proof of having been somewhere else than at the scene of the crime.

• To **allege** is to make an assertion, most often by way of accusation, without giving proof that it is true. An **allegation** may be true or false until proved one way or the other. In a legal context, to *allege* is to give statements in evidence that may still be rebutted or contested.

• **All right** means unharmed or entirely correct. In colloquial speech and informal writing, *all right* is widely used to mean "okay" or "Hey, why not?" *Alright,* though gaining some currency in America, will strike fastidious readers as an ignorant misspelling.

• To **allude** is to refer to something indirectly or covertly. To **refer** implies direct mention or citation. The distinction is useful. The two words should not be confused. (See also **elude, elusive.**)

• **A lot of** is a three-word phrase commonly used (and greatly overused) to mean *much* or *many*. Its original sense has been lost (*a lot* [i.e., a batch] of dye, of silk). The fused spelling, "*alot,*" though never correct, is forgivable when used to mean *very much,* without the *of*: "I like you alot." Where possible, use *many* for countable items, and *much* or *a lot of* for an uncounted quantity (*many candidates, many donors, a lot of money, much jubilation*). Still better is to drop *a lot,* and to be specific. For "Cher's new motorcycle cost a lot of money," try: "Cher paid $18,000 for her new motorcycle." If you have *a lot of* problems, you have **myriad** troubles, not "a myriad *of*" them. If you have only *two* problems, you have a **couple of** them. (No one can have "a couple problems," although an aspiring adulterer may have "a couple problem.")

• *Already* means previously. *All ready* means "completely ready" or "everyone [is] ready": "We *already* ate lunch but we're *all ready* to eat again."

• Take him to the *altar* and he's yours forever, to have, to hold, and to *alter*.

• *Alternate*, used as a noun, denotes a substitute or second choice. As an adjective, it means "every other." To *alternate* is to occur by turns, first one, then the other. *Alternative,* as a noun, is one of precisely *two* options, plans, or possibilities. To speak of finding "a different alternative" is superfluous, as there is never more than one. When our president says "that the babies out of wedlock is a very difficult chore" and that "I believe we ought to say there is *a different alternative than* the culture that is proposed by people like Miss Wolf in society," the intended phrase is *"an alternative to* Miss Wolf's proposed culture."[6] Used as an adjective, *alternative* describes a person, place, thing, or idea that remains a second choice, or a situation allowing only one of two possibilities. If Mr. Smith, a bigamist, *alternates* between spouses, living with wife no. 1 in January, March, and May, and with her *alternate* in the *alternate* months, the second wife is an *alternative* to the first, and vice versa. If Mr. Smith prefers wife number 2, then wife number 1 is his *alternate*."

• *Altogether* means thoroughly, entirely, taken as a whole. *All together* is everyone in a group. "In the *all together*" is slang for exhibiting all of your body parts at the same time and is best avoided, at least in mixed company.

• *An ambiguous* statement, or *double entendre* (or a triple or quadruple pun, if you're Shakespeare), is a double meaning in the text, whether intended by the author, or discovered by the reader, or both. A *vague* statement is merely imprecise or unclear.

• If you are *ambivalent*, you have mixed feelings. If you're *indifferent*, you have no preference either way. Though *ambiguity* usually denotes double meaning, a cross-dressed man or bearded lady may be described as *sexually ambiguous*. *Ambidextrous* means only that you are good with either hand, or dextrous in a *ménage à trois*.

• *Among, amongst* (see *between*).

• Use *amount* (or *little—*, or *much—*) for uncountable quantities. Use *number* (or *few—*, or *many—*) for what's countable. Do not say "a large amount of people" unless, perhaps, when speaking of the carnage at the site of a plane crash.

• Reserve *analyzation* for chemists, mathematicians, and proctologists: *analysis* is the better word. When our president says that "This case has had full analyzation and has been looked at a lot," he may mean, *I think someone already studied that.*[7]

• **And/or** is a form that denotes three selections: one, or the other, or both: "Jacob will marry Leah *and/or* Rachel." Where possible, come to a decision. Then delete the distracting term, *and/or*, and recast the sentence: "Jacob will marry Leah first, then Rachel, retaining Leah as the alternate."

• An **anecdote** is a short, pithy account of a funny or pointed incident. An **antidote** is a remedy or cure. When the president explains that "A tax cut is really one of the anecdotes to coming out of an economic illness," *antidote* is the intended word.[8]

• An **antagonist** is an *adversary* or counterforce that *contends against* (the hero) or *counteracts* (a muscle, a chemical substance). A **protagonist** may or may not be the "good" guy, but he or she is always the "main contender" (the *proto-agonist*). To **antagonize** is not just to irritate but to make someone into an adversary.

• To **anticipate** is to take action in advance of an expected event. To **expect** an event is merely to suppose that it is coming. The distinction is a useful one and should be preserved. *To anticipate* an expected attack may be to strike first. An exam *expected* at end of term is *anticipated* only if you study for it. **Expectation** is not a synonym for *aspiration*. If our president says that America's "common denominator" is that our "*expectations* rise above that which is expected," *hopes* may be the intended word.[9] If the president says, "I'm the master of low expectations," he may mean, *I am good at making pessimistic forecasts*, or perhaps, *Of all the Bush politicians from whom you might expect zero achievement, I am the supreme example.*[10]

• **Anxious** means worried, nervous, fidgety. You are *anxious* to take an exam if the thought of it makes you nervous. If you mean **eager**, say so: "Mom is *eager* to take a vacation, though *anxious* to fly."

• **Anymore,** in its negative or limiting sense, means (not) *any longer* or (not) *at this time*, or (not) *now:* "One cannot buy vinyl records anymore." It does not mean *lately*. Such statements as "*Anymore* the traffic is getting worse," or "*Anymore* a new microwave is expensive" do injury to the language. (If you cannot substitute "as used to be true" for "anymore," you have used the word incorrectly.) *Any more* can also be a two-word phrase: "Are there **any more** cookies?" "I'm not *any more* tired now than I was hours ago."

• Do it **any way** you like: the choice is yours. Or a sign may say, "Don't do it," and you do it **anyway**. **Anyway** at the beginning of a sentence (a device not to be used in formal prose) indicates that the speaker or story-teller has resumed a narrative thread after a digression or interruption: "Anyway, as I was saying..." *Anyways* is illiterate.

• *Apostasy* denotes an improved understanding of one's religion. *Heresy* denotes an opinion or belief not sanctioned by one's co-religionists. An *apostate* leaves the church and is condemned for his *unbelief.* A *heretic* stays on until she is reformed, excommunicated, or burned at the stake for her *misbelief.* An *apostle* is a first-century true believer on whose supposed authority the Church assumes the right to behave in such a fashion.

• To *appraise* is to assess, to set a value on. To *apprise* is to inform: "Ms. Davis of Century 21 *appraised* Mr. Kaczynski's backwoods property and *apprised* potential buyers of its colorful history."

• *Apropos* (in French, *à propos*, "to the purpose") means relevant, pertinent, connected with what has gone before. Rhymes with "Pop, go slow." If you mean "appropriate," write *appropriate.*

• *Apt* (see *prone*).

• An *ark* is a large, flat-bottomed boat, such as the one on which Noah is believed to have housed representatives of the Earth's ten million animal species for a year. An *arc* is a curved line or structure, such as the rainbow that the god Yahweh is said to have placed in the firmament as a sign that He would not again drown the entire planet.

• *As* and *like* are a source of much confusion. Use *as* for that which happens or exists in the same way, and *like* for a similarity between two people, places, or things: "When I die, I want to go peacefully in my sleep, *as my grandfather did,* not screaming in terror *like his passengers*" (or: "*as his passengers did*"). If you are *as* hungry *as* a lion, you may eat *like* a lion. If you speak *as* an authority, you are one. If you speak *like* an authority, you're only faking it.

To make comparison, *like* is always to be followed by a noun (*like thunder, like tar, like strawberries, like sandpaper*). To use *like* as a conjunction is to risk sounding illiterate, at least to grammar pundits: "Pundits ridiculed my campaign speech, *like I expected*" (better to say "*as* I expected" or "*as* usual"). When a presidential candidate says, "There needs to be debates, like we're going through," he may mean, "There must be televised debates such as those we are having now."[11] If he says, "We must all hear the universal call to like your neighbor just like you like to be liked yourself," the second "like" should be an *as.*[12] Never is it necessary to say "like in" or "like on," nor ever correct to say, "like for example." Products at the department store are not "*like on TV,*" but "*as seen on TV*" or "*like the ones seen on TV.*"

For formal writing, it is best to avoid even such commonplace solecisms as "It looks like rain." Water from a drippy faucet may *look like rain,* but when an overcast sky threatens a storm, it *looks as if* it *may* rain. "Like I said" may, one day, become fully idiomatic. Until then, it's "as I said" (or "as I was saying"). Write and say "as in

London," not "like in London" (or: "as in the 14th century," "as in my previous example," "as they do in China").

As well as. To say that "Taylor Swift golfs *as well as* Tiger Woods" implies not only that Taylor Swift is a golfer but that she's as good a golfer as Mr. Woods. Try: "Like Tiger Woods, Taylor Swift golfs, though not *as well*." Avoid putting *as well as* at the beginning of a sentence. "*As well as* singing, Taylor golfs," is a weird construction.

As can be followed by a conjunction (**as if, as when**) but take care not to saddle an *as* with unneeded prepositions. **As to** can usually be replaced by *about*. **So as to** can usually be replaced by *to.* **As of** often means *by* or *since*. It is never correct to say "**as of yet**," which makes no sense. Try: "*As of* noon today, the hostage was still alive" or "The hostage is not *yet* slain," but not: "*As of yet,* the hostage has not been slain." The idiom will make no great difference to the hostage, but that is a weird way for the newscaster to have said it.

To write, "I could not finish the essay on time, *as* I had a headache," will give your English teacher a headache as well. *As* is not a synonym of *because* or *while*; it is a conjunction, meaning *in the same manner*.

• Use an **augur** to predict if you will go to heaven when you die, or an **auger** to drill your way in.

• **Autarchy** means absolute sovereignty. **Autarky** indicates economic self-sufficiency. Don't use either word unless you're sure your audience knows the difference.

• **Average** (see **mean**).

• An **awesome** athlete or fireworks display or performance is **awe-inspiring**. An **awesome** enemy may be **awful** (terrible) or make you feel **awful** (unpleasant). A **fearsome** enemy makes you **fearful**. **Frightening** and **frightful** mean pretty much the same thing, although *frightful* is sometimes used figuratively, such as a "frightful liar" or your child's "frightful grade report." For informal writing, *awfully* can be used to mean *very*: "Rubber Ducky, I'm awfully fond of you."

• **Awhile** (as an adverb) and **for a while** (three words) are synonymous, as in "Stay *awhile*" and "Stay *for a while*." A **while** is an unspecified period of time, as in the phrase, "a while ago."

• Wheels turn on an **axle**. The Earth turns on its **axis**. Skaters who can jump and turn like Axel Paulson can perform an **axel**—or a "triple axel" if they can turn three axels in one mighty leap.

• **Barbed** wire (see **duct** tape).

• **Basically** is an overused word: When the president says, "What I am against is quotas [because] they basically delineate based upon whatever," the thought is unclear.[13] From such sentences as "Basically, I grew up in Midland, Texas," or "I basically hope to be more like my dad," omit *basically*. Even when used correctly, the word can usually be deleted. The same goes for *essentially* and *totally*.

• ***Basis***, another overused word, is rarely necessary. If it happens *on an annual basis*, it happens *annually* or *every year*. Use *basis* as a synonym for *grounds* or *foundation*, or not at all: "Fascism was really the basis for the New Deal" (Ronald Reagan).[14] *Groundwork* is the foundation of a project, and denotes the *preliminary* activity; do not confuse it with *framework*, which denotes the structure. If our president speaks of "the framework—the groundwork—not framework—the groundwork to discuss a framework for peace, to lay the—all right," he may mean that adversaries must lay the groundwork for peace before they can discuss a framework for peaceful relations.[15]

• ***Bear*** the pain or responsibility (He *bears*, he *bore*, he has *borne* the burden). To ***bear*** a child is to carry it in the womb until birth (The child is *borne* [carried] for nine months before being *born*, after which it may be *borne* in your arms or on your shoulders), until adolescence, when it must be *borne* (endured) with parental fortitude. To ***bare*** your shoulders or buttocks or soul is to expose it (*bare, bared, has bared*). "Bear with me" means *be patient*. "Bare with me" means something else.

• ***Because*** introduces a reason. It may be used in place of *since* or *for the reason that*. Begin a sentence with *because* if you wish ("*Because* of the blizzard, shops closed early"); or put the dependent clause second ("The shops closed early *because* of the blizzard"). Write a fragment, if you must, in reply to a question ("Why did shops close early? Because of the blizzard"). But do not write, "The reason is because"—which is a silly redundancy. "The reason why is because" is even worse, and may actually cause brain damage.

• To ***better*** is to improve or make better. To ***embitter*** is to make resentful. When our president urges the poor "to embetter" themselves, and promises to welcome "those faith-based programs for the embetterment of mankind**," *betterment***, not ***embitterment***, is the intended word."[16]

• ***Between*** is used when linking two persons or things: *The next race will be between Jim's rat and mine* (or: *between you and me*). It is never correct to say "between you and I." A coin may fall through one crack or the other, but it cannot fall "*between* the cracks." Nor can a thing be *between* itself. When our president boasts that "Border relations between Canada and Mexico have never been better," he seems to imply the sudden disappearance of the 48 contiguous States.[17] To say with our president that "It's a struggle between good, and it's a struggle between evil," is like clapping with one hand. [18] ***Among*** is used when at least three persons or things are involved:

"Rather than split the contested donut *between* Officers Medavoy and Sipowicz, Chief Burns divided it equally *among* the entire squad." *Between* may, however, be used for three or more persons or things closely interrelated ("A free trade agreement was formed *between* Canada, the U.S.A., and Mexico"), or for purposes of comparison, as if by successive comparison: "Voters who can see no difference *between* the Republican, Democrat, Libertarian, and Independent candidates are invited to split their donations among all four."

• *bi-* is a prefix meaning *two*. There is no such thing as a three-wheeled bicycle. *Biannual* means twice a year, and *biennial,* every two years. To avoid confusion, use *twice yearly* or *every six months* for *biannual,* and *every other year* or *every two years* in place of *biennial. Biweekly* means every other week; *bimonthly,* every other month. A *bisexual* person is not the same as a *hermaphrodite.* (See also *semi-.*)

• A *biased* person has a *bias against* someone or something. To have a *bias toward* something is to be biased in its favor. *Bias* is a bowling metaphor, indicating that an unbalanced ball is disposed to curve.

• To *foot a bill* (a statement of fees or charges) is to add it up and write a total at the bottom, but the same phrase is sometimes used informally to mean "pay the full amount." To *fill* or *fit* the bill (a statement or list of particulars), also informal, is to be quite satisfactory, meeting all requirements.

• A *bizarre bazaar* is a strange marketplace. Both words are often misspelled.

• A *blatant* child, driver, or donkey is unpleasantly loud. A *blatant* lie or plagiarism or act of fornication calls attention to itself. "Blatantly brilliant" is an ill-chosen phrase except in reference to someone whose display of genius strikes others as obnoxious.

• Take chicken *bouillon* for a cold. Take gold *bullion* for thirty years without parole.

• When you need to *breathe*, take a *breath*.

• *Cash* is what you don't have enough of to put in a *cache*, or hidden storage.

• Use *call for* to make a request ("The president called for a tax cut"), or to require ("Bart's behavior called for a detention"), or to make a pickup ("I'll call for you at 5:00 p.m."). *Call for* does not mean *predict*. A meteorologist has delusions of grandeur if he thinks he can issue a report that "calls for" good weather.

• A *callous* foot or *callused* hand has *calluses*. A *callous* person is too insensitive to care (cf. *mucous, mucus*).

• A big gun is a *cannon*. All others—whether literary, musical, Biblical, or ecclesiastical—are *canons*.

• *Canvas* is durable cloth. To *canvass* is to go around asking.

• A *capital* is an upper-case letter, or a city that serves as a seat of government. A *capitol* is a building in which a legislature meets. *The Capitol* (capital C) is the domed building in Washington, D.C., where the U.S. Congress meets. It is situated on Capitol Hill, not on a "congressional hill." [19]

• A *carrot* is an orange root, eaten by people and rabbits. Precious stones are weighed in *carats*. The *karat* is a measure comprising 24 units, denoting the proportion of pure gold in an alloy (a "12 karat" or "12K" ring is 50% pure gold). A *caret* (^) is a mark used most often by proofreaders and computer programmers.

• *Case,* except with reference to grammar or law, is an overused word. For "If it is the case that," write *If.* Instead of "in many cases," write *often.* "In any case" can usually be omitted.

• A *catalyst* remains unchanged while speeding up a reaction in the other elements. It is not a synonym for *means, mechanism, medium, method,* or *cheerleader.*

• A *causal* force changes things but never changes into *casual* attire.

• Jesus was crucified on *Calvary* hill. No *cavalry* came over the hill to rescue him.

• If you are *cavalier*, you exhibit a jaunty disregard for your critics, whom you consider mere *cavilers,* people who nitpick.

• To be *celibate* is to remain unmarried, especially by religious vow. Catholic priests, though always celibate, may not be *chaste*, in which case they may be transferred to another parish or be *chased* out of town.

• *Celsius* or *centigrade* is the metric temperature scale (adopted everywhere except in the stubborn USA) on which water freezes at zero degrees and boils at one hundred degrees. To convert *Fahrenheit* to Celsius, subtract 32, multiply by 5, and divide by 9. In prose, write out the number of degrees. In tables, a temperature can be abbreviated (*72F, 32F, -10F, 22C, 0C, -23C, etc.*), with or without a degree symbol (*72°F*), but be consistent.

• To *censure* is to reprimand or condemn. To *censor* is to remove or suppress language that is considered offensive, subversive, or harmful. As a noun, *censor* denotes the person who examines a text for approval or possible censorship. A *censer* is a container used for burning incense. A *sensor* is a device that detects and responds to physical stimuli such as movement, light, or heat.

• A *census* is a systematic count or official survey. A *consensus* means general agreement or collective opinion. The phrases, "consensus of opinion" and "general consensus," are redundant.

• **Centered on, based on, revolved around.** An airplane, army, or burglar may "circle around," and a planet may "revolve around," but no one can "center around." ("While Jack's campaign *circled around* the abortion issue, Shannon's was *centered on* a woman's right to choose." "*Lolita* is a novel that *revolves around* child sexual molestation.") When the London *Times* reports that "new ethical arguments centre around genetic manipulation," *center on* or *focus on* may be the desired phrase.[20] Nor can writing or another structure be "based around" or "based off of" its foundation: "The Oscar-winning film, *A Beautiful Mind*, is *based on* [*not* "off of"] the life of John Nash."

• To **chafe** is to make worn or sore by literal rubbing (as from a rope on the neck or from a saddle on the buttocks), or to irritate or annoy, or to become annoyed: "Justin *chafed at* his father's backseat driving." To **chaff** is to tease good-naturedly: "Mr. Dixon *chaffed* his son for running a red light."

• **Chair** (or *the chair*) can usually serve for **chairman, chairwoman, chairmanship,** and works better than *chairperson,* a word that will sound droll to many readers, such as *freshpeople* rather than *first-year students* as a gender-neutral substitute for *freshmen,* or *personhole* for *manhole.*

• *To* **charge** a person or an organization with a task, liability, expenditure, or offense is to assign responsibility. It is not a synonym for *accuse or allege.* Police officers may *charge* a suspect *with* a crime, or *accuse* him *of* a crime, or *allege that* he committed a crime, but they cannot "charge that" he committed a crime. *Charge that* is correct only in the sense, "Charge that purchase to my account" or "We shall charge that village before dawn."

• A **chic chick** (sheek chick) is either a fashionable baby chicken or a young woman (slang) whose stylish.

• To **choose** is to make a decision. Pronunciation of *choose* and *chose* differs from *loose* and *lose*: "I choose booze." "I am choosing a bruising." "I chose a rose." "I have chosen to be frozen."

• A **chorale** may sing **choral** music in church. Cattle may moo in a **corral.** **Coral** is found in the sea.

• **Circumstances** (usually plural) are those conditions that "stand round about" (circum+stance): a person or situation is said by purists to be *in*, not *under*, the circumstances. But if your hero can "rise above" the circumstances without censure, then my hero may well sink and go "under" them whenever I please. The "surrounding circumstances" is, however, a redundant phrase best avoided.

• **Cite** (see **site**).

• To **claim** is to assert one's right to take or to keep something—a piece of property, a prize, a lost article, the children's attention. Used informally, to *claim* is to say something without proof that it is true.

As used by reporters, "claim" implies that the writer is skeptical of what the speaker has said. To be safe, use *said*.

• A *click* is a small sound, as from a mechanical device. A *clique* is an exclusive circle of socialites or snobby adolescents. A *claque* is an organized group of supporters at a political or theatrical event who clap loudly and cheer to make the viewing audience think that the person on the stage must have said or done something really brilliant.

• *Climatic* means "relating to climate": "Owing to unfavorable *climatic* conditions, the wedding was postponed." *Climactic* means either "forming a climax" or "at the most exciting moment," making any postponement difficult.

• To be *coarse* is to be rough and unrefined (cloth), large-grained (sandpaper), or vulgar (humor). A *course* is a series of lessons, or a route to be followed. A *corse* is a *body* (obsolete word).

• To *coexist* is to exist together at the same time and in the same place. If the president says, "I know the human being and fish can coexist peacefully," he may mean that human beings and fish should be able to swim together without quarreling.[21]

• *Commensurate* is an adjective meaning *duly measured* or *well suited*. To *commiserate* is to express pity. When our president promises to reduce our "own nuclear capacities [*i.e.*, capabilities] *commiserate* with keeping the peace" or promises "an expenditure of money that is *commiserate* with keeping a promise to our troops," *commensurate* is the intended word.[22] *Commensurable* is an adjective meaning equal in terms of something else, such as *commensurable* systems of measurement or currency.

• A *comment* expresses opinion. To *comment* is to give an opinion, not to state facts. You may comment *on* a problem but you cannot simply *comment* something. Do not *comment that*. Just *say* it.

• *Common* (see *mutual*).

• To *compare* is to assert a likeness. Use *compare with* when describing objects, people, ideas, that are essentially similar, as when blocks of writing are *compared with* one another. Use *compare to* when describing things essentially different, as when writer's block is *compared to* paralysis or constipation. The decision may be subjective: "My dear, I cannot help but *compare* you *with* your mother." "Don't you dare *compare* me *to* my mother, you sonuvabitch!"

• *Compass points*: use *north, east, south, west* when referring to directions or compass points. Use *eastern* [*western, northern, southern*] for that which faces east (*eastern exposure*), or is situated in the east (*the eastern hills*) or that comes from the east (an *eastern* or *easterly wind*). The *eastbound* traffic heads east. Directions take caps when part of a place name: North Dakota, South Korea, West Jersey.

• A *complacent* person is smug or self-satisfied. A *complaisant* person exhibits a willingness to please.

• *Complement* and *complementary* describe that which completes or perfects something else by supplying extra features. A *compliment* or *complimentary* statement is an expression of praise. Use "with compliments" or "complimentary" to describe a small gift given as a courtesy or favor.

• To *comprise* is *to be composed of*: "The university *comprises* [*or* "is composed of'] nine colleges, a graduate school, and a law school. Women make up [not "comprise"] 54% of the total enroll-ment." *Constitute* is used in the opposite manner, to specify the parts that make up the whole: "The law school, graduate school, and nine colleges *constitute* the university." Do not write "is comprised of," which is always incorrect.

• An individual or group can make a *concentrated* effort but it takes at least two people or parties to make a *concerted* effort. To work *in concert* is to collaborate.

• *Confident, dependent, independent* are conditions. The *confidant* whom you trust to keep a secret, and the *dependant* who relies on your care, are persons.

• *Consensus* (see *census*).

• The verb, *to consider*, may be followed by *as* only when it means *discuss* or *examine*: "In this seminar we shall *consider* the her-maphrodite *as* a marker of cultural anxieties about gender." Or: "Air carriers shall *consider*, *as* a cost-cutting device, a plan to give each passenger ice water and a pretzel in place of a microwaved dinner."

• *Contemporary* (see *current*).

• The Earth's seven *continents* are Africa, Antarctica, Asia, Australia, Europe, North America, and South America. Australia is both a continent and a *country*. Antarctica belongs to humanity and has no government. When our president reports that "Africa is a *nation* that suffers from incredible disease," *continent* is the intended word. [23] When he says, "We have to work with Nigeria. That's an important continent," *country* is the intended word.[24] When our vice president describes the Holocaust as "an obscene period in *our nation's* history," he may mean *world* or *human* history.[25] When the same vice president says of Latin America that "The US has a vital interest in *that area of the country*," a better phrase would be "in Latin America" or "in the southern hemisphere" or "in that part of the world";[26] and when he says that the United States as "a part of Europe," *North America* would be more accurate. If the president says, "Natural gas is *hemispheric*. I like to call it '*hemispheric*' in nature because it is a product that we can find in our neighbor-hoods,"[27] *local* may be the word he is looking for.

• *Continual* means over and over, happening frequently, though with intervals. *Continuous* means without interruption: "My heart beats *continuously*. My back hurts *continually*." *Continuous* can refer to space as well as time: "The protesters formed a *continuous* line around the power plant." To be *contiguous* is to share a border, boundary, or edge, such as the forty-eight contiguous states. If the president warns that "Israel must make sure there's a continuous territory that Palestinians call home," he does not mean that Israel must ensure a Palestinian homeland stretching all around the globe, but only one that neighbors Israel: *contiguous* is the intended word.[28]

• *Controller* and *comptroller* mean the same thing (someone whose job it is to oversee financial matters) and are pronounced the same way. "Comptroller" is an archaic variation used today only if it is the formal title of the holder of the office (as in England, a land where many archaic spellings are still treasured).

• To *convince* is to bring someone to a firm belief, and is followed by *that* or *of*: "If you would win a man to your cause, first *convince* him *that* you are his sincere friend" (or: "convince him of your sincerity"). To *persuade* is to urge or to make somebody act or believe, and is usually followed by to: "Discourage litigation. *Persuade* your neighbors *to* compromise whenever you can" (Abraham Lincoln).

• Apples and nuclear reactors have *cores*. An elite *corps* (kor) may drink Heineken while most of the other *corps* (korz) drink Coors. If there is one *corpse* (korps), it may be a homicide; if there are thousands of *corpses* (korpzez), it may called be "a holy war," a "jihad," or a "liberation of Iraq."

• A *counsel* or *counselor* is someone whose advice is sought (*e.g.*, a lawyer). *Counsel* may also denote the advice itself. A *council* is a group of elected or appointed administrators, whose members are called *councilors*. A *consul* is a local representative of a foreign government. A *console* (KON-sole) is a storage compartment. To *console* (kun-SOLE) is to provide comfort.

• *Couple of* (see *a lot of*).

• A *credible* witness, actor, or story is *believable* and perhaps *convincing*. A *creditable* person or thing deserves acknowledgment and praise. Except in advertising copy or American slang, *incredible* always means impossible or difficult to believe. To tell an actor or a material witness that his or her performance was "incredible" is an insult. (See also *incredulous*.)

• A *crescendo* is not a peak, summit, or zenith but a passage of increasing loudness. A story, orchestra or sexual encounter may build to a *climax*, but neither Pavarotti nor the Boston Pops Orchestra can "build to a crescendo."

• A *crisis* is a decisive event or turning point that changes history or one's life (plural, *crises*). A *crisis* is not a disaster, though it may be a moment or situation in which action must be taken to avoid disaster (e.g., *Oedipal crisis*). Many ongoing economic and political troubles are wrongly described as *crises* when they are merely troubles.

• To *criticize* ("judge") someone is to find fault (*personal criticism*). To *criticize* a cultural artifact is to evaluate it (as in art or literary *criticism*). A *critical* essay is chiefly concerned, not with "good" or "bad" writing, but with the ways in which meaning and cultural value are constructed in and through the literary text. A *critique* (of a piece of writing, a golf swing, a business deal) is a detailed evaluation. *Critique* has recently come to be used as a verb meaning "to assess."

• Take your *cue,* hit a *cue* ball, stand in a *queue.*

• A *crux* is a puzzling problem that demands a decision. It does not mean *gist.* The *crux* of your argument, if you have one (and not all arguments do) is the point at which readers must decide whether you are correct, or off your nut. A textual *crux* is a variant reading that forces editors to make a difficult choice between possibilities. In ascending Half Dome or Mt. Everest, the *crux* is the toughest point in the climb.

• *Current, contemporary,* and *contemporaneous* denote that which occurs or exists at the same time or in the same period as something or somebody else. What was *current* word usage in the 16th century may not be *current* today. *Contemporary* art in the 18th century was not what we now call "modern art." *Contemporary* may also be used as a noun: "Although Chaucer was a *contemporary* of King Richard II, his Canterbury Tales are not *contemporaneous* with Shakespeare's *Richard II*, a play written two centuries later."

• *Damage* is usually singular. But in a legal context the word denotes a sum of money and is always plural: *Damages* may be awarded to the plaintiff in a civil case.

• *Data* (facts, figures) takes a plural verb, and *datum*, a singular verb. The plural noun, *data,* has been so often abused as a synonym for *information* that it is now well on its way to becoming a singular English noun. But it is still better to write "these data are," or "this information is," than to write "this data is."

• To *decimate* is to destroy a proportion of the whole (originally a tenth), not to destroy completely. To *devastate* is to inflict severe or widespread harm. To be *devastated* is to feel overwhelmed by pain or sorrow, though "I'm devastated" has acquired a slightly insincere ring, because overused. Try "sad."

• A *definitive* decision or ruling is *decisive*, not to be challenged. A *definite* answer is fixed, certain, and clearly delineated.

• To **defuse** means (literally) to remove the fuse or (figuratively) to make safe. To **diffuse** is to spread out, or to scatter over a wide area. "If the is bomb is not *defused,* the plane's wreckage may soon be *diffused* over the Atlantic." "Diplomacy may help to *defuse* border tensions." "A scrim can *diffuse* bright light."

• A **degraded** person or environment or culture has been corrupted. A **degraded** compound is decomposed. To **downgrade** is to lower status, rank, or value. If your boss berates you, you have been denigrated, not "downgraded" (although your salary may well be downgraded if you don't shape up).

• **Deliver** is a transitive verb: you must deliver *something*— letters, a message, a baby, a prisoner, the goods. You may *deliver* what was promised, or *deliver* something *as* promised, or (colloquially) *deliver on* a promise, but you can't just "deliver." And it is better to *keep* promises than to "deliver on" them.

• **Demand** has peremptory connotations and should be used with caution. Do not write that "Dockworkers have *demanded* a ten-percent increase" if they have **requested** ten but will settle for six. A *demanding* task is one that requires concentrated effort. A *demanding* mother is hard to please, and possibly to blame for your neurosis.

• To **deploy** is to spread out a force (troops, artillery) over a wide area. It does not mean *use* or *employ.*

• To **deprecate** a person or car is to speak ill of it, with **deprecatory** intent. To **depreciate** a car or business asset is to set a lower value on it than it had before. People can be appreciated but not "depreciated." To **denigrate** ("blacken") a person or reputation is to make libelous or insulting remarks. (Cf. **degraded**.)

• A **desert** is a wasteland. A **dessert** adds to your waist. **Deserts** are a *deserved* reward or punishment. "Just *deserts*" ("well-deserved deservings") is a tired phrase, and redundant: Just say, *"The villain got his deserts"* or *"got what he deserved."* "Just *desserts*" may, however, be a child's favorite dinner. (A mnemonic aid: *stressed,* in reverse, is *desserts.*)

• **Despite** and **in spite of** must be followed by a noun: *despite* his poor grades, *despite* the poor weather, *in spite of* my cold. To contrast a phrase with the rest of the sentence, use *although*: *"Although* he had poor grades in high school, he did well in the Army." When possible, use *although* or *despite,* not *in spite of.* To do or say something **in spite** is, of course, to be malicious.

• To **destruct** is military jargon meaning to destroy a missile or rocket after launch. To **self-destruct** is to destroy oneself (or itself). In all other contexts, the word is **destroy. Deconstruction** is a mode of literary criticism. It is not the opposite of **construction.** You cannot "destruct" or "deconstruct" a building. You *destroy* it.

• To **deteriorate** is to rot, or become worse, or fall apart. You cannot "deteriorate a car," though it may well deteriorate on its own, in which case it will **depreciate**, or lose value. (Cf. *deprecate*.)

• **Devaluation** denotes the act of lowering the exchange value of a national currency by lowering its gold equivalency. **Deflation** denotes only the reduction in available currency and credit that results in lower prices. On Feb. 18, 2002, President George W. Bush put the Japanese Yen into free-fall by confusing the two terms at a news conference.

• **Devise** is a verb. **Device** is a noun. "*Devise* a wise plan." "Use a nice *device*." (Cf. *advise, advice*.)

• Our opinions **differ** when you and I disagree. Our opinions **vary** only when our mind changes from one day to the next.

• **Different** is an overused word, best omitted or replaced by something specific. If you speak "five different languages," you speak *five languages*. If your boyfriend is a little *odd*, don't say that he's "a little different." Avoid generalities: a vice of student prose is the tendency to make such pointless remarks as "The societies of America and North Korea are very different" or "Chaucer's male characters are different from his female characters." Such assertions only makes your teacher wish she that had chosen a different profession.

• **Different from**: Objects or people, if not the same, are different *from* one another, not different *than*. When the president says that "accounting in Washington is a little different than the way normal— I shouldn't say 'normal' people—the average person accounts," *different from* is the intended phrase. The advertising slogan, "Dove is different than soap," should be scrubbed from impressionable minds. *Different from* is correct even when the difference is more than (or less than) one might have thought: "The children of Iraq are *less different from* our own *than* the president may have supposed." "Different than" is sometimes hard to avoid: a situation may be "*different than* it was before" if you cannot say "*different from* what it was." If in doubt, write "different from," not "different than," and you'll be wrong only once in a million tries.

• **Diffuse** (see **defuse**).

• A **dilemma** is not just any difficulty. It has two (*di-*) horns (*lemma*). A *dilemma* offers a choice between alternatives, each having unpleasant consequences. In logic, a *dilemma* is a form of argument (the *horned syllogism*) in which you are forced to accept one of two propositions, each of which contradicts your original contention.

• A **discreet** person shows good judgment or **discretion**, taking care not to attract attention, or give offense, or reveal secrets. **Discrete** circles (or variables, or areas of interest) are separate, completely distinct, unconnected. (*A mnemonic aid*: the *t* in *discrete* keeps those two *e*'s apart.)

• **Discrimination** is the ability to recognize a significant difference between two things, ideas, or people. It becomes a vice only when decisions are made unfairly or by noting such arbitrary criteria as sex, age, or race. Similarly, to **discriminate** is to exercise good judgment or taste. (To *discriminate* by race or gender is to show *poor discrimination*.) When used to express prejudice, both verb and noun require a modifier: "The restaurant chain was sued for *discrimination against* homosexuals" (or "for *racial discrimination*"). "The Army *discriminates between* homosexuals and heterosexuals." (See *bias*.)

• To be **disinterested** is to be *fair* and *impartial*. To be **uninterested** is to be *uncaring* or *bored*. *Disinterested* editors will judge your story fairly. If *uninterested*, they will not read it.

• **Disk** is correct except for the patented spelling, "compact **disc**," for CD. In a computer, the **hard drive** turns the **hard disk** on which all of your data are stored.

• To **disassemble** is to take apart. To **dissemble** is to fake, or to disguise true intentions. Responding to reports that troops were abusing prisoners at Guantanomo Bay, Cuba, George W. Bush ascribed the allegations to "people who were held in detention, people who hate America, people that had been trained in some instances to disassemble—that means not tell the truth" (George W. Bush); *dissemble* was the intended word.[29]

• To **disperse** is to scatter (a crowd, confetti, gossip). To **disburse** is to pay out (money). To **asperse** is to make false accusations.

• **Dominance** is the condition or fact of having control or ascendancy over others. The **dominant** person, nation, dog, or or gene has eminence, power, or authority over those **dominated**. If something is **predominant**, it is **preponderant** or **paramount**, having the greatest influence, importance, or **prevalence** (such as a *predominant* local crop), at least for the time being. **Dominate, domination** indicate supreme power and control while **predominate, predomination** signal only the greatest 'extent, influence, or ascendancy. A **dominatrix** is a woman who ties up her sexual partner and treats him like a slave. If she has an encounter with a (male) **dominator**, one of them is bound to be unhappy.

• To **doubt that** God and Satan are real people, or that your lover is faithful, is to lean *against* the proposition. To **doubt whether** (or, informally, to "doubt if") is *to be uncertain*: you're still mulling it over. To be **doubtless** is to be confident or assured. An **undoubted** fool (or proposition) is one that is widely accepted as such. **Doubtful** implies more doubt than its near-synonym, **dubious**. "Undoubtably" (not a word) is a common mistake for **undoubtedly**.

• A *drastic* gesture, or budget cut, or storm, is severe and likely to be harmful. If it is showy, or as exciting as a good stage play, it is *dramatic*.

• A *dribble* is a drippy rain or a bouncing ball. A *drizzle* is a gentle, misty rain. *Drivel* is foolish talk or dribbling saliva. To *dribble* is to bounce the ball, or to rain in dribs and drabs, or to drool.

• A clothes *dryer* makes the clothes *drier*.

• *Duct tape* is useful for taping ductwork or almost any inanimate object but should not be used on a broken *duck*. Wire with barbs on it is *barbed* wire, not "barb" or "bob" wire.

• *Due to* must be followed by an object. It can substitute for *because of* but not for *because*: "His homework was late due to computer problems" is fine. That it "was late due to his computer crashed" is weird. If in doubt, use *because of,* or *owing to,* or *on account of:* "His work was late *because of* computer problems."

• Do not write *earnings* when you mean *profits*. *Net income and expenses* (previously called *gross earnings*) is a phrase denoting the annual net income and all operating expenses. *Operating earnings* are after-tax profits related to the company's regular activities, *exclusive* of net realized investment gains or losses. *Net earnings* are profits after taxes that *include* realized investment gains or losses. A company's bottom line may be referred to as *net earnings, net profits,* or *net income.*

• Take an *economics* course, study an *economic* system (or theory or problem), live *economically*, and drive an *economical* car.

• To *effect* is to bring about or accomplish, a word best avoided (see *affect*). But it is always better to effect or to bring about than "to effectuate." Used as a noun, *effect* means result or impression, and it is a better word than *impact.* To be *effective* is to produce an intended or expected change. To be *effectual* is to be fully adequate in producing a desired change. Do not mistake *effectively* or *effectually* with *in effect*, which is used to mean "in essence," "more or less," "for all practical purposes."

• Police may *elicit* (cull) from witnesses a description of an offender who did something *illicit* ("not allowed"), such as running naked through a schoolyard. *Elicit* is always a verb, sometimes implying information culled through deceptive interview techniques. *Illicit* is always an adjective, most often with reference to sexual transgressions.

• To *elide* is to omit or delete a part of the whole. In a standard contraction, elided letters or syllables are marked by an apostrophe (*don't, 'em, 'tis*). An *elision* is an act or instance of *eliding*. Elided words in a quotation are marked by an *ellipsis* (spelled with a double consonant, *-ll-*, but typed as three consecutive dots [...]). As if to confuse matters further, *ellipsis* may also denote the omission of one or more words from a sentence though unmarked by the three-dot ellipsis. In the sentence, "Bill told us he's the richest man in the world," the relative pronoun, *that,* has been elided after "us" without injury to the sense. If speech or writing is ***elliptical*** it has been made so concise through omission as to make the sense difficult or impossible to understand. Unrelated to these editing terms is an ***ellipse,*** or oval-shaped figure.

• To ***elude*** is to escape being caught, as if by cunning: "For seventeen years the Unabomber *eluded* the FBI." If a joke *eludes* you, it was too clever: you didn't get it. To ***evade*** is to escape or avoid, usually with a sense of irresponsibility, as per someone's ***evasion*** of arrest, taxes, or the truth.

• An ***elusive*** criminal is hard to catch. An elusive fact is hard to remember. An elusive concept is hard to grasp. An ***allusive*** text, such as a James Joyce's *Ulysses,* is full of allusions to other texts. An *allusive* remark refers inexplicitly to something, such as sex, money, or death. (See also ***allude, illusive, illusionary, illusory.***)

• ***Emergent*** diseases or technologies or problems are newly ***emerging.*** An ***emergency*** requires ***urgent***, not *emergent*, attention.

• To be ***eminent*** is to be distinguished, elevated, superior, or especially noteworthy. To be ***pre-eminent*** is to be *most eminent* of all. If an event or action is ***imminent,*** it's about to happen any minute now, or is well on its way. To be ***immanent*** (a theological term) is to exist within or to extend into all parts of the material world. The respective nouns are ***eminence, pre-eminence, imminence,*** and ***immanence***.

• ***Emotionality*** may denote the emotional character or temperament of a person or a piece of writing. When our president says he can "understand the *emotionality of* death penalty cases," *emotions aroused by* would be more clear.[30]

• To ***enervate*** is to cause something to lose energy or vitality. It does not mean ***energize*** or ***invigorate***, nor is it a synonym for ***inebriate***, though an inebriated person may indeed be enervated. When George W. Bush speaks with nostalgia of growing up in Midland, Texas—"It was just inebriating what Midland [Texas] was all about then"—*invigorating* may be the word intended, although not necessarily.[31]

• An ***enormity*** is a monstrosity, a great wickedness. It has nothing to do with size. (Involuntary castration may an enormity but the thing it removes, is not.) If you wish to impress your readers with the "enormousness" or "hugeness" of a thing, or if it's a concept too big to understand, try ***immensity.***

• To **envelop** (en-VEL-up) is to cover or surround. An **envelope** (AHN-vel-ope) is a paper container used to enclose a letter or document.

• You are **envious** if others have it, and you want it. You are **jealous** if you already have it (a wife, a boyfriend, a chosen people) and are fearful of losing it. The distinction, though useful, is all but lost in American English, so that **possessive** and **possessiveness** may have to be used in place of *jealous* and *jealousy.*

• **Environment** is an overused noun. **Surroundings** may do the job. "In a business environment" often means simply "business"; if not, try "conditions for business." For "in the home environment" try saying *at home.* If you must use *environment*, at least spell it correctly (it's *–vi-ron-*, not *–vi-orn-*). **Environs** is a plural noun that means *the surrounding area.* To **environ** is to surround. **Ecology** does not mean "natural environment" but denotes the interrelatedness of living organisms in a habitat.

• **Epigram, epigraph, epitaph, epithet, epitome.** An *epigram* is a concise, pithy saying or poem: "What is an epigram? A dwarfish whole, / Its body brevity, and wit, its soul." An *epigraph* is a brief quotation used to introduce a piece of writing (such as a chapter in the book, *How to Write*), or the inscription on a statue or building. An *epitaph* is a short poem or tombstone inscription that memorializes a dead person: "Here lies Anne Mann: she lived an / Old maid and died an old Mann." An *epithet* is a term used to characterize a person or thing ("bright-eyed Athena," "Richard the Lion-Hearted," "tricky Dick," "slick Willie"). A racial or ethnic epithet characterizes a person or race with a term of contempt (such as "hymie" for Jew or "raghead" for Arab). An *epitome* (rhymes with "a bit of me") is a summary, abridgment, or abstract (an epitome of *Paradise Lost*), or the consummate representative of an entire class or type ("Hitler is the epitome of evil"); *epitome* signifies the *essence* of something, not a *climax* or *peak*, as when President George H. W. Bush observed that his wife Barbara "epitomizes a family value." [32]

• If it is **equitable**, it is fair and just; if **equable**, it is equal or uniform throughout. When our president asserts that "The Constitution of the United States says we're all—you know, it does not say that. It does not speak to the equality of America," **equitability** may have been intended; or perhaps: "Some Americans are not equal to others" (George W. Bush). [33]

• **Equivalent** takes different prepositions if used as a noun or an adjective. If A is equivalent *to* B then it may also be the equivalent *of* B.

• To **equivocate** is purposely to avoid making a clear and explicit statement, as when the president says, "I did not have sex with that woman" while holding in his head the image of, let's say, Mamie

Eisenhower while his audience thinks that he's speaking of not having sex with Monica Lewinsky. An *equivocal* remark is not just ambiguous but intended to be vague or misleading. When George W. Bush promises to "carry out this equivocal message to the world: markets must be open," *unequivocal* is the intended word.[34]

• An *erring* statement or child or sinner must be corrected. An *errant* knight or spy or teenager wanders about, without a set destination. *Arrant* is an adjective applied to someone who serves as an extreme example of something disapproved of, such as an *arrant* knave, whore, thief, lecher, lobbyist, or tort lawyer.

• To *escalate* does not mean simply to increase. Unlike, say, *acceleration* or *exacerbation,* worlds that implies willed activity, *escalation* entails an element of increasing without effort and against one's wishes.

• *Evolution* is a gradual process by which something changes into a significantly different, usually more complex, form. *Evolutionary* change is slow or gradual, though not always "better." If a presidential candidate says, "It's *evolutionary*, going from governor to president, and this is a significant step, to be able to vote for yourself on the ballot," he may mean "exciting." [35]

• The prefix, *ex-*, takes a hyphen. Latin phrases with *ex* in them (*ex dividend, ex parte, ex officio*) do not. Your *ex* is your divorced spouse or former lover. To describe a job no longer held by someone, use *former*, not *ex-* (former president, judge, commander).

• *Exact* is a much overused word. When tempted to say "the exact opposite" or "the exact same," omit *exact*. If emphasis is needed, try *identical* for "the exact same."

• To *exalt* is to elevate, honor, glorify, or extol ("Tiger Woods is the greatest golfer in the history of the world"). To *exult* is to jubilate or rejoice ("—but I beat him yesterday by four strokes.")

• To *except* (see *accept*).

• *Exceptional* means quite untypical or unusually good. *Exceptionable* means open to objection or likely to give offense. An *exceptional* writer or bedpartner is first-rate. An *exceptionable* one may not be.

• An *expatriate* is someone who has left his or her homeland to live or work elsewhere. To call someone an "expatriot" is defamatory.

• *Expect, expectation* (see *anticipate*).

• To *exploit*, in a favorable sense, is to employ people or things to the greatest advantage (an opportunity, computer technology, your own experience). In a pejorative sense, *exploit* indicates the taking of unfair advantage ("Shame is an unhappy emotion invented by priests in order to exploit the human race"), or may indicate the seizing of an opportunity for selfish and unethical purposes. In neither sense is *exploit* a synonym for **explore.** If the president says that "We've got hundreds of sites to exploit, looking for the chemical and biological weapons that we know Saddam Hussein had prior to our entrance into Iraq," he seems to imply that he will use those supposed sites for his own political advantage.[36] (Cf. *Freudian slip.*)

• Use such phrases as **exponential growth** and **order of magnitude** only if you understand them. An order of magnitude is an estimate of size or magnitude expressed as a power of ten—as on the Richter scale, which measures the power of earthquakes. If your company sales this year are up 100%, they have merely doubled. A hundredfold increase represents two orders of magnitude. Growth or spending or population increases "exponentially" only when it repeatedly grows by multiples of some factor in a rapidly accelerating fashion, as in the sequence, 5, 25, 125, 625, 3125, 15625.

• *Extrapolate* (see *interpolate*).

• A *fact* is true and capable of direct verification: That "the sun rises each morning" is a pleasant illusion. That "flowers are lovely" is a sentiment. That "democracy is preferable to tyranny" is a conviction. That "water boils at 100°C"; and that "the square root of 16 is 4"; and that "many Americans celebrate Christmas on December 25": *these* are facts. Use the word, *fact,* sparingly. Avoid such redundancies as *actual fact, real fact, true facts.* Strike "The fact" from sentences beginning, "The fact that—." Just begin with "That."

• *Fahrenheit* (see *Celsius*).

• A *fallacy* is a false belief or spurious line of reasoning. *Fallibility* is a tendency toward error. When our president describes himself as "a person who recognizes the *fallacy* of humans," *fallibility* is the intended word.[37]

• *Farther* refers to physical distance. *Further* indicates additional degree, time, or quantity. You may *proceed further* with a design or may *proceed farther* down a path. You may *drive* farther *without* further *speed,* or walk *farther* without *further* thought. If tempted to drink *farther* and drive *further,* stop yourself.

• A *fawn* is a baby deer, such as Bambi. A *faun* has the body of a man and the legs and horns of a goat, such as Pan or Satan.

• *Faze* (see *phase*).

• "I *feel*" does not mean "I think" or "I believe."

• *Female* and *male* denote the sex of a person or animal. *Feminine* and *masculine* refer to that which is socially conditioned. What is defined or viewed as *feminine* behavior or dress in one society may be considered *masculine* (or ungendered, simply human) elsewhere. Use *female* and *male* as nouns ("the females" and "the males") only when speaking of animals. For people, use *men, women, the male sex, the female sex.*

• *Few* and *a few* have a different emphasis. The first, as Fowler puts is, means "some but not many," while the second means "some and not none."[38] To make a comparison, use *fewer*, not "more few." If our president asks, "Will the highways on the Internet become more few?" he probably means, "The Internet's 'information superhighway' can only grow."[39] (See also *less*.)

• *First, firstly, first of all, second,* etc.: When enumerating items or ideas, use the forms *first, second, third* (not "firstly," "secondly," "thirdly"). "First of all" and "last of all" should be used sparingly and only when your list or outline has at least four items. Never write "second of all."

• Do not use *fix* to mean *repair* unless the mending entails putting something back that has come loose or fallen out of place. To fix a thing in the mind is to put it there and keep it there, not to heal a schizophrenic delusion. A lighting *fixture* is attached to the wall or ceiling while a lamp may be moved around. A corporate vice president or college dean or custodian is said to be a fixture when it seems as if he will never retire. To *affix* a person to a wooden cross is to perform a *crucifixion*. The common misspelling, "crucifiction," implies a measure of religious skepticism or levity no less than the misspelling, "reserection."

• A *flack* is a press agent or publicist. To *flack* is to perform that service for someone. *Flak* denotes either *anti-aircraft artillery* or the attendant *bursting of shells*, or, figuratively, excessive criticism or opposition. If you're catching *flak* from the press, hire yourself a *flack*.

• To *flaunt* is to display something (body, clothes) ostentatiously. To *flout* is to show scornful disregard. "Miss Gabor *flouted* the anti-fur demonstrators by *flaunting* her mink coat, alligator purse, sealskin gloves, and coonskin cap."

• To *flounder* is to proceed clumsily, or with confusion. To *founder* is to lose one's bottom, and sink. A *floundering* CEO may cause the company to *founder*.

• To *forbid* is to prohibit. A *forbidding* task or financial report is off-putting, grim, or ominous. A *forbidding* neighbor may be unfriendly, perhaps scary. To *forebode* is to signal misfortune. *Foreboding* may indicate a dark premonition or an evil omen. A *formidable* task or adversary induces dread but may yet be conquered through concentrated effort.

• A *forceful* argument, effort, or blow is powerful, vigorous, full of force. A *forcible* one is able to force a result: "With a *forcible* blow, Mike punched a hole in the wall." "Floyd punched the wall with a *forceful* blow that broke his fingers." A *forced* entry or landing or smile or confession is one achieved by *forceful* or *forcible* effort. A bad law is *unenforceable*. Weak writing is *forceless*.

• A *forebear* is an ancestor. To *forbear* is to abstain. A *forbearing* parent is tolerant, slow to punish.

• To *forgo* is to *do without* or *to relinquish*. To *forego* or *forgo* (variant spelling) can also to mean *precede*, but its use may cause confusion and is best avoided. A *foregone* conclusion is one that is inevitable from the outset.

• *Former* (as in "former police chief") may refer to a position no longer held, though the person is still alive. *Late* ("the late mayor") is used when the person is either dead, or overdue. (See also *ex-*). *Latter* is best reserved for something further advanced in time or sequence, as in "the latter part of the book." It is bad writing to use "the former," "the latter," or "the last-named" like pronouns, as a way to reference items or names in the preceding sentence or paragraph.

• *Fortuitous* means happening by chance, or accidental. *Fortunate* means lucky. A *fortunate* event may seem *fortuitous*, but a *fortuitous* event (e.g., a stroke of lightning) may not be *fortunate*.

• To be *free* is to be without something (chains, inhibitions, cost). You may give or receive something *free of charge*, or *for a price*, but not "for free," a nonsense phrase that cannot be stomped out but is best avoided in your own speech and writing.

• A *Freudian slip* denotes a misstatement in which repressed thoughts of aggression or desire are supposed to escape unwittingly, as when President Reagan spoke (often) of the United States assisting "the third world war" (for third world nations), or when George H. W. Bush spoke affectionately of Mr. Reagan, saying, "For seven and a half years I've worked alongside President Reagan. We've had triumphs. Made some mistakes—we've had some sex—uh—setbacks"; or when his son, George W. Bush asked how anyone, looking at his foreign policy "could have possibly envisioned an erection" (election) in Iraq; or when Bush's unmarried Secretary of State, Condoleezza Rice, inadvertently spoke of Mr. Bush as "my husb—"; or when George W. volunteered the information, "Sometimes when I sleep at night I think of 'Hop on Pop!'" with intended reference to a children's book of that title.[40]

• *Fulsome* (odors, praise) is excessive, offensive, disgusting. It does not mean *full* or *fullest*, or *to the full*.

• To *fund* and to *pay for* are not synonymous. If you do not understand the distinction, use *pay for*, not *fund*.

• *Further* (see *farther*).

• A *gaffe* is a clumsy social error, a *faux pas*. A *gaff* is a hook or spur. A *gaffer* is an old man.

• *Gage* and *gauge,* except in the sense *plum* or *to pledge*, are interchangeable. *Gauge* is often misspelled "guage." If in doubt, use *gage*.

· **Gender,** as a grammatical term, applies only to words, not to sex. In German, *das Mädchen* (the girl) is neuter, but the girl herself is of the female sex. As a cultural or literary term, *gender* denotes *masculinity* or *femininity* as a set of social codes and expectations. (See **female, male.**)

· **Genus** and **species** are categories in the taxonomic classification system of related organisms. The *genus* comes first and takes a capital letter, followed the *species* in lower-case: *Homo sapiens* (human), *Equus caballus* (horse). Do not confuse *genus* with *gender* or *species* with *sex*. Do not write "the female species" even to be cute.

· Take a **geology** course, study **geologic** formations, and join a **geological** society.

· The **gist** (often confused with **crux**) is the essential point of a story or argument, or the essential grounds for a legal action. **Grist** is grain to be ground into flour or, figuratively, material processed to someone's advantage. When our president complains of his father being made "the gist for cartoonists," he means *grist* or *jest*.[41]

· To **glean** is to gather fragments of grain, food, or information overlooked by others. To **garner** is to *store*, not to *gather*, though one may *glean* first and *garner* afterward.

· **Good** and **bad** are useful words though vague and overused. Where possible, find more specific adjectives than *good* or *bad*, *positive* or *negative*.

· **Good** and **well.** Martin Luther King, Jr., did good, Bill Gates did well. An attractive person looks good, a healthy person looks well. A grilled chicken smells good though not well. A farting beagle smells well though not good.

· A **gourmet** is a *connoisseur* or *epicure*. A **gourmand** is a **glutton.**

· To be **graceful** is to exhibit poise, elegance, or smooth movement. To be **gracious** is to be tactful and kind. To be **grateful** is to feel gratitude. And "greatful" is a misspelling. When the president says, "I'm so thankful, and so gracious. I'm gracious that my brother Jeb is concerned about the hemisphere. [...] I'm very gracious and humbled," *grateful* is the intended word. [42]

· If it is **gratis**, it is given freely, without charge. If it is **gratuitous**, it is undeserved (a gratuitous award), unearned (a promotion), unnecessary (an assignment), or unwarranted (criticism).

· If it is **grisly**, it's gruesome (*grisly* roadkill). If it is **grizzly** or **grizzled**, it's gray, or gray-tipped, or going gray (a *grizzly* bear, a *grizzled* beard).

· You can **grow** a beard or a zucchini but not a company or a child. **Growth** is development or increased size. A **growth** is an abnormal formation of tissue, such as a brain tumor. When our president says,

"I understand small business growth—I was one," his intended meaning is something like, "I have had experience developing a small business." 43

• A **guerrilla** movement is a paramilitary campaign. A **gorilla** movement is a migration of apes.

• **Half** takes a singular verb for uncountable nouns, and a plural verb for countable quantities: "*Half* the herd is gone. *Half* the cowboys are drunk.*"* To **halve** is a transitive verb. A deficit can double or triple, or *fall by half*, but it cannot simply *halve*. It takes a thrifty government to *halve* it.

• A extra **hanger** is something you look for in your bedroom closet and cannot find. If it's an extra airplane you need, look for it in a **hangar**.

• A woman may **head** the company or team but neither she nor anyone else can "head it up."

• **Healthy** is best reserved for that which is either physically robust or **healthful**. For "healthy profit," try *big* or *satisfactory*.

• A **hearty** lover is lively, passionate, sincere. A **hardy** lover does not want to quit. A *hearty* meal is deeply satisfying. A *hardy* meal may not be, but at least it will be healthful.

• **Heresy** (see **apostasy**).

• **High technology,** in architecture, denotes a style that makes use of metal, glass, and plastic in a simple, useful way. The word is more commonly used today to denote advanced technology, especially in electronic engineering: "High tech is potent, precise, and in the end, unbeatable. The truth is, it reminds a lot of people of the way I pitch horseshoes. Would you believe some of the people? Would you believe our dog? Look, I want to give the high-five symbol to high tech" (George H. W. Bush).44

• A **hippy** woman is big in the beam. A **hippie** woman is devoted to flowers, universal love, tie-dyed clothing, good dope, and the Grateful Dead.

• A **hoard** is found in attics, dragon's caves, or ancient tombs. **Hordes** are found roving the land with their minds set on murder, rape, pillage, or on equal economic opportunity and a liveable wage.

• **Hoi polloi** ("the many") is a snotty term for the common people as viewed from a position of wealth or intellectual advantage. From down below, the rich may seem **hoity-toity** (or **highty-tighty**), a term meaning *snobbish, pompous, prim, pretentious,* or *tight-assed.*

• **Hopefully** is used (illogically, though without loss of clarity) to mean "It would be good thing if" or "Let us hope that." Except for the purpose of informal conversation or fictional dialogue, use *hopefully* in its strict sense (full of hope): "Martha Twitty entered marriage *hopefully,* and Billy Bob, reluctantly, with Mr. Twitty's shotgun at his back." Always make clear who's doing the hoping, e.g., "*I hope* that Burt passes the Wasserman Test," or "*Burt hopes* to pass the Wasserman Test," or "It *is hoped by many* that Burt passes the Wasserman Test"; but not: "*Hopefully*, Burt will pass the Wasserman Test."

• To be **horrid** or **horrendous** is to be dreadful or disgusting. To be **horrible** is to be unusually bad. To be **horrific** is to cause horror. **Terrific** used to mean "causing terror," but the word, in that sense, got ruined: use **terrifying.**

• To be **hostile** is to show or feel enmity, hatred, or anger. A **hostel** is a place to stay. A **hostage** stays until ransomed or rescued. When our president says, "We cannot let terrorists and rogue nations hold our nation *hostile* or our allies *hostile*," *hostage* is the intended word.[45]

• **However:** use it sparingly and punctuate it correctly (see 1.8.2c Adverbs, and 1.8.3e. Semicolons). *But* is usually the better word.

• **Hyper-** is a prefix meaning *over, above, beyond, excessive*. **Hypo-** is a prefix meaning, *under, below*, or *not enough*. **Hypothermia** is a health threat in winter, and **hyperthermia**, in summer. "Hyper," short for *hyperactive*, is slang for manic or excitable.

• **If** (see **whether**).

• **Illicit** (see **elicit**).

• If it is **illusive,** such as a government's balanced budget, it lacks reality. If it is **illusional**, **illusionary**, or **illusory**, such as a desert mirage, you may be deceived. (See also **elusive, allusive.)**

• **Immanent, immanence** (see **eminent, eminence**).

• **Impact** denotes the action of one object hitting another, or the physical force of the blow. **Influence** (a "flowing-in") denotes the affective power of a person, thing, or idea to shape people, events, or cultural discourse. The two words are often confused. When the vice president remarks, "People that are really very weird can get into sensitive positions and have a tremendous impact on history," *influence* is the intended word.[46] (See also **affect.**)

• An **impertinent** remark is not only **irrelevant** but quite possibly impudent, presumptuous, or rude.

• **Implication** (see **inference**).

• To **imply** (see **infer**).

• **Important** is a tired word: "It's important for us to explain to our nation that life is important" (George W. Bush). [47] Don't say that something or someone is *important*. Be specific. Show us how.

• To be **incarcerated** is to be imprisoned; to be **incinerated** is to be burnt to ashes. When our president urges adult Americans "to mentor [*sic* ...], to start a ministry which will find the children of those who are *incarcinated* and love them," *incarcerated* is the word intended to describe the children's imprisoned parents.[48]

• **Incredible** does not mean either *excellent* or *skeptical*. An *incredible* actor has no talent. (See **credible** and **incredulous**.)

• To be **incredulous** is to be skeptical, unbelieving, unconvinced. When you hear a fish story, you may be **credulous** (gullible) or *incredulous*, but you are not **incredible** unless you profess to have caught a fish even bigger than the fish in the incredibly fishy fish story.

• To **infer** is to reach an opinion through reasoning. To **imply** is to make something understood without saying it directly, as through hints, signs, or innuendo. (That a man has bad taste may be *implied* in comments made by his wife, or by his pumpkin-orange necktie.) *Infer* is often used where *imply* is intended. It is the speaker or writer who *implies*, and the reader or listener who *infers*: "Iago *implies* that Cassio may be sleeping with Othello's wife. Othello *infers* as much from the circulation of his favorite handkerchief."

• An **inference** is a conclusion drawn from evidence or logic, or (sometimes) the process of thought that leads to a conclusion. An **implication** is an unstated consequence, or the act of suggesting a proposition without actually stating it. In logic, *implication* denotes a relationship between two propositions that holds when both A and B are true, and fails when A is true but B is false.

• **Inflammable** and **flammable** mean the same thing, "easily **inflamed,"** but are put to different uses. Both may denote burnable material, but *inflammable* is more often reserved for figurative use: Your drill sergeant has an *inflammable*, not a *flammable*, personality. An **inflammatory** remark may enkindle anger. "Flammatory" is not a word.

• **Ingenious** means clever, brilliant, inventive. **Ingenuous** means open, frank, sincere; or, sometimes, naive, unsophisticated. To be **disingenuous** is either to convey a false impression of innocence or sincerity, or to withhold known information. An **ingénue** denotes a sexist stereotype, the stock role of a naive young woman who requires a manly gallant to rescue her from shame, cruelty, or ruin.

• An **inheritance** is the act of inheriting, or the thing inherited. A **heritage** is a legacy, tradition, property, or inheritance that has been passed down through successive generations and is always singular. When our president promises a "common-sense vision for good forest policy" by working with "the United Nations Senate to preserve these national heritages," "United States Senate" and "our natural heritage" are the intended phrases.[49]

• An **inkling** is a hint or vague idea. When our president says, "Any time we've got any kind of inkling that somebody is thinking about doing something to an American and something to our homeland, you've just got to know we're moving on it—to protect the

United Nations Constitution," *intelligence* or *information* would be a better word than "inkling."[50]

• **Innocent,** in a legal context, is not the same as **not guilty**. A verdict of "not guilty" means only that the prosecution has failed to prove the defendant's guilt. The defense is not obliged to prove that the accused is indeed innocent.

• Save **input** for data entry. For human "input," be specific and personal. Try *suggestion, help, comments,* or *contribution.*

• **Inquire** and **enquire** are variant spellings of the same word. Many British writers use *enquire* and *enquiry* for matters of *asking,* and reserve *inquire* and *inquiry* for matters of *investigation;* but this potentially useful distinction has not caught on in the United States. If in doubt, use the *in-* spelling, which is never wrong. One makes an inquiry *into* a matter, or undertakes an investigation *of* it.

• If it's **insidious,** it is slowly and subtly harmful; if it's **invidious** it produces resentment or ill feeling. Undetected cancer is insidious, and a public insult, invidious.

• To **insure** is to guard against loss. To **ensure** is to make certain. To **assure** is to convince or to make certain. You may *insure* your car against theft, but to *ensure* that no one steals it, lock the doors. To *assure* yourself that you have not locked yourself out, check your pocket or purse for your car keys. ("You may be rest assured" is gibberish—but even the correct form ("You may rest assured that") is a tired phrase, so give it a rest.

• A scary movie or a headache may be **intense**. A six-week course in a foreign language, or a fertilized, closely planted crop, may be **intensive**. Words such as *very* and *extremely* are **intensifiers.**

• To **interact** is to act on or with others. If our president says, "I'm more interacting with people," **interactive** may be the intended word (or *sociable*).[51] In computer science, an **interface** is the point of **interaction** between a computer and some other entity or equipment. If the president says, "This is what I'm good at—I like meeting people, my fellow citizens, I like *interfacing* with them," *chatting* may be the intended word.[52] Save *interface* for computer technicians.

• **Interesting** is an overused word, as when the president announced, "One of the interesting initiatives we've taken in Washington, D.C., is we've got these vampire-busting devices. A vampire is a cell-deal you can plug in the wall to charge your cell phone."[53] Don't just say that a person, problem, or political platform is important or interesting, *show* it.

• **The Internet** is a large computer network linking smaller computer networks worldwide. Although the term properly denotes only the hardware of the network, "the Internet" is commonly used to describe the information sources that reside on **servers** linked *through the Internet*, as when our president spoke of "children living in, you know, the dark dungeons of the Internet."[54] The **World Wide Web** is a system of Internet servers that support documents formatted in a script called **Hyper-Text Markup Language** (HTML), facilitating links to other documents, as well as graphics, audio, and video files. Not all Internet servers are part of the Web.

• An **interment** is a burial. An **internment** is an incarceration, usually denoting the detention of civilians during wartime. An **intern** is an advanced student or recent graduate or unpaid worker who receives supervised training during a specified period of **internship.**

• To **interpolate** is to insert or introduce something (often something unnecessary) between other things or parts, such as to add one's own phrase or comment to a text, thereby altering its sense or emphasis. It does not mean simply to **interrupt.** To **extrapolate** is to infer or estimate (unknown values or information) by extending or projecting known values or information. One may *interpolate between* (this and that), or *extrapolate from* (these data).

• **Interpretative.** Use **interpretive.**

• **Invigorate** (see **enervate**).

• An **inviolate** place or right or belief is one not violated. An **inviolable** one is secure from violation or infringement. If the president asserts that the chief executive's right to grant pardons is "inviolate, as far as I'm concerned," and one to be "preserved" for his "predecessors," **inviolable** is the intended word (see also **predecessors**).[55]

• **"Irregardless"** (a conflation of **regardless** and **irrespective**) is not a word. When Jeb Bush, governor of Florida, reports that "They'll constantly slam conservatives *irregardless* of their record," *irrespective* may be the intended word. When Jesse Ventura, WWE wrestler and governor of Minnesota, remarks that "You should go into that booth and vote for someone *irregardless* of what the pundits say," *regardless* may be the intended word.[56]

• The contraction, **it's**, always means *it is* or *it has*. The possessive form of *it* is **its** (just as the possessive of *he* is *his*): The bus rolled onto *its* side. *It's* lucky no one got hurt.

• A **jerry-built** car or dike is shoddily constructed. A **jury-rigged** sail or dike is makeshift, for emergency or temporary use.

• **Jive** is jazz or swing music, and to *jive* is to dance to it. As slang, *jive* denotes nonsense or deception. To **gibe** is to taunt or tease. To **jibe** or **gybe** is to "come about," to change directions when sailing.

• A **key** person, decision, or industry is indispensable. A musical **key** may be *major* or *minor*, but not *low*. For "low-key," substitute *simple, modest, discreet*.

• **Kind of** and **sort of** should not be used, except informally, as a substitute for *rather,* and should not be spelled "kinda," "sorta," except for cuteness. Restrict these phrases to their literal sense: "Ricotta is a kind of cheese." When President George H. W. Bush says, "I *kind of* think I'm a scintillating *kind of* fellow," the second "kind of" is correct, but the first should be omitted.[57] When his son says that his campaign staff "doesn't need to be manufacturing *kind of* subliminable messages to get my message out," *kind of* is superfluous: he has no need to manufacture subliminal messages.[58]

• **Koran** (see **Qur'an**).

• **Kudos** (*KOO-doze*) means acclaim or praise for noteworthy achievement. The word has no plural. You receive *kudos* or you don't. There is no such thing as a "kudo."

• A **lama** is a priest. A **llama** is a beast.

• **Last, latest.** Do not speak of "the last" issue of a periodical until it has gone belly up. The *latest* issue is the one most recently published. "Last year," when spoken on New Year's Eve, does not mean the same thing as "last year" when spoken the next morning. But "the past year" will always denote the previous 12-month period. (See also **former, latter.**)

• To **lead** (leed) is to be in front; to **have led** (led) is to have been in front at one time; to **have lead** (led) is to be in possession of a heavy gray metal.

• A **legacy** is something bequeathed or handed down from an ancestor or predecessor, either literally (as from a will) or figuratively (a legacy of religious freedom). **Mandate** denotes the will of the electorate (as expressed most clearly in a landslide election). When George W. Bush, speaking of the 2000 presidential election, says "There's no such thing as legacies—at least, there is a legacy, but I'll never see it," *mandate* is the intended word.[59]

• One **lens**, two **lenses.**

• Use **less** (or **less than**) for countable nouns (less hair, money, talk). Use **fewer** (or **fewer than**) for countable quantities (fewer teeth, people, cars, ideas): *fewer* steers, *less* beef, *fewer* steaks. "Less" is often used in error for *few*: "Fewer than [*not* "less than"] twenty teens attended the Wayne Newton concert." Do not use "under" with numbers ("under twenty teens"), except perhaps to describe a hogpile ("The rock star was found under twenty teens"). Similarly, use **more than** for quantifiable figures and amounts ("more than $20 thousand"; "more than forty students"). Save **over** to indicate spatial relationships ("over the roof," "over our capacity").

• If you **libel** someone, you are **liable** (susceptible, likely) to be sued and may be held **liable** (legally responsible). A **liability** is something for which you are *liable* (such as an obligation or debt), and it may therefore be viewed as a hindrance or handicap.

• The verbs, to **lie** and to **lay**, can be confusing. To *lay* is to set something down: *I* will lay [now lay; am laying; have laid; laid] *the pizza on the table*; or to have sex (*Joe got laid; Molly laid Joe.*) To *lie* is to remain still in a place: *The pizza* will lie [now lies; is lying; has lain; then lay] *on the table*. If you *lie down* and get up again, you *have lain down*. Even presidents occasionally confuse these two verbs: "We understand where the power of this country lay [i.e., *lies*]. It lays [*lies*] in the hearts and souls of Americans. It must lay [*lie*] in our pocketbooks. It lays [*lies*] in the willingness for people to work hard. But as importantly, it lays [*lies*] in the fact that we've got citizens from all walks of life, all political parties, that are willing to say, 'I want to love [lay waste, etc.] my neighbor.'" [60] As for the matter of speaking untruly (something a U.S. president would probably never do), the words are *He will lie, he lies, he is lying, he has lied, he lied.*

• **Like, as** (see **as**). **Would like, should like** (see **would, should**).

• **Lightning** accompanies thunder. At dawn the sky may be **lightening** without any *lightning*.

• **Literal** and **literally** are synonymous with *actual* and *actually*. A *literal* translation is rendered word for word. A *literal* mind is one incapable of figurative thought and expression. A *literal* expression is neither figurative nor exaggerated, but factual. *Literal* and *literally* are often used incorrectly to support exaggeration or cliché: "It literally rained cats and dogs" (which is impossible unless the animals poured from on high.) "A literal army of ants invaded our kitchen" (*What, they came out shooting?*) "Macbeth's hubris literally explodes in his face" (*Hubris as trick cigar?*). "Literally" can often be cut.

• **Loan** is a noun, and **to lend** a verb. One does not *loan* money, but *lends* it to the *borrower* (not to a "loanee").

• To be **loath** is to be *averse* or *reluctant*: *Jack is* loath *to visit the dentist*. To **loathe** is to hate or dislike, and is best avoided because hard to pronounce without lisping: *Seth loathes his theory professor*. (The adjective, *loath*, rhymes with *oath*. *Loathing* rhymes with *clothing*.)

• To **loose** is to release. To **loosen** is to make or become less tight or rigid. To **lose** (often misspelled) is not to find, or not to win. One may "play fast and *loose*" (ignoring the rules) and yet *lose* the game. (*Lose* rhymes with *choose, losing* with *choosing*, and *loose* with *caboose*; but *chose* rhymes with *hose*).

• A *lousy* person or dog or motel room is one infested with lice. (Rhymes with *mousy,* not *drowsy.*) When our president says, "I need to be able to move the right people to the right place at the right time to protect you, and I'm not going to accept a lousy bill out of the United States Senate," *inferior* may be the word intended. [61]

• A *lusty* person is full of spunk, and desirable. A *lustful* one is full of desire. Only rarely do these two epithets apply to the same love-object at the same time, but when they do, it's a beautiful thing.

• If a mansion is *luxurious* (*lavishly furnished*), its garden may be *luxuriant* (*growing thickly or profusely*). In Shakespearean texts, "luxurious" means lustful or uninhibited.

• *Malfeasance* denotes wrong or illegal conduct, especially in politics or the civil service. *Misfeasance* denotes the improper and unlawful execution of an action that is in itself lawful and proper. *Nonfeasance* denotes the failure to perform an act that is an official duty or a legal requirement. When our president alleges "malfeance," or says of his own role that "There was no *malfeance* involved, [...] no *malfeance,* no attempt to hide anything," *malfeasance* is the intended word. [62]

• *Male* (see *female*).

• A *mantle* is an article of clothing worn by Zorro, Batman, Batboy, and Superman. A *mantel* is where they may hang it to dry.

• It is best not to confuse *marital* (*relating to marriage*), with *martial* (*relating to war*). Your electronic spellchecker cannot tell the difference. A *marshal* is a person in charge.

• Catholic *mass* does not require a capital letter. To denote the *Eucharist*, most protestants use the word *communion*, not *mass*. When used to denote the general public, *the masses* (always plural) signals an allusion to Marxism. As an adjective, *mass* can denote that which pertains to a large number of people or things, or a large number, broadly general (*mass communication, mass extinction, mass leisure, mass media*) or to physical mass or quantity (*mass defect, mass balance, mass number, mass noun*). If our president warns against foreign "weapons of mass production," his intended reference is probably to weapons of *mass destruction* and not to accident-prone sport-utility vehicles.[63]

• If he rubs your back in a soothing way, he's a *masseur* (rhymes with *assure*). If she does it, she's a *masseuse* (rhymes with *kazoos*).

• *Masterly* is usually a better word than *masterful* for that which is *highly skilled* or *done with the skill of a master*. *Masterful* may mean imperious or domineering.

• *Material*, as a noun, denotes *matter, substance, fabric*. *Materiel* denotes the supplies and equipment associated with a military force.

• *May* and *might* are not identical. You may want *may* more often than you suppose. If in doubt, try *may* first: "I may die from this illness" becomes, later, "I might have died from that illness." As indirect past speech, it becomes "I said I might die." Conditional sentences using the subjunctive (conditional) also need *might*: "If I were to die, I might go to heaven" means about the same thing as "If I die, I may go to heaven." Conditional sentences stating something not already factual need *might*: "If I were dead, my wife might marry my brother." *May* and *might* are interchangeable in a hypothesis that may or may not be true: If these fine points of usage matter to you, you *might* (or you *may*) need to get a new life. I may have it right, but I really don't care. You might get it right if you study.

• *Mean,* as an adjective, may mean *average, base, cruel, ignoble, inferior, low, miserly, paltry, poor, shabby,* and more. Substitute a more specific word. Used as a noun, *the mean* is the middle term, or the middle point between extremes, or an average. To obtain the arithmetic *mean* of a set of values, divide the sum of the set of values by the number of values in the set. The *median* of a distribution is the middle value, with an equal number of values above and below; and the *mode* is the value that appears most frequently. Only in a *normal distribution* are the *mean, median*, and *mode* the same.

• *Meantime* and *meanwhile*, as nouns, denote *an interval*, and as adverbs, *during an interval*: "We all owe Time a death: *meanwhile*, let's party"; "Rather, *in the mean time*, let us pray."

• A *medium* is a means of conveying ideas or information, such as the medium of television or email (plural, *media)*. When our president observes that "Our society is a good, solid democracy because of a good, solid media," *because of our independent news media* may be the intended meaning. [64]

• *Mediocre* means "halfway up the mountain." To call some people *mediocre* may be giving them more credit than they deserve: in a cone-shaped hill of sand, only an eighth of the grains are above the level of mediocrity.

• If you show *mettle* (courage), you may win a *medal* made of *metal*. To *meddle* is to interfere.

• *Midnight*, by tradition, means the end of a day, not the beginning of the next. When speaking or writing on Sunday morning, *midnight yesterday* is Saturday night and *midnight tomorrow* is Monday night. *12:00 a.m.* denotes *noon* or *middday*; *12:01 p.m.* marks the first minute of the *afternoon*, and *12:00 p.m.* is *midnight*.

• *Minuscule,* used as an adjective, may mean either *lower-case* or *tiny*. It is often misspelled as "miniscule."

• To **miscalculate** is to make a wrong tabulation, or wrong assessment. If our president remarks, "They have miscalculated me as a leader," he probably means only that he was misjudged, not that someone mistook him for a leader. [65]

• To **mitigate** is to ease, to mollify, or to a make a difficulty less severe. To **militate against** is to act as a counterforce. To "mitigate against" makes no sense. *Mitigate* and *mitigation* are rarely useful outside a legal context (*e.g.*, a statement in *mitigation* of sentence, to urge leniency). Otherwise, a plain style "militates against" using words against such words as *mitigate* and *militate*.

• To **moot** is to debate, or to introduce a topic for debate. A *moot* is an imaginary case argued by law students as an exercise. That which is *moot* is arguable, unresolved, a subject for debate; or it may be an issue that was previously settled but is no longer of legal significance. *Mute* means *silent*, and rhymes with *cute*.

• **More** and **most** are used to express, respectively, the comparative and superlative of an adjective that does not end in *–y* and that has two or more syllables: *sweeter, sweetest; funnier, funniest; more handsome, most handsome; more beautiful, most beautiful.* If our president promises to make America "a literate country and a *hopefuller* country," *a fully literate and more hopeful country* is probably his intended meaning.[66] You were hopeful yesterday, and even **more so** (not "moreso") today.

• **Most, "almost."** Do not use **most** for *almost*: "Most everyone in rural Mississippi eats grits," should read, *Almost everyone.* "I've seen most all of North Dakota" should read *I've seen most of North Dakota.* For "most always," write *almost always*, or (better), *usually*.

• **Mucous** is an adjective, as in *mucous-yellow*. **Mucus**, a noun, comes from a *mucous* gland and gets blown into a tissue.

• What is **mutual** is shared by, or reciprocally exchanged between, two persons or things, such as *mutual* property or *mutual* respect. What is **common** may be had or held by all.

• **Myriad** (see **a lot**).

• If you are **nauseated**, you feel ill. If you are **nauseous**, you make other people feel ill. Roadkill is *nauseous*. You probably are not.

• **Necessitate** is a silly word. Use **require, need,** or **demand.**

• **Niggard** (miser) and **niggardly** (miserly) have no historical or etymological or connotative association with the racist epithet, *nigger.* The "beauteous niggard" of Shakespeare's *Sonnets* is a good-looking cheapskate. When the reader encounters *niggard* and *niggardly*, no offense should be taken—but neither will a writer use words that, in his own cultural moment, may distract the reader's attention. That includes *beauteous*.

• *Nobody*, as a pronoun, is one word, and *no one*, two. Both are singular. *Nobody is perfect* means that we all have faults. *No body is perfect* means that we could all benefit from a little dieting, exercise, makeup, cosmetic surgery, depilatory, soap, or embalming fluid.

• *Noisome* means harmful, offensive, or offensive, such as *noisome fumes*. It does not mean *somewhat noisy*.

• *Notwithstanding* is a long, distracting word. Try *but, despite, for all that, in spite of,* or *yet*.

• A *nuance* is a very slight difference in expression or implication; a *nuanced* discussion is attentive to subtle shades of meaning. When Pres. Bush was asked about the prospect of Russia joining NATO, and replied, "I haven't thought about the *nuance* of it," *nuisance* may have been his intended meaning.[67]

• The plural of *nucleus* is *nuclei*. *Nuclear* power and nuclear weapons are so-called because they involve a reaction that alters the energy and structure of atomic nuclei. The adjective is pronounced *noo-kle-ur*, not *noo-kyoo-lur*.

• To be *officious* is to be pushy in offering assistance or advice to others, and does not mean *official*.

• *Often*. A bad writer may be tempted to use *oftentimes* or even *ofttimes* as a quaint substitute. Don't. When George W. Bush says, "Oftentimes we live in a processed world," *oftentimes* may be deleted altogether, since we only live once. (See *process*.)

• Use *okay* except in a direct quotation, saving *OK* for informal use. "O.K.," "ok," and "O-K" are always incorrect.

• *One* can be used as a personal pronoun to avoid the universal "he," but where possible, it's more direct and personal to use *you* for *one*, and *your* for *one's*. (*If* one *is not careful with "one,"* one's *writing may sound stuffy*.) Be careful with the phrases, *one of the* and *one of those*, which are typically followed by a plural subject and a plural verb: "Ms. Imbrie is one of *those professors who have* [not "has"] a natural gift for teaching."

• *Only*: to avoid ambiguity or confusion, place "only" immediately before the word or phrase that it modifies: "*The polar bears mated only in June*" (but not in other months); "*The polar bears only mated in June*" (without pausing to eat or sleep). "*Martin only said he loved the screenplay*" (but he did not elaborate); "*Martin said only he loved the screenplay*" (but no one else did); "*Martin said he loved only the screenplay*" (but not the novel).

• *Onto* may be one word or two, depending on whether the action of the verb is moving *onto*, or just moving *on*: "Go *onto* the bridge" means *get on the bridge*. "Go *on to* the bridge" means *proceed to the bridge*.

• To be **opportunistic** is to seize opportunities without regard for principles or consequences. An **opportune** moment or situation or event is advantageous, right and apt for a particular purpose. If the president urges American children "to learn to have the skills necessary to take advantage of our fantastic opportunistic society," his intended advice may be to *take advantage of the fantastic opportunities offered by our society.*[68]

• The **optimum** is the most favorable, not the biggest, longest, fastest, hottest, or coolest. A car's optimum speed is that which provides the best combination of speed, safety, and economy.

• **Oral** activities are done with, to, or through the mouth (sex, surgery, medication). If it's **aural**, it is done with, to, or through the ears (lesson, surgery, medication). An *oral agreement* is one that is not written down. Do not use "verbal agreement." All agreements, whether written or unwritten, are **verbal**.

• **Ordnance** denotes military materiel, or that branch of a force that procures and stores materiel. An **ordinance** is a regulation, law, injunction, or decree (usually municipal).

• **Overall** is one word when used as an adjective (*the overall effect*) and two words when used to mean "in summary": "*Over all*, expenses held steady though profits were down." **Overalls,** in the sense "work jeans," is always one word and always plural.

• To **overwhelm** is to surge over, submerge utterly, crush, bring to sudden ruin. An "overwhelming majority" is a tired metaphor.

• The **palate** is the roof of the mouth. Artists mix colors on a **palette**. A **pallet** is a machine part, or a potter's or printer's tool, or a portable platform for moving cargo, or a hard, narrow bed.

• A **paradigm shift** is bureaucratese for a change in a conceptual model or ideology, indicating a new way of thinking about an old problem. When the president says, "You also got to measure in order to begin to affect [*effect*] change, that's just where it's more than talk; there's just actual, a paradigm shift," no one, anywhere, knows what he means—which means that linguistics scholars may need a paradigm shift before undertaking close study of presidential syntax.[69]

• A **parameter**, in math or science, is an arbitrary constant. A **property** is an explicit value or characteristic. The **perimeter** is a line bounding a closed figure or area, or the length of such a boundary. **Periphery** denotes the outermost edge of an area. **Circumference** is the perimeter of a circle (though one may go *in circuit* about a parcel of real estate that is not actually round).

• Use **partially** when you intend the opposite of **impartially**. Do not use *partially* to mean **partly**, as when the car is *partly* rusted or the pie *partly* eaten. If "Chuck is a *partial* fool," make clear whether he's only part fool, or a biased fool.

• **Passed** is a past-tense verb. **Past** can be a noun (the *past*), adjective (*past* lover), adverb (*past* due), or a preposition (go *past* the sign), but never a verb. **Pastime**, as a noun, is a leisure activity. That which is **past time** is *late* or *overdue*.

• **Payload** in its original sense denotes the revenue-producing part of a cargo. It has since come to mean total weight, including passengers, or (by way of military euphemism), the size of the explosive charge carried in the warhead of a missile. A **paydown** denotes repayment of part of an outstanding loan balance. **Payroll** denotes either a list of employees receiving wages or salaries, with the amounts due to each, or the total sum of money to be paid out to employees at a given time. If the president says of the Space Shuttle Columbia that it "carried, in its payroll, classroom experiments from some of our students in America," *payload* is the intended word.[70]

• **Pedagogue** (teacher), though not so pejorative a term as **pedant,** has lately acquired connotations of dogmatism, as if by tainted by the term, **ideologue.**

• Put the **pedal** to the metal, or **pedal** as fast as you can. One who **peddles** is a **peddler** (US) or **pedlar** (UK). The fastest **pedaller** (UK) or **pedaler** (US) wins the bike race, and the fastest **paddler**, a canoe race. **Petals** are found on flowers.

• **per, a**. The French eat **600** million snails **a** *year*. The Swiss eat more cheese **per** *person* than any other nation.

• **Percent** (US) is the same as **per cent** (UK), but not the same as a **percentage**. **Percent** is always specific and should be used with a number (*15%* or *fifteen percent*), whereas **percentage** is not specific and is never used with a number ("A small percentage of students were expelled for plagiarism." "A large percentage of the citrus crop is frost-damaged." "The percentage of undocumented aliens is on the rise.") If something trebles or triples, it increases by 200%. But if advertisers say their new toothpaste will "decrease plaque by 200%," they're lying through the teeth. Nothing can fall or be decreased by more than 100%.

• A **perk** is a common term for **perquisite**, a benefit of one's office or employment. To **perk** is to **percolate**. Whether it's through a coffee filter or a septic field, to *perk* or to *percolate* is to pass through, not to go up and down.

• To **permeate** is to spread throughout or pervade. A chill may permeate your winter clothes, and water may permeate the sheet rock, but it does not "permeate through."

• To **perpetrate** is to commit a harmful or criminal act. To **perpetuate** is to make something continue (an idea, an epidemic, a religion, an economic crisis). A president does not "perpetrate" a recession, though his policies may *perpetuate* one.

• To **persecute** is to oppress or harass with persistent ill treatment. To **prosecute** a plan is to carry it out. To *prosecute* a crime or accused criminal is to initiate and carry out legal proceedings. When Pres. Bush warns that an enemy soldier who obeys orders "will be treated, tried, and *persecuted* as a war criminal," *prosecuted* may be the intended word.[71]

• **Persevere, perseverance, perseveration** (see **preserve**).

• The plural of **person** is people. The possessive form is **person's** (house, car, grades). There is rarely a need to write "persons."

• To be **perspicacious** is to have or show insight. **Perspicuous** means easily understood or lucid.

• A **phase** is a step, stage, or period of development. To **faze** is to cause embarrassment, upset, or discomposure, most on the model, "was not fazed by" (criticism, broken equipment, a slip of the tongue).

• A **picturesque** story or phrase is as striking as a picture. A **picaresque** novel is a satirical tale of clever, swashbuckling rogues, such as one set in Washington, D.C.

• A **pillared** building has columned support. A **pilloried** person is one held up for ridicule, as if put in a wooden pillory for punishment. If our president asks, "Why the heck am I [...] getting *pillared* in the press and cartoons," *pilloried* is the intended word.[72]

• A **pipe dream** is not something you see far down the road or imagine will be a long time coming. A *pipe dream* is what you saw in your head while smoking dope.

• A **podium** ("small foot") is a small platform (as for a speaker or orchestra conductor), or any structure resembling a foot, such as a low wall or footing for a foundation. A **lectern** is the reading desk or stand used by a speaker for his books or script. One speaks *on* a *podium*, but *at, with*, or *behind* a *lectern*.

• A **populous** (adjective) county or region is well populated. To denote the general public or population, use **populace** (noun).

• One is **possessed** *of* information, or *by* a devil, or *with* good looks.

• If it is **practical**, it is useful in actual practice. If it is **practicable**, it's capable of being put into practice. The distinction is worth observing. That which is *practicable* is not always *practical*.

• A **precipitous** hill or **precipice** is quite steep. A **precipitant** or **precipitate** action is rash and impulsive, speeding headlong as if over a cliff without pausing to consider the consequences.

• A **precedent** is an action or decision that can be used thereafter as to justify a similar action or decision. A **president** is someone who holds the top position in an organization, club, corporation, or society. When President Richard Nixon, speaking in 1974 of alleged grounds for impeachment, said, "That is a discredited president," *discredited precedent* was the intended phrase.[73]

• *Precise* and *precision* (see *accuracy* and *accurate*).

• A *predecessor* precedes, or goes before. A *successor* follows: When our president says, "I am mindful not only of preserving executive powers for myself, but for *predecessors* as well," *my successors* is the intended phrase (or, better, "future presidents").[74]

• *Predominance, predominant, predominate, pre-eminence, pre-eminent, preponderance, preponderant, prevalence, prevalent* (see *dominance, dominant, dominate*).

• That which is *premier* has the highest status or importance, or may be the earliest, the first in time. A *première* is the first public presentation of a movie or play.

• A *prerequisite* is a necessary condition: *A passing grade in English 101 is a* prerequisite *for Literary Theory.* A *perquisite* (cf. *perk*) is a benefit or privilege that comes with one's job or rank.

• *Presently* is soon, but not *at present.*

• To *preserve* is to keep, protect, or store. *Preservation* is the act or process of preserving. To *persevere* is to persist, endure, carry on. *Perseverance* is dogged determination, in action or belief. And *perseveration* is a tendency to repeat one's response to an experience in a later situation where it is not appropriate. When George W. Bush remarks, "I appreciate *preservation*—it's what you do when you run for president, you gotta *preserve*," *perseverance* and *persevere* are the intended words.[75]

• A *presumptive* conclusion or statement is based on what is thought likely and reasonable. A *presumptuous* statement or action or person is thoughtlessly assertive, overconfident, audacious. If a presidential candidate says, "It is incredibly *presumptive* for somebody who has not yet earned his party's nomination to start speculating about vice presidents," *presumptuous* is the intended word.[76]

• To *prevaricate* is to *evade the truth*, not to lie outright. (Cf. *equivocate.*)

• *Preventative* is a poor substitute for *preventive.*

• A *principle* is a basic law, truth, assumption, or moral standard, and is always a noun, not an adjective. To be *unprincipled* is to ignore basic moral principles. *Principal,* used as a noun, means *head, chief,* or *main part*; and, as an adjective, *highest* or *best.* (A school *principal* is the head or *principal* instructor.) If a presidential candidate describes his campaign as one without "cynicism and polls and principles," he probably intended something different.[77]

• *Prior* means *previous* (*prior* arrangements, by *prior* agreement). Do not use "prior to" ("prior to that"). Use *before.*

• **Pristine** means *original* or *former*, not *spotless*: "Billy restored his '57 Chevy to *pristine* condition."

• **Problem** and **problematic** are much overused words.

• To **proceed** is to go forward or continue. To **precede** is to go before or to come earlier. The respective nouns are **procedure** and **precedence**. When our president remarks, "We have struggled to not *proceed*, but to *precede* to the future of a nation's child," he may mean: *As we proceed, let us struggle for our children's future, just as preceding generations have done for us.*[78] A **precedent** is an act or decision that may be used as an example or standard when dealing with a subsequent similar case.

• **Process**, though used today as a verb with a wide variety of meanings, is best reserved for use as a noun. A processed application is one that has been acted on, and a processed subpoena one that has been served. Processed data has been formatted or computed. Pasteurized, "processed" or "process" cheese, such as Cheez Whiz, is an orange substance almost, but not quite, entirely unlike real cheese. If the president says, "Oftentimes, we live in a processed world—you know, people focus on the process and not results," he may mean that we live in a world in which voters should not look too closely at the means by which a desired political goal was achieved.[79]

• To be **prodigal** is to be rashly wasteful of money or resources. A **prolific** writer or worker is highly productive, and a *prolific* couple is one with many children. If something is **prodigious**, it is amazing. When our president says that "it's time to change that attitude about how prolific we're going to be with the people's money," *prodigal* is the intended word.[80]

• A **prodigy** is a person or event so rare as to be marvelous. A **protégé** is a person whose instruction, welfare, or career is promoted by an influential mentor.

• To be **prone** is to lie with the front or face downward, or to have a tendency, usually a tendency to fall or to breakdown or to err. To be **supine** is to lie on one's back. To be **prostrate** is to be lying down. Men have a **prostate**, not a "prostrate," gland. To be **apt** is to be exactly suitable, with a natural tendency toward. An *apt* student is one *prone* to miss the frat party. A *prone* student is *apt* to fall asleep.

• **Propaganda** (which always takes a singular verb) is a systematic effort to influence public opinion. It may be true or false: *The U.S. Government will never win the trust of the Arab nations without sensible and culturally sensitive propaganda.* When President George W. Bush says, "See, in my line of work you got to keep repeating things over and over and over again for the truth to sink in, to kind of *catapult the propaganda*," he may have meant exactly what he said, for once.[81]

• **Prophecy** is a noun. To **prophesy** is a verb, often misspelled and often mispronounced. (The noun rhymes with *sophistry*, and the verb with *softest sigh*). A prophet *prophesies*, or he may utter *prophecies*, but he never "prophecies."

• To **proscribe** is to banish, exile, prohibit, condemn. To **prescribe** is to recommend a course of action or treatment, or to lay down rules or laws. (See also **ascribe** and **subscribe**.)

• **Prostrate, prostate** (see **prone**).

• **Protagonist** (see **antagonist**).

• **Proved** may be a verb or adjective ("He *proved* his case"; "a *proved* hypothesis"). **Proven** may be used as an adjective (a *proved*, or a *proven*, argument). *Proven* is often used where *proved* is preferred. It is never wrong to use *proved*.

• Do not use **providing** for **if** or for **provided that**: *Providing* health insurance for every American is a reachable goal, **provided that** [i.e., **if**] Congress restrains its pork-barrel military spending.

• To act **purposefully** or **on purpose** is to *have* a purpose, to act with intention. To do something **purposely** is to have a *specific* purpose (as in "purposely to annoy"). **To good purpose** means "with good results."

• **Quality** is a noun. By itself it cannot modify anything, unless you are a writer of advertising copy. Form a compound adjective by adding high- or top- or poor- "The Army offers a high-quality education."

• A **quantum leap** is an abrupt jump or step, not a big one. Save the phrase for a discussion of quantum physics. For the meaning, *big step*, try: "big step" (cf. **exponential**).

• A **quiche** (pronounced *keesh*) is a savory pie filled with eggs and cream. A **quickie** (pronounced *kwickee*) is something done in haste, especially a hurried act of sex. The two words should not be confused, most especially when telling a restaurant waitress what you want for breakfast.

• The **Qur'an** is the sacred text of Islam, believed by Muslims to contain God's revelations to Muhammad. Use *the Qur'an* or *al Qur'an* (with or without the preferred apostrophe), not the obsolete spellings, "Koran" or "Alcoran." "The al Quran" is redundant (*the al* = *the the*). By editorial convention, sacred texts such as the Qur'an, Bible, and Talmud are capitalized but not italicized.

• **Rack** (see **wrack**).

• **Rapprochement** (a renewal of cordial relations) is a good thing, but a word to be avoided unless your audience knows what it is and can pronounce it correctly.

• **Rate** (see **per cent, percentage**).

• A *rationale* provides the fundamental reasons for something. A *rationalization* is the practice or process of making something conformable to reason; the word is sometimes used to denote a self-satisfying but incorrect justification of one's own behavior. A *rationale* must be logical, and a *rationalization* must seem so. When our president speaks of "the logic *behind* the rationale" for his pledge to abrogate the 1972 Anti-Ballistic Missile treaty, he seems to imply that there is no logic *in* his rationale, that it is just a rationalization.[82]

• *Ravage, ravish, ravenous. Ravenous* (insatiable) pirates *ravage* (pillage) the town and *ravish* (rape) the women. A *ravishing* (rapturous) woman *ravages* a lecher's *ravenous* heart.

• *Real* is a much overused word and rarely needed. Same for *really*. Really.

• To *recur* is to happen repeatedly, sometimes according to a pattern. To *reoccur* implies a one-time repetition.

• To *refute* a statement or opposing argument is to disprove it. To *rebut* is to present a contrary argument. To *deny* a statement is merely to say that it is untrue. The corresponding nouns are *refutation, rebuttal, denial.*

• To be *regretful* is to feel or show regret. A *regrettable* event or statement is one that *causes* regret. A person is *regretful*, an action *regrettable*.

• To be *regular* is to follow a set pattern, schedule, or scheme. It is not a synonym for *ordinary* or *normal*: John Grimond has put it this way: "Mussolini brought in the *regular* train, All-Bran the *regular* man; it is quite *normal* to be without either."[83]

• To be *reliant* is to depend on someone or something. To be *reliable* is to be trustworthy and dependable. If our president demands "more extensive and more reliant rail service," he may mean *a more extensive rail system and more reliable service.*[84] If our president says that "The key to foreign policy is to *rely* on *reliance*" he may mean that America must rely on its *alliance* with other nations.[85]

• *Remuneration* is a recompense or payment. A *renumbering* is the act of numbering again, or in a different order. An *enumeration* a detailed list of items, or the act of enumerating. There is no such word as "renumeration" or "renumberation."

• To *rend* is to tear. To *render* is to give or provide. When our vice president remarks that the destruction from an earthquake is "just very heart-rendering," *heart-rending* or *heart-wrenching* is the intended word.[86]

• ***Repellent*** things include bug spray, Gortex fabric, and bad breath. Road kill, violent pornography, and racism are ***repulsive***. You may ***repel*** an invasion or an electric charge or a sexual advance. When drunk, your behavior may ***repulse***.

• A ***resister*** is found at a sit-down strike or an antiwar protest. A ***resistor*** is found in an electrical device.

• ***Restaurateur*** (no "n") is the correct spelling for the owner or manager of a restaurant, though the word is misspelled so often that some dictionaries now allow *restauranteur* as an English adaptation of the French.

• To ***restrain*** someone is to prevent him or her from speaking or acting. To ***refrain*** from acting or speaking is to restrain oneself. To ***retain*** is to keep. When our president promises "to *retain* aggression and evil, by force," *restrain* is the intended word.[87]

• To ***retch*** is to vomit, which may make you feel like a ***wretch***, though less ***wretched*** after you have finished, if all goes well.

• If you are ***reticent,*** you are ***reluctant*** to speak.

• To ***retort*** is to make a sharp or witty reply. To ***resort*** is to find recourse, as in "resort to dirty tricks." If a presidential candidate promises he will not "*retort* to personal attacks and negative ads," *resort* was probably intended.[88]

• ***Right*** and ***left***. When using *right*, be clear whether you mean "not to the left" or "not incorrect" or "not liberal." On a boat or plane, ***port*** relates to the left-hand side, facing forward; ***starboard***, to the right; ***fore***, forward; and ***aft***, to the rear. In the theater, ***stage left*** and ***stage right*** refer to the left- and right-hand side when facing the audience. ***Upstage*** is toward the rear, and ***downstage***, toward the audience. You may be said to "upstage" your colleagues or fellow actors when you attract attention to yourself by moving to the rear, forcing them to turn their backs on the audience so that all eyes are on you.

• ***Risky*** means dangerous. A ***risqué*** remark or joke is one that alludes to sex in a manner not welcome in polite society. A "poor risk" is a person, action, or thing that is deemed vulnerable to loss or calamity. An "at risk" person or group is one vulnerable to future illness, hardship, or disadvantage. When our president says that "at-risk children...means basically they can't learn," he is mistaken.[89] Poor children may be poorly served by our schools, but they are not innately stupid.

• A ***role*** is a part to be played. A ***roll*** is something you eat (bread), call or take (a list of names), or what you do to a round object.

• A *runner-up* is one that takes second place, as in a race, game, election, or other competition (plural, *runners-up*). The second runner-up comes in third. An *also-ran* is one that does not win, place, or show (plural, *also-rans*). George W. Bush, during his 2000 presidential campaign, promised not to take money from Social Security unless there was a war, recession, or national emergency during his administration. Shortly after 9/11, he joked, "Lucky me. I hit the trifecta."[90] That may be a sick joke, but it was not a malaproprism. To win a *trifecta* is to repulsive big by betting rightly on the first, second, and third horses.

• A *sea change* is not a change in the sea but a substantial change in something caused by the sea, literal or figurative. The *Titanic* has had a sea change.

• *Second, secondly* (see *first, firstly*).

• If it is *secondary*, it's of the second rank or inferior or acts in a subordinate way or auxiliary capacity. If a presidential candidate says that "Farmers are not going to be *secondary* thoughts [but] in the forethought of our thinking," he may mean that *farming is not just an afterthought but a top priority.*[91] *Secondarily* is dumb.

• *Semi-* is a prefix meaning half. *Semi-weekly* means twice a week, *semi-monthly* twice a month, and *semi-annual*, twice a year. Cf. *bi-*.

• A *sensuous* experience (a concert, a spring day, a lavish meal) is one that satisfies the senses. A *sensual* experience or person is one that appeals or pertains to your physical appetites, most especially to your appetite for sex.

• A *serial* killer slays one person after another; a *cereal* killer ate all of the Cheerios. A journal or magazine is a *serial* because it is published *serially*, as a series of issues.

• *Sequestered* means secluded. *Sequestrated* means confiscated or made bankrupt.

• *Sewage* is the stuff that goes down the pipes. A *sewer* is a conduit to dispense with it. *Sewerage* is a system of sewers.

• To *shear* is to cut the wool from sheep, to fleece; or, figuratively, to swindle or divest. (One may be *shorn* of either wool or dignity.) To *sheer* or *sheer away* is to swerve suddenly, or to avoid an unpleasant topic. A *sheer* cliff is perpendicular. *Sheer* nonsense is *nothing but*. A *shear* is a cutting tool, often called *shears* by analogy with its synonym, *scissors*.

• To *sic* is to attack someone physically and is used most often as a command to a dog. When appearing in brackets, [*sic*] is a Latin meaning *thus* or *just so*, and is used by editors to indicate that what precedes it has been reproduced verbatim from the original, even if it looks like a mistake. Expressing his concern for working mothers,

President George W. Bush assured them, "as far as I'm concerned [...] you're working hard to put food on your family [*sic*]." [92]

• *Sight* (see *site*).

• *Silicon* is a nonmetallic element, found in the earth's crust in *silica* and *silicates*, having a wide variety of industrial uses, as for glass, pottery, and semiconductors. A *silicone* is any of a group of semi-inorganic polymers used for adhesives, lubricants, protective coatings, prosthetic limbs, and breast-implants.

• *Simple* may mean either easy or foolish. A simple argument is easy to follow. If it is *simplistic*, it has been *over-simplified*. To be *simple-minded* is to be stupid or naive.

• A *site* is a place or URL. *Sight* is vision. You may *cite* a statistic, authority, or reference work.

• *Situation* is a much overused word. No sentence ever needs to end with the dull phrase, "of the situation." Be specific. "In a crisis situation" is superfluous (omit *situation*).

• To *slight,* to treat *slightly,* as if it has only *slight* importance. A *slight* is an action that shows contempt. A *sleight* is an instance of trickery or cunning.

• To *smooth* a wrinkle or problem is to make the thing *smooth.* The verb and the adjective are spelled the same, without final *–e.*

• *Societal* means relating to the organization, structure, or function of society, such as societal distinctions in gender. Whether denoting society and its organization, or relating to the way people in groups behave and interact, *social* is usually the better term.

• *So* is one of the most overused words in the language. In formal prose, avoid using *so* as an intensifier ("so sad") unless the thought is completed with a relative clause beginning in *that* ("so sad that even a U.S. Marine would have wept"). *So* does not mean *very.* "The pizza is greasy" is a complete thought. "The pizza is so greasy" is a sentence fragment.

• *So as to* (see *as*).

• If it is *soluble,* you can dissolve it; if *solvable,* solve it.

• *Sometime, some time,* like *everyday* and *everyday*, depend on context: An *everyday* event may happen *every day. Everyday* clothes may be worn at *any time.* "Mike Tyson is a *sometime* world boxing champion." "*Sometime,* let's visit Paris." "When we go, let's spend *some time* there." *Any time* and *every time* are always two-word phrases.

• To *soothe* a wound or injury, or to provide a soothing touch, is to make it feel better. *Sooth* is an old-fashioned noun meaning (and rhyming with) *truth.*

• *Sort of* (see *kind of*).

• A **spoonerism** (so named for Rev. William A. Spooner), transposes the initial sound of two or more words, muddling the thought—as when a distinguished scholar is praised inadvertently as "a whining shit" instead of a *shining wit*, or an usher says, "Let me *sew* you to your *sheet*," or when a preacher says, "Jesus Christ is a *shoving leopard*," or when a nervous student tells his professor, "I'm sorry I *hissed* your *mystery* lecture," or when an Oxford professor inadvertently calls her majesty, Elizabeth II, "our *queer* old *dean*." A *spoonerism* mangles the sound of words, unlike a **malapropism**, which mangles the sense. When our president says "We cannot let terriers and rogue nations hold this nation hostile or hold our allies hostile," *terrorists* and *hostage* are malapropisms for "terriers" and "hostile"; when he says that the economy will grow "if *terriers* and *bare ifs* are torn down," and that his economic "*pan plays* down an unprecedented amount of our national debt," or promises to hold to account those who "*lie, steat or cheal*," such statements are *spoonerisms*, not *malapropisms*.[93] (See also **Freudian slip**.)

• To be **stationary** is to stay in one place. **Stationery** is writing paper.

• **Steady** may mean regular, uninterrupted, reliable. **Steadfast** may mean firm, fixed, loyal. If our president says, "We are making *steadfast* progress, "*steady* is the intended word.[94] In his speech to the people of Senegal during a visit to Africa, **steadfastness** may have been the his intended word: "It's very interesting when you think about it, the slaves who left here to go to America, because of their *steadfast* and their religion and their belief in freedom, helped change America." [95]

• A **story** is a tale or anecdote. A **storey** (storage-level) is a floor in a building.

• **Straight** means direct or uncurved. A **straight face** shows no hint of a smile. **Strait** means narrow or tight and may be a noun (*Straits of Gibraltar*) or an adjective (a **strait-jacket**). To be **strait-laced** is to be repressed, as if wearing your corset too tight. A **straight arrow** is someone who walks the **straight and narrow**, and enters the **strait gate** to Christian Heaven.

• **Stuff** is an overused word. Delete "and all that stuff" from the end of a sentence: "You cannot be president of the United States if you don't have faith. Remember Lincoln, going to his knees in times of trial and the Civil War and all that stuff. You can't be. And we are blessed. So don't feel sorry for—don't cry for me, Argentina" (George H. W. Bush).[96] Elsewhere, try substituting *material*: "This foreign policy stuff is a little frustrating" (George W. Bush).[97]

• A **subliminal** stimulus is below the threshold of conscious perception. A **sublime** experience or work of art is not to be excelled.

A *sublimated* drive or instinct is one that finds expression in an altered and socially acceptable form. If our president speaks of "putting *subliminable* messages into ads" *subliminal* is the intended word.[98] When he promises not to be "*subliminable* about the differences" between himself and his opponent, *unclear* may be the word intended.[99]

• To *subscribe* is to pledge or contribute money to a charitable campaign, or to sign up for something (as for a magazine *subscription*), or to sign one's name to a written document. To *ascribe* is to assign someone else the responsibility for an act or document, or to assign a motive. If our president complains that "some doctrine gets *subscribed* to me," or that people "*subscribe* politics" to him as a motive, *ascribe* is the intended word.[100]

• To *subside* is to sink or settle down or to ease off. To *subsidize* is to provide a *subsidy* (monetary assistance). That which is *subsidiary* assists, or is of secondary importance. To *subsist* is to exist (as with bare necessities, mere *subsistence*). "Subsidation" is not a word. When our president says he "will not stand for the subsidation of failure," he may mean that he will not *subsidize* failing schools, workers, or neighborhoods.[101]

• A *substitute* is something or someone that stands in place of another. To *substitute* item (or person) B *for* item (or person) A, is the same as to *replace* item (or person) A *with* item (or person) B. But you cannot say that "*B* substituted *A*."

• *Such* is an overused word. "Betty had such a good time" is fragmentary. Either delete "such" ("Betty had a good time"), or complete the thought (e.g., "Betty had such a good time at church Bingo that she soon became a gambling addict").

• To *suck* is draw in or by, as if by suction. To *suckle* is to breastfeed. When our president speaks out against an education system that "suckles kids through," *sucks* is the intended word. *Suck* is a word best avoided except in its literal sense.[102]

• *Supersede* (replace, supplant) is often misspelled by way of confusion with *intercede*.

• *Supposed to, used to,* and *old-fashioned* are often misspelled "suppose to," "use to," and "old-fashion" because the writer does not hear the *-d*. "Supposably" and "supposingly" are mistakes for *supposedly*.

• *Syntax* denotes the way in which words are put together to form phrases and sentences. *Sin tax* is a surcharge on such items as alcohol and cigarettes.

• When you see an old photograph, you are *taken back*. When you see the estimate for repairing your car, you are *taken aback*.

• *Target* is best used as a noun. If you are tempted to *target* your efforts, try to *direct* them instead. (In its original sense, *to be targeted* is to be supplied with a shield.)

• To have or keep a *temper* is to maintain self-control, not to lose it. People who are often irritable may have a *poor temper* or a *bad temper,* or may *lose* their *temper* altogether. To be *temperate* is to show restraint.

• A *tenant* is a *renter.* A *tenet* is an *opinion, doctrine,* or *principle.* When Pres. George H. W. Bush, says, "I don't have to accept *their* tenants, I was trying to convince those college students to accept *my* tenants," *tenets* is the intended word.[103]

• *That* (see *which*).

• Use *then* to express what is next. "And then" is usually redundant—use one word or the other ("We shopped, then watched a movie"). Use *than* for comparisons. Never write "less then" or "more then" except in those rare instances when *than* immediately follows ("I owed the bank more then than I do now").

• *They're* always means *they are.* *Their* (house, idea, problem) is possessive: it is *theirs,* not yours or mine. *There,* like *here,* is a word that identifies, introduces, or situates. In conversation or informal writing, *there is* or *there has* may be contracted to *there's* (There's *been an accident*). "Their's" is never correct. There is no such word as *"theirself"* or *"theirselves."* If our president promises "whatever it takes to help Taiwan defend theirself," *itself* is the intended word; or else, "to help the people of Taiwan to defend themselves."[104]

• *Therefore*: use sparingly, punctuate correctly (see 1.8.2c Adverbs, and 1.8.3e. Semicolons).

• *Thus* is a stuffy conjunctive, overused and rarely necessary. *Thusly* the silliest word in the English language. (see 1.8.2c Adverbs, and 1.8.3e. Semicolons).

• *Throes* are pangs or struggles (of fortune, of childbirth, of indecision). *Throws* are what a baseball pitcher sends to the plate.

• A *tidal wave*, as scientists point out, is a misnomer: a *tsunami* is not tidal. But neither does the sun really rise at sunrise or set at sunset.   Use whichever word will be best understood by your audience. For metaphorical purposes, as use the better known term, as in the president's advice to those who must snorkel through a crime wave: "So tomorrow there'll be another tidal wave, so keep your snorkel above the water level and do what you think is right. [...] Got to keep that paper moving or you get inundated. Your snorkel will fill up and there will be no justice" (George H. W. Bush).[105]

• *Times*: take care. "Three times more than" X means *four times as much as* X. If our president says, "We've tripled the amount of money—I believe it's from $50 million up to $195 million," his intended meaning is that we now have nearly *quadrupled* the original sum.[106] Times indicates multiplication, not diminishment. "Your house is worth three times less than mine" or "Tom Thumb is twice as small as Gina Davis" are nonsensical statements. Try: "Your house is a third as large as mine," "Tom Thumb is half the size."

• *Torturous*, which entails pain as if from torture, is often confused with *tortuous* (severely twisted) or with *tortured* (subjected to torture). Work or punishment may be *torturous*. Roads or logic may be *tortuous*. Prisoners or logic may be *tortured*.

• *Totally* is overused. Delete. (Cf. *basically*.)

• *Towards* has no advantage over *toward*.

• To *transpire* is an overused and often misused verb. It does not mean to *happen* or *occur* or *turn out*. It means to give off water vapor, or, metaphorically, to become apparent by a similar process of minute disclosure.

• *Trivia* is a plural noun that has no singular. For just one *trivial* item, use *trifle*.

• A *troop* is a large group of similar people, animals, or things, or an organized body of soldiers. A *troupe* is a team of actors, circus people, or other entertainers, applied most often groups that travel. If the president says, "I do think we need for a *troop* to be able to house his family—that's an important part of building morale in the military," *soldier* is the intended word. [107]

• To *try and hang* the mayor is to put him on trial, and to hang him. To *try to hang* the mayor is to make an effort to hang him. Americans often say *try and* when they mean *try to*.

• A *turbid* liquid (or, figuratively, situation) is murky, as from mud or stirred-up sediment. A *turgid* body is bloated. *Turgid* writing is pompously ornate or tediously complex.

• To *undo* is to cancel or reverse what has been done; to *overdo* is to do too much. If it's *overdue* (payment or essay), it's late; if it's *undue* (influence, punishment), it goes beyond what's appropriate.

• *Undoubted, undoubtedly* (see *doubt*).

• If it is *unimaginable*, it is incomprehensible, impossible to grasp; if *unthinkable*, it is deemed hardly possible (though *unthinkable* may also mean "out of the question," "not something you'd think seriously about doing"). If something is *inexpressible*, it may be felt but cannot be put into words. If *unutterable*, it is inexpressible or else (if written down) impossible to pronounce (such as a tongue-twister). If our president says of the White House, "I'm sure you can imagine, it's an *unimaginable* honor to live here," *inexpressible honor* is the intended phrase.[108] If something is *ineffable*, it is *indescribable* (or, sometimes, by way of taboo, cannot be spoken). The *ineffable* quality of the White House was borne out on a presidential visit to Britain. When an English child asked President George W. Bush what the White House is like, he thought for a moment, then said, "It is—white."[109]

• *Unique*: If a thing (event, feature) is *unique*, it's one of a kind, unexampled, nothing else quite like it, snap it up while you've got the chance and you'll be the only person who's got one. A thing may be "almost unique" or "unique in some respects." One of five sisters may be "uniquely pretty." But nothing is ever "very" or "pretty" *unique*. When advertisers boast of a "unique offer" or a "unique opportunity," they're lying to you, almost always.

• *Unlike* must be followed by a noun, not by a verb, nor by *in* or *on* or by any other preposition. Say "Unlike my house, yours is tidy" or "In my house, unlike yours...," but do not say, "Unlike in my house,..." (See *as, like.*)

• **"Upmost"** is a common mistake in American English for *utmost*, meaning at the greatest degree or amount; at the most distant point or extremity. If it's on top, or of the highest rank, use **uppermost.**

• *Usage* denotes the manner or amount of *use* (word usage, water usage). For other purposes, use *use* (rhymes with *moose*).

• To *utilize*, a much-abused word, means *to find a use for.* In all other instances, use *to use*.

• A *value* denotes the worth, meaning, or importance assigned to something. To be *valuable* is to be highly valued. If a sign at the hotel says, "Management not responsible for theft. Please leave your values at the front desk," *valuables* is the intended word.

• To be *venal* is to be corruptible, open to bribery, susceptible to venal behavior. A *venial* sin is a small one, easily forgiven.

• *Venerable* means worthy of reverence. It is not always a synonym for *old*. If our president speaks of combating "venerable disease" with condoms, *venereal* may be the intended word.

• *Verbal, verbal agreement* (see *oral*).

• In law, *versus* is abbreviated "v" with no period (*Roe v Wade*). *Verses* are poetry.

• *Via* means *by way of*, not *by means of.* You can go to Hell, Michigan, via Route 96. A sinner may go to the other Hell via the grave. No one can get to either place "via" train, plain, bus, or car.

• *Viable*, which means capable of living, is an overused word, often in a nutty way, such as a "viable economy" or a "viable farm." To *vie* means to contend or strive for victory. A silly word, *vie* is not a synonym for *try* or *aim*. When our president says that "It's in our strategic interests to have a peaceful and economically *vile* hemisphere," *viable* is the intended word, or perhaps *vital*.[110]

• Your dog is *vicious* (vishus), and your eyedrops, *viscous* (viskus). A *vicious circle* is a situation in which the solution of one problem in a sequence leads to a new problem that makes solving the original problem more difficult than ever.

• A *warranty* is a guarantee on purchased goods or a condition in an insurance contract. A *warrant* authorizes somebody to do something and has a wide variety of applications. A *warrantee* is the person to whom a *warrantor* gives a *warrant* or *warranty*.

• *Well* (see *good*).

• *Which* informs, *that* defines. Use *that* for a restrictive (defining) clause: "In the kitchen drawer is *a flashlight that* I use as a case to hold dead batteries." Use a comma + *which* to introduce a "nonrestrictive" (inessential, parenthetical) clause: "My *flashlight, which* I use as a case for dead batteries, is in the kitchen drawer." If you cannot tell the difference between one clause and another and are unsure whether to use *that* or *which*, have no despair, life will go on. Try Shakespeare's method: plug in whichever one sounds best. No one but your editor or English professor will care if you get it wrong.

• *While* means *during* or *at the same time* and should not, strictly speaking, be used for *although, whereas, and,* or *but*. It's generally best to use *while* only with strict literalness, meaning *during the time that*. Otherwise, try *and* or *but*: "A group of frogs is called an army, and a group of kangaroos, a mob, *and* [not: *while*] a meeting of military officers is called a mess." (See also *awhile*.) *Worth while* means worth the time. The phrase is overworked as a term of vague approval or (with *not*) disapproval; it is strictly applicable only to actions that will take time: "Is it worth while to visit the Corn Palace?" The strictest authorities consider it worth their while to say that *worthwhile* as an adjective (a "worthwhile" book, lesson, trip) is an inexcusable barbarism.

• Use *who* for the nominative case, saving *whom* for the objective: "*Who* will dance?" "*Who* do you think you are?" "*Whom* do you love?" "*Who* cares?" "To *whom* was your love poem addressed?" "To *whom* it may concern." If you're unsure when to use *who* or *whom*, just make a guess and hope for the best. (If you err, as in this sentence, whom do you think will notice?) But if you confuse *who's* with *whose*, most educated readers will be distracted by the mistake. Like *he's* and *it's* (*he is* or *he has, it is* or *it has*), *who's* is a contraction: *Who's on first?* Like *his* and *its*, whose is possessive: "Find out *whose* car is parked in my spot." "*Whose* goldfish is floating in my soup?"

• *Will, shall.* A fine point of traditional usage, observed by the fastidious: *will* in the first person (*I, we*) suggests volition (an act of the will), while *shall* is merely predictive; *will* in the third person (*he, she, they, it*) indicates that which someone wants to do, and *shall*, that which someone must do ("Juliet *shall* marry Mr. Paris" [whether she *will*, or no, because her father commands it]): "Falling one dark night into a muddy castle moat, the frightened Princess Barbie cried out, "No one will save me! I shall drown!" And drown she did. Her fiancé, Prince Ken, upon learning of his loss, jumped into the moat after her, bellowing in despair, "I will drown! No one shall save me!" (Use *will* if you will. No one will condemn you. See also *would, should.*)

· **Will, would.** Use **will** for simple future tense (it *will* happen), and **would** for future events that are conditional (it *would* happen if): *The California bill, if passed, would outlaw the use of cigarettes. The California Bill, when passed, will outlaw,* etc. (See also **may, might.**)

· **Within** is often used when *in* will do.

· **Worth while** (see **while**).

· **Would, should.** Grammarians, speaking strictly for themselves, use "should," not "would, for conditional statements in the first person ("Madam, were it not for this vile champagne, I should not have belched so loudly." "My darling, I should not have been able to kill Duncan without your help.") Purists note also that the verb, *to like*, when used to mean **enjoy** or **find pleasant,** takes *should*, not *would*, for conditional statements ("would like" implies a *will or desire to like*). *Fastidiously correct:* "I should like a martini, if you please." *Also correct*: "I would have another martini, please." *Correct as well*: "I'd like another martini." *Incorrect*: "I would like another martini." (But by the fourth martini, who cares?) When in doubt, use *I'd*, which will serve for either "I would" or "I should." (See **would, should.**)

· A **wrack** is a *wreck*, or *wreckage*, except when it means *seaweed*. A **rack** is a frame used for hanging clothes or stacking hay or arranging billiard balls or torturing heretics. A "wracked brain" is a wrecked one; a "racked brain" is merely stretched beyond its normal workaday capacity and may yet recover.

· A **wreath** is a circular arrangement (of flowers, greenery, pipe smoke). To **wreathe** is to surround or encircle. (Cf. *smooth, smoothe.*)

· A **yea** (yay) is either a cheer, or a yes ("yeas and nays"). A **yeah** is an informal *yes*.

· **You're** always means *you are*. **Your** (house, idea, spelling) is possessive: it's **yours.**

3.2. *The Queen's English*

> *The Americans are identical to the British in all respects*
> *except, of course, language.* —Oscar Wilde [111]

When writing for an international audience, be attentive to differences in American and British usage. In American English, 1 x 10^9 is a *billion* and 1 x 10^{12} is a trillion; in Britain, the corresponding terms are *milliard* and *billion*. (The British usage is slowly giving way to the American, but do not use *billion* if the figure will be unclear. Write "a million million" or 1 x 10^{12}.) To *table* an issue, in America, is to set it aside for future debate; in Britain it means to bring an issue forward for action. A *saloon,* in Britain, is a sedan; in America, it's a drinking establishment. A *tinkle*, in Britain, is a telephone call; to *tinkle*, in America, is to urinate. To be *knocked up*, in Britain, is to be awakened, and in America, to be impregnated. A *rubber*, in Britain, is an eraser, and in America, a condom. To be inattentive to such differences may lead to unfortunate transatlantic misunderstandings, as when your prospective son-in-law, a British chap, tells you over the phone, only months before the wedding, "Oh, dear! I think I may have just knocked up your daughter by taking a tinkle in bed." The young man will be stunned by your displeasure, not least by your remark that he should have used a pencil eraser.

British spellings include *aeon, aeroplane, colour, centre, defence, favour, favourable, glamour* (but *glamorous*, not *glamourous*), *grey, harbour, honour, honourable, humour* (but *humorous*), *hotch-potch* (for *hodge-podge*), *to install, instalment, to instil, instilling, jewellery, labour, licence* (noun), *to license* (verb), *manoeuvre, manoeuvring, mould, offence, paediatric, paediatrician, programme* (*program* only with reference to computing; but *kilogram*, not *kilogramme*), *practice* (noun), *practise* (verb), *soyabean, storey* (floor), *titbits, yogurt* (not *yoghurt*) The British use *-ise, -isation* (organise, realisation) where Americans use *-ize, -ization*.

The **metric system** or **Systeme Internationale**, standard throughout the world except in the stubborn United States, starts with seven basic units to measure length, time, mass, temperature, electric current, luminous intensity, and amount of substance. U.K. spelling distinguishes between **metre** (a unit of length equivalent to 39.37 inches) and **meter** (a device for measuring, such as a gas meter). In America, both terms are spelled **meter.**

3.3. *Names*

> *The beginning of wisdom is to call things by*
> *their right names.*   —Chinese proverb

Many cities and some countries have a name used in English that is not the one used by natives of the place. Consider your audience when writing place-names, and be consistent. Don't vacillate between *Bruges* and *Brugge, Mumbai* and *Bombay, Germany* and *Deutschland, Canton* and *Guangzhou.*

If a place has a proper adjective, use it: the Alaskan legislature, Texan boots, Welsh hospitality, the Iraqi minister of tourism.

When referencing racial or ethnic groups, your chief concern should be to avoid giving offense, as when President George W. Bush thoughtlessly used a colonial epithet to denote the people of Pakistan that he did not realize was a white British term of contempt. Your next concern is to be accurate. Here are some proper nouns and adjectives that may cause trouble:

· *Africans* may be black or white. If you mean blacks, write *blacks. Afrikaans* is a language of South Africa, derived from 17th century Dutch. An *Afrikaner* is a person or thing identified with Afrikaans. People of mixed race in South Africa are *coloureds.* In the U.S., many blacks prefer to be called *African-Americans*, while blacks, Latinos, and Asians are sometimes referenced, collectively, as *people of color.*

· *America* and *American* are commonly used with sole reference to the United States. It is best to be specific when speaking of *Latin, Central* or *South America* (or *Americans*). Most Canadians are content to be called *Canadians*, not *North Americans*. Although anyone born in America is a *native American*, only the aboriginal peoples are called *Native Americans*.

· A *Celt* (or *Kelt*) is one of an ancient people of western and central Europe. *Celtic* (or *Keltic*) denotes the language or culture of the Celts. In America, these terms are widely mispronounced "selt" and "seltic," thanks to a team of Boston athletes who are better at bouncing than pronouncing.

· *Columbia, Colombia.* Although both places are named after Columbus, the U.S. capital is the District of *Columbia*, whereas the South American country is *Colombia.*

· *Confucianism* is a philosophy of life based on the teachings of Kong Fu Zi a.k.a. Confucius (551-479 BC). *Confusionism* is a funny misspelling.

· *Far East* is a Western term that takes the U.S. or western Europe as planet central, which bothers many east Asians. To avoid giving offense, use *East Asia.* The *Middle East* denotes a region extending from Turkey to Iran. If our president says that "unrest in the Middle East creates unrest throughout the region" he may mean that unrest in the Middle East fuels unrest throughout the Islamic world.[112]

• A *Filipino* or *Pilipino* (m.), like a *Filipina* or *Pilipina* (f.), is from the *Philippine* islands, where the Filipino language is spoken.

• *Greeks* live or come from *Greece* (Hellas). "Greek" is also a slang term, in America, for the member of a college fraternity or sorority. That which is *Grecian* relates to the culture of ancient Greece. "Grecian Formula" is a patented hair dye for men. "Greek" or "Grecian" love is a euphemism for an older man's affection for a fair youth. If our president speaks of his "good relations with the Grecians," he probably means good relations, not with pederasts, but with the people of modern Greece.[113]

• *Indians* are a people of south Asia. *American Indians* should be referenced where possible by nation (*Apache, Blackfoot, Cherokee, Cheyenne*). Otherwise, use *Native Americans* (sometimes awkward in that everyone born in America is a native American), or *American Indians*.

• *Islam* is the religion of Muslims, based on the teachings of Muhammad. *Islam* may also denote Muslim peoples and culture collectively. (See also *Muslim* and *Quran*.)

• *Jewish* is the proper adjective. To use *Jew* as an adjective ("Jew doctor") is an ethnic slur. Ditto for *jew* or *gyp* (gypsy) to mean "cheat."

• A *Latino* is a *Latin American* male. A *Latina* is a Latin American woman. *Hispanic* encompasses Spanish-speaking peoples in both hemispheres. *Chicanos* and *Chicanas* are Mexican Americans. If our president speaks of "*Hispanos* and African-Americans," Latinos or Hispanics may be the intended word."[114] If the president vows to answer a reporter's question "neither in French, nor in English, nor in *Mexican*," nor in "Hispanical," or if our vice president regrets "that [he] didn't study Latin harder in school so [he] could converse with those people" in Latin America, *Spanish* is the intended word.[115] Latin is the language of ancient Rome.

• A *Muslim* is a person, a follower of *Islam* (q.v.).

• The people of *Scotland* are *Scots*: a *Scot* is a *Scottish* person, and *Scotch whisky* is a *beverage*. To be *scot-free* is to be *free from payment of a fine* (or *punishment*), not to be free from *Scotsmen*.

3.4. *Latin abbreviations*

Illiud Latine dici non potest.[116]
—Latin saying

Wherever possible, use the English equivalent:

• *AD* (*anno domini,* "year of our Lord") and *BC* ("before Christ") should be in caps with no points. AD is placed before the year (AD 1492), and BC, after (55 BC). For a secular, mixed-faith, or non-Christian audience, use *CE* ("common era"), not AD; and *BCE* ("before the common era") not BC.

• *cf.* (in Latin, *confer*): "compare."

• *e.g.* (*exempli gratia*), "for example."

• *et al.* (*et alii*), "and others." Unlike etc., *et al.* may be used of persons.

• *etc.* (*et cetera*), "and the rest," is pronounced as spelled (et-**set**-ra, *not* ek-**set**-ra). *Etc.* may be used to represent the last terms of a list otherwise given in full, but it should be avoided in formal writing and should never be used of persons or personal names. A list of examples is best introduced with *such as* or *for example*, omitting *etc.*: "In Environmental Studies 101 we shall study such problems as acid rain, deforestation, and ozone depletion." (Never tack an *etc.* to the end of a list introduced by *such as* or *for example*). *Etc.* may also be used to take the place of immaterial words at the end of a quotation, but a bracketed ellipsis is less distracting: "To be or not to be, that is the question [...]." To say or write "etc., etc." is nonsense unless used to mean, "blah, blah, blah!"

• *i.e.* (abb. for Latin, *id est*) means "that is," or "in other words," and is used for elucidation, i.e., to clarify.

• *op. cit.* (abb. for Latin, *opere citato*), "in the work cited," *ibid.* (*ibidem*), "in the same place," and *loc. cit.* (*loco citato*), "in the place cited," are used in footnotes to indicate texts already noted; *q.v.* (*quod vide,* singular) and *qq.v.* (*quae vide,* plural), "which see," are usually inserted in a parenthesis after a cross-reference.

If you *must* use such Latin abbreviations such as *cf., et al., ibid., op. cit., loc. cit., q.v.,* and *qq.v.,* at least use them correctly. If it gives you *pleasure* to use them, *Fac ut vivas* (get a life).

Part Four: INDEX AND READY REFERENCE

Part One: Ten Commandments

1.1. BE INTERESTING

1.1.1.   **Angle: *Find your best hook, line, and bait***
   1.1.1a. *Begin with a bang, not a whimper*
   1.1.1b. *Choose a subject that grabs you*
   1.1.1c. *Choose a title that will grab readers.*
   1.1.1d. *"Fit audience find, though few"*
   1.1.1e. *Exhibit some gusto*
   1.1.1f. *It's not really about you*
   1.1.1g. *If you want to write well, be well read.*

1.1.2.   **Tone: *Stay on pitch***
   1.1.2a. *Be confident*
   1.1.2b. *Don't lecture*
   1.1.2c. *Don't be pretentious*
   1.1.2d. *De-escalate the technobabble*
   1.1.2e. *Don't be glib*
   1.1.2f. *Don't be quaint*
   1.1.2g. *Avoid cuteness*
   1.1.2h. *Avoid sentimentality*
   1.1.2i. *Take responsibility for your own conclusions*

1.1.3.   **Variety: *Get out of the rut***
   1.1.3a. *No gimmicks*
   1.1.3b. *Vary your structure*
   1.1.3c. *No drumbeat repetition*

1.1.4.   **Vitality: *Choose lively verbs***
   1.1.4a. *To be or to act? No question*
   1.1.4b. *Prefer the active to the passive voice*

1.1.5.   **Freshness: *Be inventive***
   1.1.5a. *Avoid clichés like the plague*
   1.1.5b. *Avoid over-familiar figures of speech*
   1.1.5c. *Consider the sense of every trite phrase*
   1.1.5d. *Reinvigorate tired language*

1.1.6.   **Image-ination: *Be visual***
   1.1.6a. *Picture it*
   1.1.6b. *What's your story?*

1.2. BE ORGANIZED

1.2.1.   **Foundation and structure:** *Sketch out a plan*
    1.2.1a. *Architectural vision*
    1.2.1b. *Say goodbye to the "five-paragraph" theme*
    1.2.1c. *Write toward an outline, not from it*

1.2.2.   **Research:** *Reading precedes Writing*
    1.2.2a. *Get to know your library*
    1.2.2b. *Keep organized notes*
    1.2.2c. *Trace information to its source*
    1.2.2d. *Discover your argument as you go*
    1.2.2d. *Know when to quit looking*

1.2.3.   **Introduction:** *Jumping in*
    1.2.3a. *Find your point of departure*
    1.2.3b. *Don't dawdle*
    1.2.3c. *If you get stuck, come back later*
    1.2.3d. *Pace yourself*

1.2.4   **Navigation:** *Get past false starts and detours*
    1.2.4a. *Dig and hurl.*
    1.2.4b. *Keep moving forward*
    1.2.4c. *Transitions*
    1.2.4d. *Wrong turns*
    1.2.4e. *Footnote detours*
    1.2.4f. *Writer's block*
    1.2.4g. *The insurmountable roadblock*

1.2.5.   **Development:** *From sketch to masterpiece*
    1.2.5a. *Paragraph development*
    1.2.5c. *Experiment*

1.2.6.   **Conclusion:** *Draw down the curtain*

1.3. BE SPECIFIC

1.3.1.   *The life is in the details*
    1.3.1a. *Support, or cut, every general remark*
    1.3.1b. *Develop one or more examples.*

1.3.2.   *What and who?*
    1.3.2a. *Show, don't just tell*
    1.3.2b. *Prefer the concrete to the abstract*
    1.3.2c. *Destroy "things"*
    1.3.2d. *Kill "people"*
    1.3.2e. *Do something about "the situation."*
    1.3.2f. *"This," "these," and "that": just say no.*
    1.3.2g. *Who's speaking?*

Notes

1.1. BE INTERESTING

[1] H. L. Mencken, attrib. Unverified.

[2] George W. Bush, *Hardball*, MSNBC (31 May 2000).

[3] J. Danforth ("Dan") Quayle, Alameda Naval Air Station, speaking of the Lomo Prieta earthquake (18 Oct. 1989), qtd. *Washington Post* (14 Jan. 1990).

[4] George W. Bush, Orlando, FL, *FDCH Political Transcripts* (4 Dec. 2001).

[5] William Shakespeare, *A Midsummer Night's Dream* 1.2.70-3, *Riverside Shakespeare* (Boston: Houghton Mifflin, 2d ed., 1997); except as noted, all Shakespeare citations are to this edition.

[6] George W. Bush, *20/20*, ABC News (15 Sep. 2000).

[7] Dan Quayle (4 May 1989), qtd. *Esquire* (Aug. 1992): 119.

[8] Dan Quayle (20 Oct. 1988), qtd. *Esquire* (Aug. 1992): 124.

[9] George W. Bush, at a White House Menorah lighting ceremony, Washington, D.C., *FDCH Political Transcripts* (10 Dec. 2001).

[10] Alexander Pope," *Windsor Forest, Works* (1736), 1.13.

[11] George W. Bush, Albuquerque, N.M. (31 May 2000), qtd. *The Guardian* (London) (4 Nov. 2000).

[12] *Webster's Seventh New Collegiate Dictionary* (Springfield, Mass.: G & C. Merriam, 1967), 938.

[13] Lewis Caroll, *Through the Looking-glass*, chapter 6.

[14] George W. Bush, speaking of education (April 2000), attrib. Unverified.

[15] Jesse Jackson (19 Jul. 1988), *Frontline*, PBS, www.pbs.org. Feb. 2004.

[16] George W. Bush, Washington, D.C. (29 March 2001), qtd. *Washington Post* (30 March 2001).

[17] Marilyn Quayle, addressing the Republican National Convention, Kansas City, Missouri (2 Sep. 1992), qtd. *New York Times* (3 Sep. 1992).

[18] George W. Bush, *Nightline*, ABC News (28 July 2000); Washington, D.C., *Federal News Service* transcript (17 Sept. 2004).

[19] Dan Quayle, on the forced resignation of John Sununu (6 Dec. 1991); qtd. *Esquire* (Aug. 1992): 122.

[20] George W. Bush, on Sen. John McCain, Florence, S.C., *Nightly News*, NBC (17 Feb. 2000); Bush, Presidential debate, Winston-Salem, N.C., *NBC Debate Transcripts* (11 Oct. 2000).

[21] George W. Bush, LaCrosse, Wisconsin (18 Oct. 2000), *Morning Edition*, NPR (19 Oct. 2000).

[22] George Orwell, "Politics and the English Language," *Horizon* (April 1946).

[23] Samuel Johnson, qtd. in James Boswell, *Life of Johnson*, vol. 1, note to entry for 20 March 1776.

[24] George Bernard Shaw, attrib. Unverified.

[25] Winston Churchill, attrib. Unverified.

[26] Apollo (eighth century B.C.E.), attrib. A.P. English; unverified.

[27] H. L. Mencken, *A Mencken Chrestomathy* (NY: Knopf, 1949), chap. 622.

[28] George W. Bush, Washington, D.C., qtd. *FDCH Political Transcripts* (25 July 2003); Bush, Washington, D.C., qtd. *FDCH Political Transcripts* (10

June 2003); Bush, St. Louis, Missouri, qtd. *FDCH Political Transcripts* (22 Jan. 2003).

[29] George W. Bush, Nashua, N.H. (13 Jan. 2000), qtd. *Washington Post* (15 Jan. 2000).

[30] George W. Bush, Fritsche Middle School, Milwaukee, Wisconsin, qtd. *CNN Live Event Transcript* (30 March 2000).

[31] Dan Quayle, qtd. *Newsweek* (18 Sep. 1988).

[32] George W. Bush (22 Feb. 2001), qtd. *Washington Post* (23 Feb. 2001).

[33] George W. Bush, South Carolina Republican Debate, *Federal News Service Transcripts* (15 Feb. 2000).

[34] George W. Bush, Washington, D.C. (28 March 2001), qtd. *New York Times* (1 April 2001).

[35] George W. Bush, Homeland Security Council, qtd. *FDCH Political Transcripts* (29 Oct. 2001).

[36] This anecdote is the world's funniest joke, according to the British Association for the Advancement of Science. "Science Cracks Secret of World's Funniest Joke," *The Times* (London) (4 Oct. 2002).

1.2. BE ORGANIZED

[1] E. B. White, *The Elements of Style* (NY: Macmillan, 2d ed., 1972), 63.

[2] Zora Neale Hurston, *Dust Tracks on a Road* (1942; repr. NY: Harper, 1996), 143.

[3] Kurt Vonnegut, attrib. "We have to continually be..." Unverified.

[4] William Strunk, "Elementary Principles of Composition," *Elements of Style*, p. 10.

[5] Ernest Hemingway, *Death in the Afternoon* (1932), chap. 16.

1.3. BE SPECIFIC

[1] Rudyard Kipling, following the story "Elephant's Child" in " *Just So Stories* (London, 1902).

[2] Frank Rizzo, qtd. *Washington Post* (26 Oct. 1980).

[3] George W. Bush, Washington, D.C., qtd. *CNN, MSNBC* transcripts (14 January 2005).

[4] Lewis Carroll, *Through the Looking-glass,* chapter 6.

[5] George W. Bush, Bentonville, Ark. (6 Nov. 2000), qtd. *New York Times* (17 Jan. 2003).

[6] Abbot and Costello, "Who's on First," skit first performed on Kate Smith's radio show (1938); ed. A. P. English.

[7] William Carlos Williams, attrib. Qtd. Loren Webster, online, www.lorenwebster.net/In_a_Dark_Time/category/poets/william-carlos-williams/. Unverified.

[8] William Carlos Williams, "The Red Wheelbarrow," (1923), from *Selected Poems*, ed. Charles Tomlinson (NY: New Directions, 1985).

[9] George W. Bush, Interview, *Washington Post* (23 March 2000).

[10] Dwight D. Eisenhower (n.d.), *Boston Globe* (16 Sep. 1992).

[11] Gerald Ford, *Buffalo News* (New York) (22 Sep. 1993).

[12] Walter Mondale and George H. W. Bush (1984), qtd. *The Observer* (London) (1 Dec. 1991).

[13] Dan Quayle (23 Aug. 1988), qtd. *Washington Post* (24 Aug. 1988).

[14] George W. Bush, Oklahoma City, Okla., qtd. *FDCH Political Transcripts* (29 Aug. 2002).

[15] George W. Bush, to Israeli PM Sharon, Washington, D.C., qtd. *White House Press Releases* (7 May 2002).

[16] Dan Quayle (15 Sep. 1988), qtd. *The New Yorker* (10 Oct. 1988).

[17] George W. Bush, media roundtable discussion, qtd. *U.S. Newswire Transcripts* (13 March 2001).

[18] George W. Bush, Washington, D.C., qtd. *FDCH Political Transcripts* (27 Oct. 2003).

[19] George H. W. Bush, Washington, D.C., qtd. *Federal News Service Transcripts* (30 March 1989).

[20] Thomas Paine, Introduction to *The Crisis* (Dec. 1776).

[21] George W. Bush, President's Economic Forum Plenary Session in Waco, Texas, *FDCH Political Transcripts* (13 Aug. 2002).

[22] George W. Bush, Washington, D.C., *20/20*, ABC News (13 Dec. 2002).

[23] George W. Bush, Dallas, Texas (April 1986), qtd. *Washington Post* (25 July 1999).

[24] Abbot and Costello, "Who's on First," skit first performed on Kate Smith's radio show (1938); ed. A. P. English.

[25] George W. Bush, *FDCH Political Transcripts,* Ontario, California (5 Jan. 2002); Mt. Lemmon, AZ, *FDCH Political Transcripts* (11 Aug. 2003).

[26] George W. Bush, Washington, D.C. (16 July 2001), qtd. *Daily Telegraph* (Sydney, Australia)

[27] Abbot and Costello, "Who's on First," skit first performed on Kate Smith's radio show (1938); ed. A. P. English.

[28] Dan Quayle, Washington, D.C. (8 Oct. 1991), qtd. *Washington Post* (9 Oct. 1991).

[29] George W. Bush, Interview, Crawford, Texas (20 Aug. 2002), qtd. *Washington Post* (19 Nov. 2002).

[30] George W. Bush, aboard Air Force One, *Federal News Service* (4 June 2003).

1.4. BE CLEAR

[1] George W. Bush, Washington, D.C., *Congressional Quarterly* transcript (23 Sept. 2004).

[2] George W. Bush, Beaverton, Oregon, *FDCH Political Transcripts* (13 Aug. 2004)

[3] Edmund G. (Pat) Brown on the North Coast flood (19-24 Dec. 1964), qtd. *Los Angeles Times* (18 Apr. 2005).

[4] George W. Bush, White House Press Conference, CNN (11 May 2001).

[5] George W. Bush, Albuquerque, N.M., qtd. *FDCH Political Transcripts* (15 Aug. 2000); Bush, after a meeting with congressional leaders, Washington, D.C. (2 Oct. 2001), qtd. *Washington Post* (3 Oct. 2001)

⁶ George W. Bush, Washington, D.C. (10 June 2002), qtd. *Washington Post* (11 June 2002).

⁷ George W. Bush, Philadelphia, PA, *FDCH Political Transcripts* (14 May 2001).

⁸ George W. Bush, Washington, D.C., Federal News Service Transcript (7 Feb. 2001); Interview, *Meet the Press*, NBC (21 Nov. 1999).

⁹ George W. Bush, qtd. *San Francisco Chronicle* (25 Jan. 2000); South Carolina (14 Feb. 2000), qtd. *Daily Mail* (London) (16 Feb. 2001).

¹⁰ Richard Guindon, *Cartoons of Guindon* (NY: Putnam Group, 1982).

¹¹ Dan Quayle (17 Aug. and 2 Sep. 1988), qtd. *Washington Post* (21 Aug. 1992), from ABC transcript.

¹² Dan Quayle (2 Sep. and 17 August 1988), qtd. *Esquire* (Aug. 1992): 124; repr. CNBC News Transcripts (9 June 2000).

¹³ George W. Bush, Washington, D.C., qtd. *FDCH Political Transcripts* (1 May 2001); Bush, Des Moines, IA, qtd. *FDCH Political Transcripts* (8 June 2001).

¹⁴ George W. Bush, Washington, D.C., *FDCH Political Transcripts* (29 Jan. 2004).

¹⁵ George W. Bush, Washington, D.C., qtd. *FDCH Political Transcripts* (10 April 2001); Bush, on the Elián González controversy, qtd. Associated Press (26 April 2000).

¹⁶ George W. Bush, President's Economic Forum, Waco, Texas (13 Aug. 2002), qtd. *FDCH Political Transcripts* (13 Aug. 2002).

¹⁷ Dan Quayle (22 May 1989); qtd. Esquire (Aug. 1992): 119.

¹⁸ Dan Quayle (22 Sep. 1990), qtd. *Esquire* (Aug. 1992): 121.

¹⁹ Dan Quayle, CNBC News Transcripts (9 June 2000).

²⁰ George W. Bush, *Time Magazine* (3 July 2000).

²¹ Dan Quayle, Washington, D.C., press conference (8 Feb. 1990).

²² George W. Bush, Washington, D.C., qtd. *FDCH Political Transcripts* (4 Oct. 2001).

²³ George W. Bush, South Bend, Indiana, qtd. *FDCH Political Transcripts* (5 Sep. 2002).

²⁴ Abraham Lincoln, *The Gettysburg Address* (19 Nov. 1863).

²⁵ George W. Bush, Nashville, Tennessee, *FDCH Political Transcripts* (27 May 2004); quietly corrected, *Federal News Service* transcript.

²⁶ George W. Bush, New Britain, Connecticut, qtd. *FDCH Political Transcripts* (18 April 2001).

²⁷ George W. Bush, Bentonville, Arkansas, qtd. *FDCH Political Transcripts* (4 Nov. 2002).

²⁸ George W. Bush, Interview, CNN (30 Aug. 2000)

²⁹ George W. Bush, Washington, D.C., qtd. *FDCH Political Transcripts* (2 Nov. 2001).

³⁰ George W. Bush, Powell Lecture, Texas A&M Univ. (6 Apr. 1998).

³¹ George W. Bush, televised presidential debate (17 Oct. 2000).

³² George W. Bush, Washington, D.C., qtd. *FDCH Political Transcripts* (2 Oct. 2001).

³³ George W. Bush, Washington, D.C., qtd. *FDCH Political Transcripts* (2

Jul. 2003).

34 George W. Bush, White House news conference, *NBC News* transcript, Washington, D.C. (28 April 2005).

35 George W. Bush, Washington, D.C. (5 Aug. 2004), qtd. *Washington Post* (6 Dec. 2004); Marlton, New Jersey, *Congressional Quarterly* transcript. (18 Oct. 2004).

36 Dan Quayle (8 Oct. 1991), addressing the Christian Coalition, qtd. *Esquire* (Aug. 1992): 122.

37 George W. Bush, Pella, IA, qtd. *San Antonio Express-News* (30 Jan. 2000).

38 George W. Bush, on the Kyoto accord, Washington, D.C. (24 April 2001), qtd. *Washington Post* (25 April 2001).

39 George W. Bush, Kananaskis, Canada, qtd. *FDCH Political Transcripts* (26 June 2002).

40 George H. W. Bush, Columbus, Ohio (16 Sep. 1988), qtd. *The Toronto Star* (17 Sep. 1988).

41 George W. Bush, Hilton Head, South Carolina, qtd. *Hardball with Chris Matthews,* MSNBC (14 Feb. 2000).

42 George W. Bush, to Swedish Prime Minister Goran Perrson, unaware that a live television camera was still rolling (15 June 2001), qtd. *New York Times* (16 June 2001).

43 George W. Bush, Milwaukee, Wisconsin, qtd. *FDCH Political Transcripts* (3 Oct. 2003).

44 George W. Bush, South Carolina, qtd. *Financial Times* (14 Jan. 2000).

45 George W. Bush, Erie, Pa., *FDCH Political Transcripts* (4 Sept. 2004).

46 Albert Einstein, *Reader's Digest* (Oct. 1977).

47 William Shakespeare, *All's Well That Ends Well,* 1.1.39-45.

48 George W. Bush, on his Democratic opponent's proposed tax plan, qtd. *Associated Press* (10 Oct. 2000).

49 George W. Bush, Poplar Bluff, Missouri (6 Sept. 2004), recording, online, http:// politicalhumor.about.com/library/ blbushism-obgyn.htm.

50 George W. Bush, *Fox Special Report,* Fox News (4 Jan. 2001).

51 William Shakespeare, *Measure for Measure,* 1.1.3-4.

52 George W. Bush, presidential debate (17 Oct. 2000), NBC News Transcripts (17 Oct. 2000).

53 George Bush, on recent terrorist attacks in Israel, qtd. *FDCH Political Transcripts* (4 Aug. 2002).

54 Ralph Waldo Emerson, attrib. Unverified.

55 Harold Coffin, attrib. Unverified.

56 John Updike, "On Reading, Writing and Rabbit," Interview with Clyde Haberman, *New York Times* (6 March 1996).

57 George W. Bush, speaking of Iraq, Manchester, New Hampshire, qtd. *FDCH Political Transcripts* (5 Oct. 2002).

58 George W. Bush, Washington, D.C., qtd. *FDCH Political Transcripts* (10 April 2002).

59 George W. Bush, Crawford, Texas, qtd. *FDCH Political Transcripts* (13 Aug. 2001).

⁶⁰ George W. Bush, Little Rock, Arkansas, qtd. *FDCH Political Transcripts* (29 Aug. 2002).

⁶¹ George W. Bush, second presidential debate, St. Louis, Missouri (8 Oct. 2004); qtd. *New York Times* (9 Oct. 2004).

⁶² George W. Bush, *CNN Live Event* (14 Jan. 2000).

⁶³ Lewis Carroll, *Alice's Adventures in Wonderland*, chap. 7.

⁶⁴ Groucho Marx as Capt. Spaulding in *Animal Crackers* (1930).

⁶⁵ George W. Bush, to community and religious leaders in Moscow, qtd. *Federal News Service* (24 May 2002).

⁶⁶ *The Scotsman* (27 Nov. 1997).

⁶⁷ Dan Quayle, Inaugural Ball (20 Jan. 1989), qtd. *Washington Post* (21 Jan. 1989).

⁶⁸ Dan Quayle (9 May 1989), qtd. *Esquire* (Aug. 1992): 119.

⁶⁹ George W. Bush, Washington, D.C., qtd. *FDCH Political Transcripts* (22 May 2001).

1.5. BE CONCISE

¹ William Strunk and E. B. White, *Elements of Style* (1957; part III, elementary rules of composition, no. 13)

² Brooke Shields, qtd. *St. Petersburg Times* (Florida) (6 June 1993).

³ Voltaire, "Preface," *L'Enfant Prodigue* (Paris, 1736), trans. anon.

⁴ Dan Quayle (30 Oct. 1988), qtd. *Esquire* (Aug. 1992), 118,

⁵ George W. Bush, Washington, D.C., *FDCH Political Transcripts* (19 May 2003).

⁶ George W. Bush, at the Summit of the Americas in Quebec City, qtd. *FDCH Political Transcripts* (21 April 2001); Beaverton, Oregon (25 Sep. 2000), qtd. "Morning Edition," *NPR* (26 Sep. 2000).

⁷ George W. Bush, on his meeting with John McCain (9 May 2000), qtd. *Dallas Morning News* (10 May 2000).

⁸ Dan Quayle (25 April 1989), qtd. *Esquire* (Aug. 1992), 119.

⁹ George W. Bush (12 Jan. 2001), qtd. *New York Times* (14 Jan. 2001).

¹⁰ George W. Bush, to Future Farmers of America, *FDCH Political Transcripts* (27 July 2001).

¹¹ George W. Bush, Washington, D.C., *FDCH Political Transcripts* (13 March 2002).

¹² George W. Bush, Lexington, South Carolina, Press Conference (12 Jan. 2000), qtd. *Houston Chronicle* (13 Jan. 2000).

¹³ Dan Quayle (13 Sep. 1992), qtd. *New York Times* (14 Sep. 1992).

¹⁴ George W. Bush, Washington, D.C., qtd. Assoc. Press (18 Jan. 2001).

¹⁵ George W. Bush, speaking about his Republican Congress, Washington, D.C., qtd. Associated Press (2 Dec. 2000); Bush, Orlando, Florida, qtd. *FDCH Political Transcripts* (4 Dec. 2001).

¹⁶ George W. Bush, Tampa, Florida, qtd. *FDCH Political Transcripts* (4 June 2001).

¹⁷ George W. Bush, Kalamazoo, Michigan, qtd. *FDCH Political Transcripts* (27 Oct. 2000).

[18] George W. Bush, Washington, D.C., *NBC News Special Report: Target: Iraq*, *NBC News* (13 April 2003).

[19] George H. W. Bush (8 Nov. 1991), qtd. *St. Petersburg Times* (9 Nov. 1991).

[20] Shakespeare, *Hamlet* 5.2.287.

[21] George W. Bush, Washington, D.C., *Congressional Quarterly* (29 Jan. 2004; 4 Nov. 2004; 16 March 2005).

[22] George W. Bush, interview with Brit Hume, qtd. *Fox News Transcripts* (22 Sep. 2003).

[23] George W. Bush, Washington, D.C., *FDCH Political Transcripts* (21 April 2004).

[24] George W. Bush, Crawford, Texas, qtd. *FDCH Political Transcripts* (8 Aug. 2003).

[25] George W. Bush, qtd. *Austin American Statesman* (*TX*) (18 Oct. 1998).

[26] George W. Bush, Gothenburg, Sweden (14 June 2001), qtd. *CNBC News Transcripts* (21 June 2001).

[27] George W. Bush, Bentonville, Arkansas, *FDCH Political Transcripts* (4 Nov. 2002).

[28] George W. Bush, qtd. *CNN* (16 Feb. 2002); greeting the South Korean press (17 Feb. 2002); qtd.*Washington Post* (19 Feb. 2002).

[29] George H. W. Bush, Washington, D.C., qtd. *Federal News Transcripts* (6 June 1989).

[30] George W. Bush, Interview aboard Air Force One (23 April 2003), *Dateline*, NBC News (24 April 2003).

[31] George W. Bush, qtd. *New York Times* (8 April 2002).

[32] George W. Bush, qtd. *New York Times* (4 March 2000).

[33] Dan Quayle (19 May 1992), qtd. *Esquire* (Aug. 1992): 123.

[34] Vladimir Nabokov, *Strong Opinions* (1973), chap. 1.

[35] Abraham Lincoln, attrib. Unverified.

1.6. BE CHOOSY

[1] Winston Churchill, qtd. Alistair Cooke, *America* (NY: Knopf, 1973).

[2] George W. Bush, White House press conference, Washington, D.C. (8 July 2002), qtd. *Washington Post* (9 July 2002).

[3] George W. Bush, Washington, D.C., qtd. *FDCH Political Transcripts* (5 March 2001).

[4] George W. Bush, Pittsburgh, Pennsylvania (8 Sep. 2000), qtd. Associated Press (9 Sep. 2000).

[5] George W. Bush, St. Louis, Missouri, qtd. *White House Press Releases* (5 Jan. 2004); quietly corrected in a FDCH Political Transcript.

[6] Stephen T. Tyman, "Ricoeur and the Problem of Evil," *The Philosophy of Paul Ricoeur*, ed. Lewis Edwin Hahn (Chicago: Open Court, 1995). For this splendid example of bad writing I am indebted to Jennifer Harris (Univ. of Toronto), who submitted it to *Philosophy and Literature*'s second "Bad Writing Contest." Harris's nomination took second place.

[7] Kingman Brewster, addressing the British Institute of Management (13 Dec 1977).

[8] See Tim Hamlett, "Jargon," Hongkong Online Style Tips, online, www.hkbu.edu.hk/~jour/style/host_J.html.

[9] George Carlin, *Brain Droppings* (NY: Hyperion, 1997).

[10] George W. Bush, Washington, D.C., qtd. *FDCH Political Transcripts* (16 Jul. 2003).

[11] Carl Sandburg, qtd. *New York Times* (Feb. 13, 1959).

[12] Gilbert Chesteron, *The Defendant* (NY: Dodd, 1901).

[13] William Shakespeare, *Love's Labor's Lost* 5.1.36.

[14] George W. Bush, speaking at the Radio & Television Correspondents dinner, Washington, D.C., qtd. *FDCH Political Transcripts* (30 March 2001).

[15] George H. W. Bush, qtd. *Federal News Service Transcript* (3 Dec. 1989).

[16] George W. Bush, Crawford, Texas (20 Aug. 2001), qtd. *USA Today* (22 Aug. 2001).

[17] George W. Bush, qtd. *NBC News Presidential Debate* (17 Oct. 2000).

[18] George W. Bush, Chicago, Illinois, qtd. *FDCH Political Transcripts* (30 Sep. 2003)..

[19] George W. Bush, Portsmouth, N.H. (1 Nov. 2002), qtd. *The Independent* (*London*) (7 Nov. 2002).

[20] George W. Bush, Washington, D.C. (13 Nov. 2001), qtd. *New York Times* (14 Nov. 2001); Rome, Italy, press conference, *Federal News Service Transcripts* (23 July 2001).

[21] George W. Bush, Texas Meeting With Tony Blair (7 April, 2002), qtd. *New York Times* (8 April 2002).

[22] Dan Quayle, standing in front of the collapsed section of highway caused by the Loma Prieta earthquake (18 Oct. 1989), qtd. *The Guardian* (London)(5 Nov. 1996); *St. Petersburg Times* (Florida) (30 Dec. 1989); *CNN* (19 Oct. 1989).

[23] George W. Bush (1 March 2000), qtd. *New York Times Debate Transcript* (2 March 2000).

[24] George W. Bush, Berlin, Germany, *FDCH Political Transcripts* (23 May 2002).

[25] George W. Bush, qtd. *Bulletin's Frontrunner News Wire* (24 Mar. 1999).

[26] George H. W. Bush, on his negative campaign ads, White House press conference, *Federal News Service transcript* (7 Nov. 1989).

[27] Tom Stoppard, *The Real Thing* (NY: Faber and Faber, 1982): 49.

[28] Richard J. Daley, qtd. *Pittsburgh Post-Gazette* (Pennsylvania) (29 Jan. 2000); original source unk.

[29] Dan Quayle, qtd. *U.S. News and World Report* (10 Oct. 1988).

[30] Dan Quayle (3 Feb. 1989), qtd. *Chicago Tribune* (4 Feb. 1989).

[31] George W. Bush (26 Sep. 2000), *San Francisco Chronicle* (27 Sep. 2000).

[32] George W. Bush, Manhattan Institute for Policy Research (New York) (5 Oct. 1999; Bush, Portland, Oregon (31 Oct. 2000), qtd. *The Financial Times* (*London*) (2 Nov. 2000); Bush, qtd. *Fresh Air, NPR* (1 Oct. 2001).

[33] George W. Bush, CNN (13 Sep. 2000); qtd. *Boston Herald* (3 Oct. 2000); Bush, on his anti-Gore ad (1 Sep. 2000), qtd. *NY Times* (2 Sep. 2000); Bush, qtd. *Hardball with Chris Matthews*, CNBC News Transcripts (12 Sep. 2000).

[34] George W. Bush, Washington, D.C. (26 Sep. 2001); qtd. *Washington Post* (27 Nov. 2001); Bush, Langley, Maryland, qtd. *Federal News Service* (26 Sep. 2001); Bush, press conference with King Abdullah of Jordan, qtd. *Federal News Service Transcripts* (1 Aug. 2002).

[35] George W. Bush, *CNN online*, www.CNN.com (30 Aug. 2000).

1.7. BE ACCURATE

[1] Charles Simmons, attrib., elsewhere ascribed to Nathaniel Hawthorne. Unverified—and therefore, perhaps, inaccurate.

[2] George W. Bush, Washington, D.C., *FDCH Political Transcripts* (19 Sept. 2002); Austin, Texas, *FDCH Political Transcripts* (Nov. 22, 2000); Chicago, Illinois, *FDCH Political Transcripts* (30 Sept. 2003); Aberdeen, S.D. (31 Oct. 2002), quietly corrected in *FDCH Political Transcripts*; Washington, D.C. *Federal News Service* transcript (18 Dec. 2000).

[3] Johann Wolfgang von Goethe, qtd. Ralph Waldo Emerson, "Goethe," in *Representa-tive Men: Seven Lectures* (1850).

[4] Ronald Reagan (Aug. 1980); repeated in *Sierra* (10 September 1980): "Approximately 80% of our air pollution stems from hydrocarbons released by vegetation, so let's not go overboard in setting and enforcing tough emissions standards from man-made sources."

[5] See Dana Milbank, "For Bush, Facts Are Malleable," *Washington Post* (22 Oct. 2002).

[6] George W. Bush, Elizabeth, New Jersey, qtd. *FDCH Political Transcripts* (16 June 2003).

[7] E. B. White, "An Approach to Style," *Elements of Style,* 72.

[8] Ibid.

[9] George W. Bush, *UPI Transcript* (5 Feb. 2001).

[10] George W. Bush, Thurgood Marshall Elementary School, Washington, D.C., qtd. *FDCH Political Transcripts* (25 Oct. 2001)

[11] Ronald Reagan, addressing the Republican National Convention, New Orleans, Loiusiana, *Washington Post* (16 Aug. 1988).

[12] Dan Quayle (17 Aug. 1989), qtd. *Esquire* (Aug. 1992): 120.

[13] George W. Bush, in Tokyo, qtd. *FDCH Political Transcripts* (18 Feb. 2002); the White House transcript was altered to "half a century," to amend the president's historical error.

[14] William Shakespeare, *The Winter's Tale* 3.3; George W. Bush, Washington D.C. (29 May 2003).

[15] Dan Quayle, CNBC News Transcripts (9 June 2000).

[16] Dan Quayle, qtd. *Times-Picayune* (New Orleans) (14 June 1998).

[17] Dan Quayle, qtd. *The Daily Telegraph* (Sydney, Australia) (20 Nov. 2000).

[18] Dan Quayle (5 Sep. 1990), qtd. *Esquire* (Aug. 1992): 121.

[19] George W. Bush, Washington, D.C., *FDCH Political Transcripts* (24 June 2004).

[20] George W. Bush, qtd. *Los Angeles Times* (8 April 2000); Interview, Spokane, Washington, ABC News (25 Sep. 2000).

[21] George W. Bush, qtd. Charlotte Church, *MSNBC* (30 Oct. 2001).

22 George W. Bush, National Security Agency, Fort Meade, Maryland, qtd. *Federal News Service Transcript* (4 June 2002).

23 George W. Bush, Aberdeen, S.D. (31 Oct. 2002), quietly corrected in FDCH Political Transcripts.

24 George W. Bush, South Bend, Ind. (31 Oct. 2002); quietly corrected in FDCH Political Transcripts.

25 George W. Bush, Washington, D.C., qtd. *FDCH Political Transcripts* (8 Feb. 2001).

26 George W. Bush, Sioux Falls, South Dakota (8 March 2001), qtd. *Washington Post* (9 March 2001).

27 George W. Bush, Bridgeport, Connecticut, *FDCH Political Transcripts* (9 April 2002).

28 George W. Bush, Marlton, New Jersey (18 Oct. 2004), http://www. whitehouse.gov/news/releases/2004/10/20041018-11.html. Accessed 15 Sep. 2005. Some online transcripts have quietly corrected "fourth" to "14th."

29 Al Jaffee, "Future Quayle Quotes We Can Expect to Hear," *Mad* (Oct. 1991): 10-11.

1.8. PLAY BY THE RULES

1 George W. Bush (12 June 2001), qtd. *Washington Post* (13 June 2001).

2 George W. Bush, Conestoga, Pa. (18 May 2001), White House Bulletin transcript (18 May 2001.)

3 Dan Quayle (12 Oct. 1990), qtd. *Esquire* (Aug. 1992): 121.

4 George W. Bush, Cleveland, Ohio (30 June 2000), qtd. *New York Times* (1 July 2000).

5 George W. Bush, Washington, D.C. (13 March 2002), qtd., *Globe and Mail* (7 Sep. 2002).

6 John Donne, "Meditation," *Devotions upon Emergent Occasions* (London, 1623), xvii.

7 Andrea Dworkin, *Life and Death* (NY: Free Press, 1997), 169.

8 Bodie Thoene, *Munich Signature* (Minneapolis: Bethany House, 1990),

9 George W. Bush, Interview, NBC (4 Sep. 2003).

10 George W. Bush, Little Rock, Arkansa (18 Nov. 2004), qtd. *The Guardian* (London) (25 Nov. 2004)/

11 George W. Bush, qtd. *Federal News Service* (21 Dec. 2001).

12 George W. Bush, qtd. "Talk of the Nation," *NPR* (2 Jan. 2001).

13 George W. Bush, Washington, D.C., qtd. *FDCH Political Transcripts* (8 Jan. 2003).

14 George W. Bush, Crawford, Texas, qtd. *FDCH Political Transcripts* (15 Nov. 2001).

15 George W. Bush, Washington, D.C., qtd. "Nightline," *ABC News Transcripts* (18 June 2003).

16 George W. Bush, Milwaukee, Wisconsin, qtd. *Federal News Service* (2 July 2002).

17 George W. Bush, on why he spent so little time in New Hampshire, qtd. *New York Times* (23 Oct. 1999).

[18] George W. Bush, White House Press Release, www.whitehouse.gov /news/releases/2003/02/20030224-1.html (24 Feb. 2003).

[19] George W. Bush, Interview with Tom Brokaw, NBC (23 Jan. 2002).

[20] George W. Bush on "parental empowerment in education," qtd. *FDCH Political Tran-scripts* (12 April 2001).

[21] George W. Bush, Interview with David Bloom (22 Feb. 2000), "The Today Show," NBC (23 Feb. 2000).

[22] George W. Bush, White House press conference, qtd. *New York Times* (23 Feb. 01).

[23] George W. Bush, Crawford High School, Crawford, TX (15 Nov. 2001).

[24] George W. Bush, Interview, ABC News (4 Dec. 2001).

[25] George W. Bush, Nashville, Tenn. (10 Feb. 2003), *White House Press Releases* transcript (10 Feb. 2003).

[26] George W. Bush, Knoxville, Tenn., qtd. *FDCH Political Transcripts* (8 April. 2002).

[27] George W. Bush, Ruch, Ore. (22 Aug. 2002), qtd. *Washington Post* (25 Aug. 2002).

[28] George W. Bush, Washington, D.C., qtd. *FDCH Political Transcripts* (6 Nov. 2001).

[29] George W. Bush, Atlanta, Georgia, qtd. *FDCH Political Transcripts* (27 March 2002).

[30] George W. Bush, third Presidential debate, St. Louis, Missouri, qtd. *Federal News Service* (17 Oct. 2000).

[31] George W. Bush, Washington, D.C., qtd. *FDCH Political Transcripts* (20 Dec. 2001).

[32] George W. Bush, Washington, D.C., qtd. *FDCH Political Transcripts* (8 Jan. 2003).

[33] George W. Bush, third Presidential debate, St. Louis, Missouri, qtd. *Federal News Service* (17 Oct. 2000).

[34] George W. Bush, New York City, qtd. *FDCH Political Transcripts* (19 Dec. 2001).

[35] George W. Bush, Grand Rapids, Michigan (29 Jan. 2003).

[36] George W. Bush, *Hardball* (31 May 2000).

[37] George W. Bush, qtd. *Chicago Sun-Times* (24 Oct. 2000).

[38] George W. Bush, *Good Morning America*, ABC (25 April 2001).

[39] George W. Bush, second Presidential debate, Winston-Salem, North Carolina (11 Oct. 2000), qtd. *New York Times* (12 Oct. 2000).

[40] George W. Bush, Interview, "Live with Regis" qtd. *The Weekend Australian* (23 Sep. 2000).

[41] George W. Bush, qtd. Samuel Tucker Elementary School, Alexandria, Virginia, qtd. *FDCH Political Transcripts* (20 Mar. 2002); Mr. Bush later corrected himself.

[42] George W. Bush, Annandale, Va. (9 Aug. 2004).

[43] Ludwig Wittgenstein, *Zettal*, Ed. G.E.M. Anscombe and G.H. von Wright. Trans. G.E.M. Anscombe (Oxford: Blackwell, 1967), 55.

[44] George W. Bush, Moscow, Russia, qtd. *FDCH Political Transcripts* (24 May 2002); Washington, D.C., qtd. *FDCH Political Transcripts* (10 Feb. 2003).

[45] George W. Bush, Columbia, South Carolina (14 Feb. 2000), qtd. *Associated Press News Wire* (15 Feb. 2000); London, England, qtd. *FDCH Political Transcripts* (19 July 2001).

[46] Dan Quayle, Hudson Institute, qtd. *Washington Post* (19 Sept. 1990).

[47] George W. Bush, LaCrosse, Wis. (Oct. 18, 2000), National Public Radio (19 Oct. 2000).

[48] George W. Bush, Interview, *Meet the Press,* NBC News Transcripts (21 Nov. 21 1999).

[49] George W. Bush, Florence, S.C., Fox News (Jan. 11, 2000).

[50] George W. Bush, CNBC, Meet the Press (April 15, 2000).

[51] George W. Bush, Washington, D.C., qtd. *FDCH Political Transcripts* (23 Jan. 2004).

[52] George W. Bush, Council Bluffs, Iowa, qtd. *FDCH Political Transcripts* (28 Feb. 2001).

[53] George W. Bush, Washington, D.C., qtd. *FDCH Political Transcripts* (24 Feb. 2003).

[54] George W. Bush, speech to students in Little Rock, Arkansas, qtd. *FDCH Political Transcripts* (29 Aug. 2002).

[55] George W. Bush, Republican National Convention, qtd. and quietly corrected, *FDCH Political Transcripts* (2 Aug. 2000).

[56] George W. Bush, Greensboro, N.C., qtd. Associated Press (10 Oct. 2000).

[57] George W. Bush, announcing his "Reading First" initiative in Reston, Va. (28 March 2000); Bush, Washington, D.C., qtd. *Chicago Sun-Times* (13 Feb. 2001).

[58] George W. Bush, Washington, D.C., qtd. *FDCH Political Transcripts* (19 Dec. 2002).

[59] George W. Bush, Washington, D.C., qtd. *FDCH Political Transcripts* (19 Dec. 2002).

[60] George W. Bush, Washington, D.C., qtd. *White House Press Release* (2 July 2001).

[61] George W. Bush, qtd. *FDCH Political Transcripts* (3 Nov. 2000).

[62] George W. Bush, Pennsylvania State University, qtd. *US Newswire* (2 Apr. 2002).

[63] George W. Bush, *Larry King Live* (16 Dec. 1999).

[64] George W. Bush, second presidential debate, qtd. *FDCH Political Transcripts* (11 Oct. 2000).

[65] George W. Bush, White House (29 Jan. 2001); qtd. *Associated Press* (31 Jan. 2001).

[66] George W. Bush, Wilton, Conn. (9 June 2000), qtd. *CBS News Transcripts* (21 Jan. 2001).

[67] George W. Bush, Chicago, qtd. *FDCH Political Transcripts* (30 Sep. 2003).

[68] George W. Bush, Washington, D.C., qtd. *FDCH Political Transcripts* (7 May 2003).

[69] George W. Bush, Bentonville, Ark., quietly corrected *FDCH Political Transcripts* (2 Nov. 2002).

[70] George W. Bush, Bartlett, Tenn., qtd. *FDCH Political Transcripts* (18 Aug. 2000); visiting the Jefferson Memorial, Washington, D.C. (2 July 2001), qtd. "This Week," *ABC News* (8 July 2001).

[71] *Games* Magazine (1984); repr. Lynne Truss, *Eats, Shoots & Leaves: The Zero Tolerance Approach to Punctuation* (NY: Penguin, 2004).

[72] George W. Bush, Ypsilanti, Mich. (7 Sep. 2000), qtd. *Washington Post* (8 Sep. 2000).

[73] George W. Bush Washington, D.C., qtd. *FDCH Political Transcripts* (1 Aug. 2003).

[74] George W. Bush, LaCrosse, Wisconsin (18 Oct. 2000), qtd. "Morning Edition," NPR (18 Oct. 2000).

[75] George W. Bush, Reuters (5 May 2000), qtd. "Crossfire," CNN (1 Nov. 2000).

[76] George W. Bush, Crawford, TX, qtd. *Federal News Service* (25 Aug. 2001).

[77] H. L. Mencken,"Gamalieliese," *Baltimore Evening Sun* (7 March 1921); repr. *A Carnival of Buncombe* (Baltimore: Johns Hopkins Press, 1956), 39.

[78] George W. Bush, Interview with David Fink of the *Hartford Courant* at the Republican Convention, 1988; qtd. Jake Tapper, "Prodigal Son," *Salon.com* (9 April 1999).

[79] George H. W. Bush, during a tour of Auschwitz, qtd. Associated Press Wire Service (29 Sep. 1987); qtd. *Washington Post* (10 March 1988).

[80] George W. Bush, Boston, qtd. *Federal News Service* (4 Oct. 2002).

[81] George W. Bush, Washington, D.C., qtd. *Fed. News Service* (4 Nov. 2004).

[82] George W. Bush, Washington, D.C., qtd. *FDCH Political Transcripts* (28 Oct. 2003).

[83] George W. Bush, Houston, TX, *FDCH Political Transcripts* (26 Sep. 2002.)

[84] George W. Bush, Fort Stewart, Georgia, quietly corrected *FDCH Political Transcripts* (12 Feb. 2001).

[85] George W. Bush, Orlando, Florida, quietly corrected FDCH Political Transcripts (21 March 2001).

[86] William Shakespeare, *The Complete Works*, ed. David Bevington (NY: Harper Collins, 1992).

[87] George W. Bush, e.g., Interview, *Time* magazine (25 Dec. 2000); Annandale, Va (9 Aug. 2004);' News conference (4 Nov. 2004).

[88] George W. Bush, to Brazilian President Fernando Cardoso (8 Nov. 2001), qtd. *Estado Sao Pauloan* (28 April 2002).

[89] George W. Bush, University of Pittsburgh, qtd. *FDCH Political Transcripts* (5 Feb. 2002).

[90] George W. Bush, New York City, qtd. *FDCH Political Transcripts* (19 Dec. 2001).

[91] George W. Bush, interview, *New York Times* (15 March 2000).

[92] Dan Quayle, California State University, Fresno (17 Jan. 1992), qtd. *Los Angeles Times* (17 Jan. 1992)

[93] George W. Bush, 60 minutes II, CBS (5 Dec. 2000).

[94] George W. Bush, CNN (18-19 Dec. 2000).

[95] George W. Bush, Burbank, Washington, KOMO-TV (22 Aug. 2003).

[96] Dan Quayle (6 Dec. 1989), qtd. *Esquire* (Aug. 1992): 120.

[97] George W. Bush, on his executive order making faith-based groups eligible for federal subsidies, New Orleans, Louisiana (15 Jan. 2004).

[98] George W. Bush, *Governing Magazine* (July, 1998).

[99] George W. Bush, Interview, *Fox News* (22 Sept. 2003); qtd. NBC News (23 Oct. 2003).

[100] George W. Bush, *Business Week* (30 July 2001).

[101] George H. W. Bush, Washington, D.C., qtd. *Star Tribune* (Minneapolis) (25 Oct. 1996).

[102] George W. Bush, on violence in Iraq, qtd. *Chicago Sun-Times* (27 April 2004).

1.9. DO NOT STEAL MUCH

[1] Mark Twain, *Notebooks* (1935).

[2] "The Oscar Wilde Sketch," *Flying Circus TV Show,* episode 39.

[3] I have stolen this thought from a remark (widely though uncertainly) ascribed to Samuel Johnson. According to the anecdote, Johnson crushed the hopes of an aspiring writer with the witticism, "Your manuscript is both good and original. But the part that is good is not original, and the part that is original is not good." No one knows where Dr. Johnson may have gotten it.

[1] H. G. Wells, qtd. *Washington Post* (28 Sep. 1980); widely attributed, original source unverified.

[2] Thomas Mann, qtd. Christopher Lehmann-Haupt, *New York Times* (12 March 1998); widely attributed, original source unverified.

1.10. JUST GET IT RIGHT

[1] George W. Bush, *White House Press Releases* (Feb. 21, 2001).

[2] George W. Bush, Detroit, Mich., *Congressional Quarterly* transcript (Feb. 8 2005).

[3] For this splendid example I am indebted to Carolyn Jacobson, "Some Notes on Gender-Neutral Language," online, http://www.stetson.edu/artsci/history/nongenderlang. html, accessed Sep. 2005.

[4] George W. Bush, *White House Bulletin* (9 Feb. 2001).

[5] Dan Quayle, news conference (17 Aug. 1988), qtd. *New York Times* (18 Aug. 1988).

[6] George W. Bush, qtd. *USA Today* (28 July 2000).

[7] George W. Bush (1999), qtd. by Molly Ivin, *Shrub* (NY: Vintage, 2000).

[8] George W. Bush, presidential campaign; "Hardball," MSNBC (31 May 2000); Des Moines, Iowa (21 Aug. 2000); qtd. *Chicago Sun-Times* (21 Aug. 2000); Wayne, Mich. (27 June 2000), qtd. *NY Times* (28 June 2000); qtd. *U.S. News & World Report* (3 April 2000); qtd. *New York Times* (23 Oct. 1999).

[9] George W. Bush, in Seattle, Washington, qtd. *Austin American-Statesman* (2 Nov. 2000); in Rome (21 July 2001), qtd. *Associated Press* (22 July 2001); Reynoldsburg, Ohio (4 Oct. 2000), qtd. *Morning Edition, NPR* (5 Oct. 2000); on his economic plan, qtd. *New York Times* (15 March 2000); Austin, Texas, qtd. *FDCH Political Transcripts* (8 Dec. 2000).

[10] George W. Bush, Davenport, IOWA, *FDCH Political Transcripts* (5 Aug. 2004).

[11] Dan Quayle, Cable News Network (11 Aug. 1989); qtd. *Washington* Post (1 Sep. 1989).

[12] Dan Quayle, North Carolina State University (9 Oct. 1988), qtd. *Washington Post* (10 Oct. 1988); responding to reports that his parents had been members of the John Birch Society, a right-wing organization that once accused even President Eisenhower of being a communist.

[13] George W. Bush, Los Angeles, *FDCH Political Transcripts* (3 March 2004).

[14] *Marin County Independent Journal*, qtd. Linda Sunshine, *All Things Oz: The Wonder, Wit, and Wisdom of The Wizard of Oz* (NY: Clarkson Potter,2003), 72.

[15] Anonymous lyric, ed. Jim Cameron, "Real Limericks," online, http://madeira.physiol.ucl.ac.uk/people/jim/crescent/Game712.

[16] Dan Quayle, Congressional hearing (6 Sep. 1988), cited *Esquire* (Aug. 1992): 124; clarified by Mr. Quayle (8 Sep. 1988) in a speech at the Chicago Civic Club: "if you read *Red Storm Rising* ..., you understand that the ASAC testing or the ASAC capability in that book won the war," excerpt, MacNeil/Lehrer NewsHour (9 Sep. 1988).

[17] Somerset Maugham, attrib. Unverified.

3.1. *A Pretty Good Guide*

[1] Tom Stoppard, *The Real Thing* (Boston: Faber and Faber, 1982), 53.

[2] Ambrose Bierce, "Academe," *The Unabridged Devil's Dictionary* (Athens: Univ. Georgia, 2000).

[3] George W. Bush, Earth Day, Wilmington, NY (22 April 2002), qtd. http://www. thedubyareport.com/quotes.html; quietly corrected *Federal Information and News Dispatch, Inc.* State Department (22 April 2002).

[4] George W. Bush, CNN (25 April 2001).

[5] George W. Bush, Press conference, Washington, D.C. (29 March 2001), qtd. *New York Times* (30 March 2001).

[6] George W. Bush, *Meet the Press,* NBC (21 Nov.1999).

[7] George W. Bush, Austin, Texas (22 June 2000), qtd. *Knight/Ridder News Service Transcript* (23 June 2000).

[8] George W. Bush, interview, *The Edge With Paula Zahn,* Fox News (18 Sep. 2000).

[9] George W. Bush, Los Angeles (27 Sep. 2000), qtd. *Herald Sun* (25 Feb. 2001).

[10] George W. Bush, aboard Air Force One (4 June 2003), qtd. *Washington Post* (5 June 2003).

[11] George W. Bush, *Larry King Live,* CNN (16 Dec. 1999).

[12] George W. Bush, qtd. *Financial Times* (14 Jan. 2000).

[13] George W. Bush, qtd. *San Francisco Chronicle* (21 Jan. 2000).

[14] Ronald Reagan, *Time* (1976), qtd. *New York Times* (24 July 1980).

[15] George W. Bush, Crawford, Texas (13 Aug. 2001), qtd. *FDCH Political Transcripts* (13 Aug. 2001).

[16] George W. Bush, Washington, D.C., qtd. *U.S. Newswire* (18 April 2002); Bush, Stockton, Calif., qtd. *FDCH Political Transcripts* (23 Aug. 2002)

[17] George W. Bush, qtd. *FDCH Political Transcripts* (24 Sep. 2001).

[18] George W. Bush to the Cattle Industry Convention, qtd. *FDCH Political Transcripts* (8 Feb. 2002).

[19] George W. Bush, *All Things Considered*, NatL. Pub. Radio (4 June 2002).

[20] "Invasion of the doom mongers," *The Times* (London) (24 Aug. 1993).

[21] George W. Bush, Saginaw, Michigan (29 Sep. 2000), qtd. *Washington Post* (1 Oct. 2000).

[22] George W. Bush, Des Moines, Iowa (23 Oct. 2000), qtd. *Chicago Sun Times* (24 Oct. 2000); NPR, *All Things Considered* (20 Dec. 2003).

[23] George W. Bush, Gothenburg, Sweden (14 June 2001), qtd. *CNBC News Transcripts* (21 June 2001).

[24] George W. Bush, presidential debate, *FDCH Political Transcripts* (11 Oct. 2000).

[25] Dan Quayle (15 Sep. 1988), qtd. *New York Times* (16 Sep. 1988).

[26] Dan Quayle (1984), qtd. *Toronto Star* (21 Aug. 1988).

[27] George W. Bush, Austin, Texas (20 Dec. 2000), qtd. *New York Times* (21 Dec. 2000).

[28] George W. Bush, Sharm El Sheik, Egypt (3 June 2003), qtd. *New York Times* (4 June 2003).

[29] George W. Bush, Washington, D.C. (31 May 2005); online, audiorecording, http://politicalhumor.about.com/library/multimedia/bush_disassemble.mp3.

[30] George W. Bush, Austin, Texas (22 June 2000), qtd. *Seattle Post-Intelligencer* (23 June 2000).

[31] George W. Bush, reflecting in 1994 about growing up in Midland, Texas, qtd. *Washington Post* (5 May 2000).

[32] George H. W. Bush, Interview with a Houston, Texas radio station, qtd. *Federal News Service* (1 Nov. 1991).

[33] George W. Bush, second presidential debate, St. Louis, Mo. *Congressional Quarterly* transcript (Oct. 2004).

[34] George W. Bush, *Federal Information and News Dispatch* (2 March 2001).

[35] George W. Bush, qtd. Associated Press (8 March 2000).

[36] George W. Bush, Mountain View, California, qtd. *FDCH Political Transcripts* (2 May 2003).

[37] George W. Bush, Interview, *Oprah*, ABC (19 Sep. 2000).

[38] H. W. Fowler, "few," *A Dictionary of Modern English Usage* (Oxford: Oxford Univ. Press, 1947), 179.

[39] George W. Bush, Concord, New Hampshire (29 Jan. 2000), qtd. *The Age* (Melbourne) (29 Jul. 2002).

[40] George H. W. Bush (1983), qtd. *St. Petersburg* Times (6 June 1993); George W. Bush, White House, Washington, D.C. (10 Jan. 2005), www.dubyaspeak.com/audio/ erection.phtml; Condolezza Rice, qtd. *New York Magazine* (26 Apr. 2004); Philadelphia, Pennsylvania, *FDCH Political Transcripts* (2 April 2002).

[41] George W. Bush, Interview, MSNBC (21 Feb. 2000), qtd. *Newsweek* 28 Feb. 2000: 30+.

[42] George W. Bush, in Miami (5 June 2001), *Federal News Service* (6 June 2001); Bush, interview with Cokie Roberts, *This Week* (20 Feb. 2000).

[43] George W. Bush, qtd. *New York Daily News* (19 Feb. 2000).

[44] George H. W. Bush, at the Ford Aerospace Systems Division, Palo Alto, California (25 April 1989), qtd. *Washington Post* (26 April 1989).

[45] George W. Bush, Des Moines, Iowa (21 Aug. 2000), qtd. *New York Times* (23 Aug. 2000).

[46] Dan Quayle to Hendrick Hertzberg (28 Sep. 1988), expressing his opinion of the book, *Nicholas and Alexandra*, qtd. *Savvy Woman* (Jan. 1989): 56.

[47] George W. Bush, Arlington Heights, Illinois (24 Oct. 2000), qtd. *Toronto Star* (2 Nov. 2000).

[48] George W. Bush, addressing the National Religious Broadcasters' Convention, Opryland Hotel, Nashville, Tennessee (10 Feb. 2003), *Federal News Service Transcripts* [transcript has been quietly corrected].

[49] George W. Bush, Aberdeen, S.D., qtd. *FDCH Political Transcripts* (31 Oct. 2002).

[50] Ibid.

[51] George W. Bush, *Meet the Press*, NBC (13 Feb. 2000).

[52] George W. Bush, Pittsburgh, Pennsylvania (8 Sep. 2000), qtd. Associated Press (9 Sep. 2000).

[53] George W. Bush, Denver, Colorado (13 Aug. 2001), qtd. *FDCH Political Transcripts* (14 Aug. 2001).

[54] George W. Bush, Arlington Heights, Ill. (24 Oct. 2000), qtd. *Toronto Star* (2 Nov. 2000).

[55] George W. Bush, qtd. *FDCH Political Transcripts* (29 Jan. 2001).

[56] Jeb Bush (Governor of Florida), " Interview with Jeb Bush," Fox News (2 June 2003); Gov. Jesse Ventura, "Good Morning America," ABC (25 Oct. 2000).

[57] George H. W. Bush, qtd. *Washington Post* (13 May 1988).

[58] George W. Bush, qtd. *Daily News* (New York) (13 Sep. 2000).

[59] George W. Bush, White House (31 Jan. 2001), qtd. *The Times (London)* (23 Apr. 2001).

[60] George W. Bush, Concord Middle School, Concord, N.C. (11 April 2001), qtd. *Washington Post* (13 Apr. 2001).

[61] George W. Bush, South Bend, Ind., qtd. *FDCH Political Transcripts* (31 Oct. 2002).

[62] George W. Bush, qtd. *Chicago Sun-Times* (11 July 2002).

[63] George W. Bush, Washington, D.C., qtd. *FDCH Political Transcripts* (27 Nov. 2002).

[64] George W. Bush, Interview with Brit Hume, Fox News (22 Sep. 2003).

[65] George W. Bush, Westminster, California (13 Sep. 2000), qtd. *The Guardian* (London) (4 Nov. 2000).

[66] George W. Bush, Washington, D.C. (11 Jan. 2001), qtd. *Chicago Sun-Times* (15 Jan. 2001).

[67] George W. Bush (24 June 2001), qtd. Peggy Noonan.

[68] George W. Bush, qtd. *Federal News Service* (30 Apr. 2002).

[69] George W. Bush, Washington, D.C., qtd. *Federal News Transcripts* (1 July 2003).

[70] George W. Bush, Bethesda, Maryland, qtd. *FDCH Political Transcripts* (3. Feb. 2003).

[71] George W. Bush. St. Louis, Missouri (22 Jan. 2003), qtd. *The Advertiser* (25 Jan. 2003).

[72] George W. Bush, qtd. *Newsweek* (28 Feb. 2000).

[73] Richard Nixon, attrib. (1974). Unverified.

[74] George W. Bush, Washington, D.C. (29 Jan. 2001), qtd. *The Times* (*London*) (23 Apr. 2001).

[75] George W. Bush, Fairgrounds Elementary School, Nashua, New Hampshire (28 Jan. 2000), qtd. *The Herald* (14 Dec. 2000).

[76] George W. Bush, qtd. *Washington Post* (24 June 1999); "incredibly presumptive" is a favored Bush phrase; cf. Keene, N.H. (22 Oct. 1999), qtd. *New Republic* (15 Nov. 1999); cf. *Boston Globe*, et al. (14 Dec. 1999).

[77] George W. Bush, Hilton Head, S.C. (16 Feb. 2000), qtd. *Washington Post* (Feb. 16, 2000).

[78] George W. Bush, Ft. Wayne, Indiana, qtd. *The Journal Gazette* (12 Nov. 2000).

[79] George W. Bush, Washington, D.C., qtd. *FDCH Political Transcripts* (29 May 2003).

[80] George W. Bush, *FDCH Political Transcripts* (20 Mar. 2001).

[81] George W. Bush, Rochester, New York, *Federal News Service* transcript (24 May 2005),

[82] George W. Bush, Brussels, Belgium (13 June 2001), qtd. *Washington Post* (14 June 2001).

[83] John Grimond, "Style Guide," *The Economist* online, available at http://www.economist.com/research/StyleGuide (accessed 2003).

[84] George W. Bush, qtd. *Columbus Dispatch* (5 Nov. 2000).

[85] George W. Bush, qtd. *The Independent* (*London*) (5 Nov. 2000).

[86] Dan Quayle, viewing earthquake damage (19 Oct. 1989), qtd. *San Francisco Chronicle* (24 Oct. 1989).

[87] George W. Bush, London, qtd. *FDCH Political Trans.* (19 Nov. 2003).

[88] George W. Bush, qtd. *Washington Post* (24 Mar. 2000).

[89] George W. Bush, speaking of the KIPP Academy in Houston, Texas (4 Oct. 2000), qtd. *New York Times* (5 Oct. 2000).

[90] George W. Bush, qtd. by Mitchell Daniels, White House Budget Director (shortly after 11 Sep. 2001, qtd. *Miami Herald* (29 Nov. 2001).

[91] George W. Bush, Salinas, California (10 Aug. 2000), qtd. *Daily News* (New York) (25 Aug. 2000).

[92] George W. Bush, Greater Nashua, N.H., Chamber of Commerce (27 Jan. 2000); transcript, NBC News (5 Nov. 2000).

[93] George W. Bush, ("*terriers...hostile*") Des Moines, Iowa (21 Aug. 2000; ("*terriers* and *bare ifs*"), qtd. *Financial Times* (London) (11 Jan. 2000); ("*pan plays*"); address to Congress, *NBC News* transcript (27 Feb. 2001); ("*steat or*

cheal") *FDCH Political Transcripts* (16 Aug. 2002).

94 George W. Bush, Wash., D.C., qtd. *FDCH Political Trans.* (9 June 2003).

95 George W. Bush, Dakar, Senegal; qtd. *FDCH Political Transcripts* (8 July 2003).

96 George H. W. Bush, Dover, New Hampshire, qtd. *Federal News Service* (15 Jan. 1992).

97 George W. Bush, qtd. *New York Daily News* (23 April 2002).

98 George W. Bush (12 Sep. 2000), qtd. *Morning Edition*, NPR (13 Sep. 2000).

99 George W. Bush, qtd. *Hardball with Chris Matthews*, CNBC (12 Sep. 2000).

100 George W. Bush, *Meet the Press,* NBC (13 Feb. 2000); Associated Press (6 April 2000).

101 George W. Bush, Florence, S.C. (11 Jan. 2000), qtd. *Boston Globe* (23 Jan. 2000).

102 George W. Bush, Beaufort, S.C. (16 Feb. 2000), qtd. *St. Louis Post-Dispatch* (22 Oct. 2000).

103 George W. Bush, *Today Show,* NBC transcript (23 Feb. 2002).

104 George W. Bush, qtd. *New York Times* (26 Apr. 2001).

105 George H. W. Bush, qtd. *Washington Post* (12 May1990); to the Disabled American Veterans in Washington D.C., qtd. *Federal News Service Transcript* (12 Sep. 1991).

106 George W. Bush, Lima, Peru, qtd. *FDCH Political Transcripts* (23 Mar. 2002).

107 George W. Bush, Tyndall Air Force Base, Florida (12 March 2001), qtd. *New York Times* (13 March 2001).

108 George W. Bush, White House, qtd. *FDCH Political Transcripts* (18 June 2001).

109 George W. Bush, London, England (19 July 2001), qtd. *The Times* (*London*) (20 July 2001).

110 George W. Bush (9 March 2000); Bush later explained, "I'm going to talk more about the vile hemisphere and America being held hostile by rogue nations. I'm not ashamed of those little slips. The hemisphere *is* vile sometimes!" *Plain Dealer* (Cleveland) (28 Aug. 2000).

111 Oscar Wilde, attrib. Unverified.

112 George W. Bush, Washington, D.C., qtd. *FDCH Political Transcripts* (13 March 2002).

113 George W. Bush, qtd. *The Economist* (12 June 1999).

114 George W. Bush, Cleveland, Ohio (1 July 2002), qtd. *Boston Globe* (2 Jul. 2002).

115 George W. Bush, Summit of the Americas, Quebec City, Canada (21 April 2001), qtd. *USA Today* (23 Apr. 2001); *FDCH Political Transcripts* (19 March 2001); again F; Dan Quayle, qtd. by Representative Claudine Schneider (R., Rhode Island), qtd. *New York Times* (28 April 1989).

116 You cannot say that in Latin.